Christmas

Taste of Home BOOKS

RDA ENTHUSIAST BRANDS, LLC
MILWAUKEE, WI

Taste of Home

EDITORIAL

Editor-in-Chief **CATHERINE CASSIDY**
Creative Director **HOWARD GREENBERG**
Editorial Operations Director **KERRI BALLIET**

Managing Editor/Print & Digital Books **MARK HAGEN**
Associate Creative Director **EDWIN ROBLES JR.**

Editor **MICHELLE ROZUMALSKI**
Art Director **JESSIE SHARON**
Associate Craft Editor **VANESSA TSUMURA**
Layout Designer **NANCY NOVAK**
Editorial Production Manager **DENA AHLERS**
Copy Chief **DEB WARLAUMONT MULVEY**
Copy Editors **DULCIE SHOENER, MARY-LIZ SHAW**
Contributing Copy Editor **VALERIE PHILLIPS**

Chief Food Editor **KAREN BERNER**
Food Editors **JAMES SCHEND; PEGGY WOODWARD, RD**
Associate Food Editor **KRISTA LANPHIER**
Recipe Editors **MARY KING; ANNIE RUNDLE; JENNI SHARP, RD; IRENE YEH**
Content Operations Manager **COLLEEN KING**
Content Operations Assistant **SHANNON STROUD**
Executive Assistant **MARIE BRANNON**

Test Kitchen and Food Styling Manager **SARAH THOMPSON**
Test Cooks **NICHOLAS IVERSON (LEAD), MATTHEW HASS, LAUREN KNOELKE**
Food Stylists **KATHRYN CONRAD (SENIOR), SHANNON ROUM, LEAH REKAU**
Prep Cooks **MEGUMI GARCIA, MELISSA HANSEN, BETHANY VAN JACOBSON, SARA WIRTZ**

Photography Director **STEPHANIE MARCHESE**
Photographers **DAN ROBERTS, JIM WIELAND**
Photographer/Set Stylist **GRACE NATOLI SHELDON**
Set Stylists **STACEY GENAW, MELISSA HABERMAN, DEE DEE JACQ**
Creative Contributors **MARK DERSE (PHOTOGRAPHER); SUE DRAHEIM, LAUREL ZIMIENSKI (FOOD STYLISTS); MEGHAN HURLEY, PAM STASNEY (SET STYLISTS)**

Editorial Business Manager **KRISTY MARTIN**
Billing Specialist **MARY ANN KOEBERNIK**

BUSINESS

Vice President, Chief Sales Officer **MARK S. JOSEPHSON**
Vice President, Business Development & Marketing **ALAIN BEGUN**
General Manager, Taste of Home Cooking School **ERIN PUARIEA**

Vice President, Digital Experience & E-Commerce **JENNIFER SMITH**
Vice President, Direct to Consumer Marketing **DAVE FIEGEL**

THE READER'S DIGEST ASSOCIATION, INC.

President and Chief Executive Officer **BONNIE KINTZER**
Vice President, Chief Operating Officer, North America **HOWARD HALLIGAN**
Vice President, Enthusiast Brands, Books and Retail **HAROLD CLARKE**
Vice President, North American Operations **PHILIPPE CLOUTIER**
Vice President, Chief Marketing Officer **LESLIE DOTY**
Vice President, North American Human Resources **PHYLLIS E. GEBHARDT, SPHR**
Vice President, Consumer Marketing Planning **JIM WOODS**

COVER PHOTOGRAPHY

Photographer **DAN ROBERTS**
Food Stylist **LEAH REKAU**
Set Stylist **MELISSA HABERMAN**

International Standard Book Number: 978-1-61765-314-8
International Standard Serial Number: 1948-8386
Component Number: 119600023H00

Printed in U.S.A.
3 5 7 9 10 8 6 4 2

PICTURED ON THE FRONT COVER: Zesty Citrus Cake (p. 152), Fudgy Mint Cookies (p. 129), Chocolate Drizzled Maple-Nut Tart (p. 160).

PICTURED ON THE BACK COVER: Buttery Lemon Turkey (p. 29), Holiday Baked Ham (p. 35), Peppermint Cheesecake on a Stick (p. 119), Pomegranate-Glazed Green Beans (p. 36).

ADDITIONAL PHOTOGRAPHY USED: iravgustin/Shutterstock.com (endpapers); shab/Shutterstock.com (p. 1); isak55/Shutterstock.com (p. 3); Gtranquility/Shutterstock.com (p. 4).

Taste of Home ❄ CHRISTMAS

Contents

Share the warmth of the season with
TASTE OF HOME CHRISTMAS

This special holiday treasury gives you exciting new ideas for making yuletide get-togethers with family and friends as memorable as can be. Enjoy scrumptious recipes, heartwarming gifts, sparkling decorations, helpful hints and much more in these 12 big chapters:

WINE-TASTING STARTERS. Host a wine-tasting party for the holidays! Along with bottles of vino, the elegant appetizers in this chapter are sure to get raves.

CHRISTMAS FEASTS. Featuring main courses of beef tenderloin, turkey and ham, these three menus feature everything you need for an unforgettable dinner.

HEARTWARMING BREADS. Golden brown goodies warm from the oven will make even a Scrooge smile. You'll find scrumptious loaves, rolls, coffee cakes and more.

SEASONAL GET-TOGETHERS. Celebrate with a fun-filled themed event, from a tropical bash and forest-inspired breakfast to an adorable reindeer party for kids.

SIDES TO MIX & MATCH. A yuletide meal will shine even brighter with standout side dishes. This chapter serves up a variety of delicious ways to round out menus.

SLOW COOKER CHRISTMAS. When welcoming friends and family for the holidays, rely on the convenience of slow cooking to make entertaining effortless.

CHEESECAKE CHEER. Who can resist? From creamy, dreamy desserts to savory appetizers, these tempting recipes will delight from the first bite to the last.

QUICK & EASY COOKIES. Festive treats are a must at Christmastime. This chapter offers fuss-free favorites that even the busiest cooks have time to bake.

SWEET SENSATIONS. Put the crowning touch on your seasonal feasts with the decadent cakes, pies, candies, tarts, bars and other family-pleasing confections here.

KITCHEN TREATS TO SHARE. Looking for a delectable way to surprise loved ones? Tins, jars or baskets of these homemade sensations are always well received.

DECK THE HALLS. Christmas merrymaking will spread throughout your home when you decorate with the simple but stunning craft projects in this chapter.

GIFTS TO GIVE. Warm hearts with presents you create yourself. You'll find creative treasures for neighbors, relatives, co-workers...everyone on your list.

*With the wonderful ideas in **Taste of Home Christmas**, your holiday-season celebrations will be filled with everything you and your family love most.*

wine-tasting STARTERS

Honey Mustard Bacon-Wrapped Chicken

These satisfying, sweet-salty dippers are a hit with kids and adults alike. Guests at my daughter's 13th birthday party couldn't get enough of the bacon-wrapped chicken and yummy honey-mustard sauce.

—KIM FORNI CLAREMONT, NH

PREP: 30 MIN. + MARINATING
GRILL: 10 MIN.
MAKES: 4 DOZEN (1½ CUPS SAUCE)

- 1 cup chicken broth
- ½ cup honey
- 2 tablespoons ground mustard
- ½ teaspoon salt
- ½ teaspoon dried rosemary, crushed
- ¼ teaspoon pepper
- 1½ pounds boneless skinless chicken breasts, cut into 1-inch cubes (about 48)

SAUCE

- 1 cup Dijon mustard
- ½ cup honey
- 4 teaspoons ground mustard
- ½ teaspoon dried rosemary, crushed

ASSEMBLY

- 16 bacon strips

1. In a small bowl, whisk the first six ingredients. Pour into a large resealable plastic bag. Add chicken; seal bag and turn to coat. Refrigerate 4 hours or overnight.

2. In a small bowl, combine the sauce ingredients; set aside. Cut bacon strips crosswise into thirds. In a large skillet, cook bacon over medium heat until partially cooked but not crisp. Remove to paper towels to drain.

3. Drain chicken, discarding marinade. Wrap a bacon piece around each chicken piece; secure with a toothpick.

4. Moisten a paper towel with cooking oil; using long-handled tongs, rub on the grill rack to coat lightly. Grill the chicken, covered, over medium heat or broil 4 in. from the heat 3-4 minutes on each side or until the bacon is crisp and the chicken is no longer pink. Serve with the sauce.

Shrimp & Feta Cucumber Rounds

I love the contrasting tastes and textures of these rounds. Each bite balances the refreshing burst and crunch of cucumber with the rich flavor and creaminess of the filling.
—**DONNA STELMACH** MORRISTOWN, NJ

START TO FINISH: 30 MIN. • **MAKES:** ABOUT 3 DOZEN

- 1 package (8 ounces) cream cheese, softened
- 1¼ cups (5 ounces) crumbled feta cheese
- 2 teaspoons snipped fresh dill
- ¼ teaspoon salt
- ¼ teaspoon chili powder
- ⅛ teaspoon pepper
- ⅔ cup peeled and deveined cooked small shrimp (about 6 ounces), chopped
- ¼ cup finely chopped roasted sweet red pepper
- 2 large English cucumbers, cut into ½-inch slices
  Fresh dill sprigs or additional chopped roasted sweet red peppers, optional

In a large bowl, beat the first six ingredients until blended. Stir in the shrimp and red pepper. Place about 2 teaspoons shrimp mixture on each cucumber slice. Refrigerate until serving. If desired, top with dill before serving.

Spinach-Cheddar Crescent Bites

My idea for stuffed appetizer rolls occurred to me on the day of a holiday gathering. The little buns were so popular at the party, they've been on my seasonal menu ever since.
—**JOSEE LANZI** NEW PORT RICHEY, FL

START TO FINISH: 25 MIN. • **MAKES:** 16 APPETIZERS

- 1 cup chopped fresh spinach
- ½ cup shredded sharp cheddar cheese
- ⅓ cup spreadable spinach and artichoke cream cheese
- ¼ cup dried cranberries
- ¼ cup chopped pecans
- ¼ teaspoon pepper
- ⅛ teaspoon salt
- 1 tube (8 ounces) refrigerated seamless crescent dough sheet
- 1 egg, lightly beaten
  Coarse sea salt

1. Preheat oven to 375°. In a small bowl, mix the first seven ingredients.
2. Unroll crescent dough into one long rectangle. Cut into 16 rectangles. Place 2 teaspoons spinach mixture in center of each rectangle. Bring edges of dough over filling, pinching seams to seal; shape into a ball.
3. Place on greased baking sheets, seam side down. Brush with egg; sprinkle with coarse salt. Bake 10-12 minutes or until golden brown. Serve warm. Refrigerate leftovers.

Curried Onion Dip

Bored with the usual vegetable dip? Kick things up a notch in just 15 minutes with a dash of curry powder and a splash of chili sauce. I serve this alongside fresh celery, cauliflower and carrots for a zippy snack.

—DOROTHY ANDERSON OTTAWA, KS

START TO FINISH: 15 MIN.
MAKES: 2 CUPS

- 1 package (8 ounces) cream cheese, softened
- 1 cup mayonnaise
- 2 tablespoons grated onion
- 2 tablespoons chili sauce
- 2 teaspoons tarragon vinegar
- ½ teaspoon salt
- ¼ teaspoon curry powder
- ⅛ teaspoon dried thyme
  Assorted fresh vegetables

In a small bowl, beat the cream cheese until smooth. Beat in the mayonnaise, onion, chili sauce, tarragon vinegar, salt, curry powder and thyme until blended. Serve with vegetables. Cover and refrigerate leftovers.

Breaded Cheddar Bites

Cubes of cheddar breaded and fried until golden brown—what's not to love? The ooey-gooey bites are always popular, and I never have to worry about leftovers.

—CLEO GONSKE REDDING, CA

START TO FINISH: 25 MIN.
MAKES: ABOUT 3 DOZEN

- Oil for deep-fat frying
- 2 eggs
- ¾ cup dry bread crumbs
- 1 tablespoon sesame seeds, toasted
- ½ teaspoon salt
- 1 pound sharp cheddar cheese, cut into ¾-inch cubes

1. In an electric skillet or deep fryer, heat oil to 350°. Meanwhile, whisk the eggs in a shallow bowl. In another shallow bowl, mix the bread crumbs, sesame seeds and salt. Dip the cheddar cheese in the eggs, then roll in crumb mixture to coat all sides, patting to help the coating adhere.

2. Fry cheese, a few at a time, 1 to 1½ minutes or until golden brown, turning occasionally. Drain on paper towels.

Parmesan Mushroom Tartlets

My easy mushroom tartlets take shape with convenient refrigerated crescent dough. They're best warm from the oven.

—BETSY KING DULUTH, MN

PREP: 25 MIN. • **BAKE:** 10 MIN.
MAKES: 2 DOZEN

- 2 tablespoons butter
- ½ pound fresh mushrooms, chopped
- 1 green onion, chopped, divided
- 1 garlic clove, minced
- ½ cup heavy whipping cream
- ½ cup grated Parmesan cheese
- 1 tube (8 ounces) refrigerated seamless crescent dough sheet

1. Preheat oven to 375°. In a large skillet, heat butter over medium-high heat. Add the mushrooms and half of the green onion; cook and stir until the mushrooms are tender. Add the garlic; cook 1 minute longer. Add cream and cheese; cook and stir 3-4 minutes or until liquids are evaporated.

2. Unroll the crescent dough into one long rectangle. Cut into 24 pieces; press lightly onto the bottom and up the sides of ungreased mini muffin cups. Fill each with 1½ teaspoons mushroom mixture.

3. Bake 8-10 minutes or until golden brown. Sprinkle with the remaining green onion. Serve warm.

Fiesta Shrimp Cocktail

Whenever I make this elegant seafood appetizer for dinner parties, it gets rave reviews. The marinated shrimp cocktail looks extra special spooned into martini glasses lined with romaine leaves.

—**LINDA STEMEN** MONROEVILLE, IN

PREP: 20 MIN. + CHILLING
MAKES: 6 SERVINGS

- 1 **pound peeled and deveined cooked medium shrimp**
- 1 **medium tomato, chopped**
- ½ **cup Italian salad dressing**
- 1 **can (4 ounces) chopped green chilies**
- 3 **green onions, thinly sliced**
- 2 **tablespoons minced fresh cilantro**
- 2 **teaspoons honey**
- ⅛ **teaspoon hot pepper sauce**
  Romaine leaves

1. Place the first eight ingredients in a large bowl; toss to combine. Refrigerate, covered, at least 1 hour.
2. Line six cocktail glasses or serving dishes with romaine leaves. Using a slotted spoon, place about ½ cup shrimp mixture in each.

Holiday Helper

Throwing a wine-tasting party? With so many varieties to choose from, selecting bottles can be intimidating for the occasional wine drinker. Familiarize yourself with the common types of wine before buying. At the party, serve an appetizer buffet to give guests ample food choices as they sip.

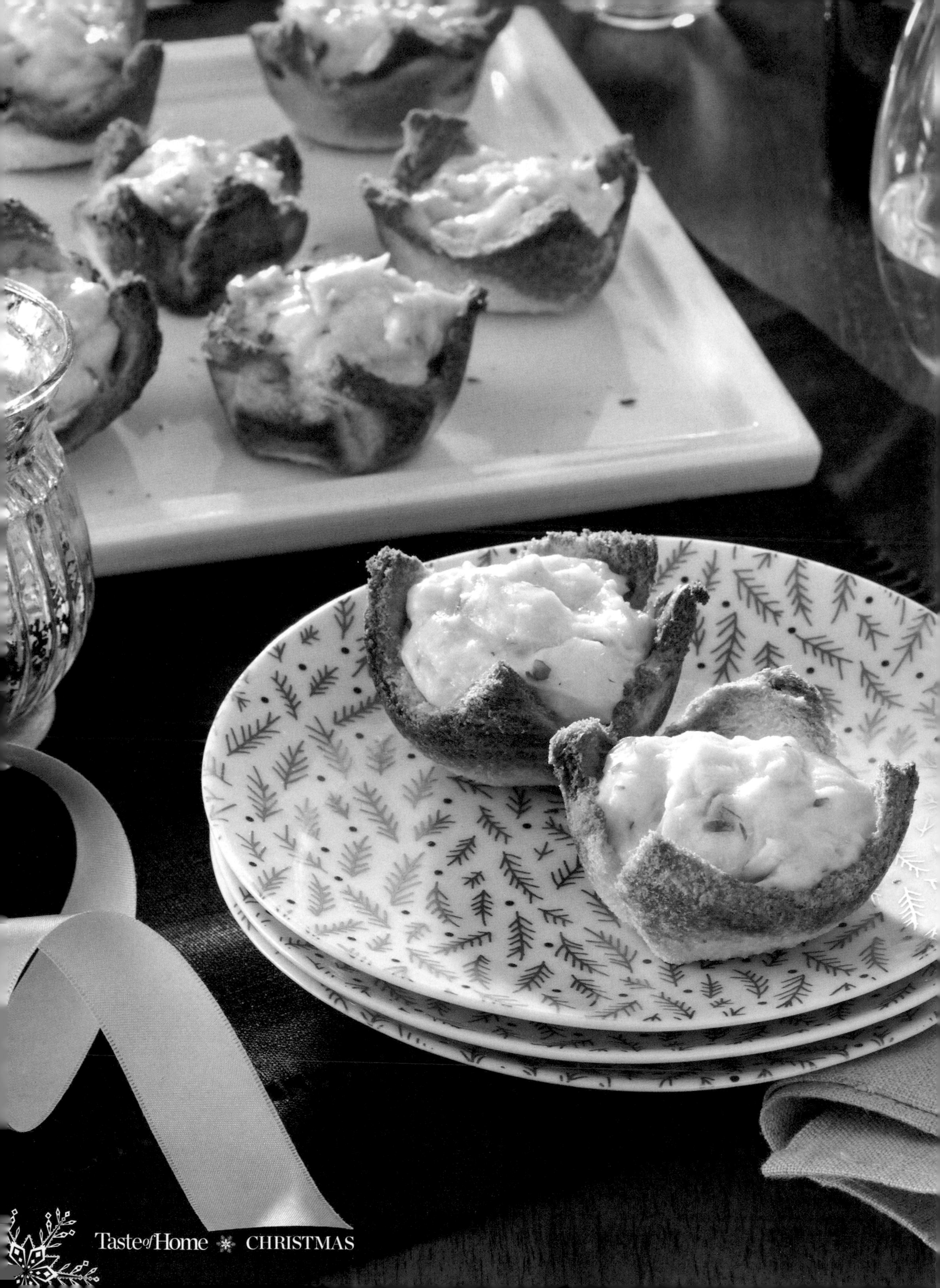

Creamy Crab Toast Cups

Seafood lovers will fall hook, line and sinker for these golden brown toasts filled with a creamy crab sauce. I use a standard-size muffin pan to quickly shape the rolled-out bread slices into little cups.

—VALERIE SCHRODER COBOURG, ON

PREP: 30 MIN. • **COOK:** 15 MIN.
MAKES: 12 SERVINGS

- 12 slices white bread, crusts removed
- ½ cup butter, melted

FILLING

- 3 tablespoons butter
- 2 tablespoons all-purpose flour
- 1¼ cups 2% milk
- 1 cup (4 ounces) shredded cheddar cheese
- 2 teaspoons lemon juice
- 1 teaspoon ground mustard
- 1 teaspoon Worcestershire sauce
- ½ teaspoon salt
- ⅛ teaspoon hot pepper sauce
- 2 cans (6 ounces each) lump crabmeat, drained
- 2 tablespoons minced fresh parsley
- 1 green onion, thinly sliced

1. Preheat oven to 350°. Flatten bread slices with a rolling pin. Brush both sides of bread with melted butter; press into muffin cups. Bake 12-15 minutes or until golden brown.
2. For filling, in a large saucepan, melt butter over medium heat. Stir in flour until smooth; gradually whisk in milk. Bring to a boil, stirring constantly; cook and stir 3-5 minutes or until thickened.
3. Add cheese, lemon juice, mustard, Worcestershire sauce, salt and pepper sauce; cook and stir until the cheese is melted. Stir in crab; heat through. Stir in minced parsley and green onion. Spoon into cups.

Holiday Helper

To easily form meatballs of equal size, lightly pat the meat mixture into a 1-in.-thick rectangle. Use a knife to cut the rectangle into the same number of squares as meatballs called for in the recipe. Gently roll each square into a ball.

Meatballs in Cherry Sauce

A cherry glaze made with pie filling gives homemade meatballs festive appeal for Christmas parties. Everyone will enjoy the zesty, sweet-tart flavor.

—RITA CHABOT-SCHULTZ BALLWIN, MO

PREP: 30 MIN. • **BAKE:** 15 MIN.
MAKES: ABOUT 3½ DOZEN

- 1 cup seasoned bread crumbs
- 1 small onion, chopped
- 1 egg, lightly beaten
- 3 garlic cloves, minced
- 1 teaspoon salt
- ½ teaspoon pepper
- 1 pound lean ground beef (90% lean)
- 1 pound ground pork

SAUCE

- 1 can (21 ounces) cherry pie filling
- ⅓ cup sherry or chicken broth
- ⅓ cup cider vinegar
- ¼ cup steak sauce
- 2 tablespoons brown sugar
- 2 tablespoons reduced-sodium soy sauce
- 1 teaspoon honey

1. Preheat oven to 400°. In a large bowl, combine the first six ingredients. Add the beef and pork; mix lightly but thoroughly. Shape into 1-in. balls. Place on a greased rack in a shallow baking pan. Bake 11-13 minutes or until cooked through. Drain on paper towels.
2. In a large saucepan, combine the sauce ingredients. Bring to a boil over medium heat, stirring constantly. Reduce heat; simmer, uncovered, 2-3 minutes or until thickened. Add the meatballs to sauce; heat through, stirring gently.

Smoked Mozzarella Flatbread Pizza

Top a refrigerated crust with portobello mushrooms, smoked mozzarella and prosciutto for a hearty starter. Made in a 15x10x1-in. pan, the pizza could also be cut into larger pieces and served as an entree.

—**EDWINA GADSBY** HAYDEN, ID

PREP: 25 MIN. • **BAKE:** 15 MIN.
MAKES: 24 SERVINGS

- 2 **tablespoons butter, divided**
- 2 **tablespoons olive oil, divided**
- ⅔ **cup sliced red onion**
- ½ **pound sliced baby portobello mushrooms**
- 1 **garlic clove, minced**
- 2 **teaspoons minced fresh rosemary or ½ teaspoon dried rosemary, crushed**
- 1 **tube (13.8 ounces) refrigerated pizza crust**
- 1½ **cups (6 ounces) shredded smoked mozzarella cheese**
- 2 **ounces sliced prosciutto or deli ham, finely chopped**

1. Preheat oven to 400°. In a large skillet, heat 1 tablespoon butter and 1 tablespoon oil over medium-high heat. Add the red onion; cook and stir 2-3 minutes or until softened. Reduce the heat to medium-low; cook 8-10 minutes or until golden brown, stirring occasionally. Remove from pan.

2. In same skillet, heat remaining butter and oil over medium-high heat. Add the mushrooms; cook and stir 2-3 minutes or until tender. Add garlic and rosemary; cook about 1-2 minutes longer or until liquid is evaporated.

3. Unroll and press dough onto bottom of a greased 15x10x1-in. baking pan. Using your fingertips, press several dimples into the dough. Sprinkle with ½ cup mozzarella cheese; top with the onion, mushroom mixture and prosciutto. Sprinkle with remaining cheese. Bake 15-18 minutes or until golden brown and cheese is melted.

Roasted Pepper & Feta Cheese Dip

Featuring roasted sweet red peppers and tangy feta, this comforting baked dip is sprinkled with panko bread crumbs. It's a crowd-pleaser I rely on again and again.

—**COURTNEY WRIGHT** BIRMINGHAM, AL

PREP: 15 MIN. • **BAKE:** 30 MIN.
MAKES: 16 SERVINGS (¼ CUP EACH)

- 4 **tablespoons butter, divided**
- ¾ **cup panko (Japanese) bread crumbs**
- 1 **shallot, finely chopped**
- 1 **package (8 ounces) cream cheese, softened**
- 2 **cups (8 ounces) crumbled feta cheese**
- ½ **cup mayonnaise**
- 1 **jar (12 ounces) roasted sweet red peppers, well drained and chopped Sliced French bread baguette or baked pita chips**

1. Preheat oven to 350°. In a large skillet, melt 3 tablespoons butter over medium heat. Add the bread crumbs and toss to coat evenly; cook and stir 2-3 minutes until golden brown. Remove from pan.

2. In same pan, heat remaining butter. Add shallot; cook and stir 1-2 minutes or until tender. Cool slightly.

3. In a large bowl, beat the cream cheese, feta cheese and mayonnaise until blended. Stir in the peppers and shallot. Transfer to an 8-in.-square baking dish. Sprinkle with toasted bread crumbs.

4. Bake 30-35 minutes or until bubbly. Serve with baguette slices.

> *"My brother shared his recipe for appetizer rolls with me years ago, and they've been a family favorite ever since. The delicate phyllo dough wraps around a zippy sausage filling."*
>
> —**KATTY CHIONG** HOFFMAN ESTATES, IL

Sausage Phyllo Rolls

PREP: 40 MIN. + COOLING • **BAKE:** 10 MIN.
MAKES: ABOUT 4½ DOZEN

- ¾ **pound bulk Italian sausage**
- 1 **small onion, chopped**
- 1 **celery rib, chopped**
- ½ **cup chopped fresh mushrooms**
- 2 **garlic cloves, minced**
- ¼ **cup chopped walnuts**
- ¼ **cup dried cranberries or raisins**
- ½ **teaspoon sugar**
- ¼ **teaspoon pepper**
- ⅛ **teaspoon cayenne pepper**
- 20 **sheets phyllo dough (14x9 inches)**
- ½ **cup butter, melted**
- 1⅓ **cups fresh baby spinach**
- ¼ **cup julienned roasted sweet red peppers**
- 1 **egg, lightly beaten**

1. Preheat oven to 400°. In a large skillet, cook the sausage, onion, celery, mushrooms and garlic over medium heat 6-8 minutes or until the sausage is no longer pink, breaking up sausage into crumbles; drain. Stir in walnuts, dried cranberries, sugar, pepper and cayenne pepper. Remove from pan; cool completely.

2. Place one sheet of phyllo dough on a work surface; brush lightly with butter. Layer with four additional phyllo sheets, brushing each layer. (Keep remaining phyllo covered with plastic wrap and a damp towel to prevent it from drying out.)

3. Arrange ⅓ cup spinach, a fourth of the sausage mixture and 1 tablespoon roasted peppers in a narrow row across bottom of phyllo within 1 in. of edges. Fold bottom edge of phyllo over filling, then roll up. Brush end of phyllo dough with butter and press to seal. Repeat three times. Place rolls on a 15x10x1-in. baking pan, seam side down.

4. Cut the rolls diagonally into 1-in. pieces (do not separate). Brush the tops with the remaining butter; brush again with beaten egg. Bake 10-12 minutes or until golden brown.

Cranberry-Raspberry Window Cookies

For elegant treats, try these lightly sweet goodies featuring a tart berry filling in a buttery sandwich cookie. They're perfect for everything from a Christmas appetizer buffet to an afternoon tea.

—**DEIRDRE COX** KANSAS CITY, MO

PREP: 50 MIN. + CHILLING
BAKE: 15 MIN./BATCH + COOLING
MAKES: ABOUT 2½ DOZEN

- 1⅓ cups all-purpose flour
- ⅓ cup confectioners' sugar
- 2 tablespoons sugar
- ¼ teaspoon salt
- ¾ cup cold unsalted butter, cubed
- 1½ teaspoons lime juice

FILLING

- 1 cup fresh or frozen cranberries, thawed
- ¾ cup seedless black raspberry spreadable fruit
- ⅓ cup sugar
- 1 tablespoon lime juice
  Confectioners' sugar

1. Place flour, confectioners' sugar, sugar and salt in a food processor; pulse until blended. Add butter; pulse until butter is the size of peas. Drizzle with lime juice and pulse just until moist crumbs form. Shape dough into a disk; wrap in plastic wrap. Refrigerate about 1 hour or until firm enough to roll.

2. For the filling, in a small saucepan, combine cranberries, spreadable fruit, sugar and lime juice. Bring to a boil, stirring to dissolve the sugar. Reduce heat to medium; cook, uncovered, 10-12 minutes or until the berries pop and the mixture is thickened, stirring occasionally. Remove from heat; cool slightly. Process in a food processor until blended; cool completely.

3. Preheat oven to 325°. On a lightly floured surface, roll the dough to ⅛-in. thickness. Cut with a floured 1¾-in. scalloped round cookie cutter.

4. Using a floured ¾-in. round cookie cutter, cut out the centers of half of the cookies. Place the solid and window cookies 1 in. apart on greased baking sheets. Bake 12-15 minutes or until golden brown. Remove from pans to wire racks to cool completely.

5. Spread filling on bottoms of solid cookies; top with window cookies. Dust with confectioners' sugar.

Sugar-and-Spice Candied Nuts

Here's a crowd-pleasing snack you'll want to have on hand for entertaining, gift-giving or munching anytime. With a sweet-spicy coating, the crunchy nuts are always a hit.
—**TONYA BURKHARD** DAVIS, IL

START TO FINISH: 30 MIN.
MAKES: 2½ CUPS

- ¼ cup sugar
- 2 tablespoons light corn syrup
- 1 tablespoon butter
- ¾ teaspoon ground ginger
- ¾ teaspoon ground cinnamon
- ¼ teaspoon salt
- ¼ teaspoon ground nutmeg
- 2 cups mixed nuts

1. Preheat oven to 350°. Line a 15x10x1-in. baking pan with foil; grease foil. In a small saucepan, combine the first seven ingredients. Bring to a boil over medium heat, stirring constantly to dissolve the sugar. Remove from heat. Add the nuts; toss to coat. Spread into the prepared pan.

2. Bake 12-15 minutes or until bubbly, stirring once. Immediately transfer candied nuts to waxed paper; cool completely. Break into pieces. Store in an airtight container.

Crisp Moroccan Appetizer Rolls

I love the distinctive flavors and textures of Moroccan food. I've also experimented many times with spring roll wrappers, so I decided to combine those two favorites into a fun fried appetizer for parties.
—**SARAH VINCH** YIGO, GUAM

PREP: 45 MIN. • **COOK:** 5 MIN./BATCH
MAKES: 3½ DOZEN

- 1¾ cups water
- 1¾ cups uncooked couscous
- 2 cups shredded carrots
- ½ cup golden raisins
- ½ cup pitted dates
- 2 tablespoons apricot spreadable fruit
- 1 tablespoon olive oil
- 1 small onion, finely chopped
- 1 garlic clove, minced
- 1 package (12 ounces) frozen vegetarian meat crumbles
- 1 teaspoon salt
- ½ teaspoon chili powder
- ¼ teaspoon ground cinnamon
- ¼ teaspoon ground cloves
- ¼ teaspoon ground cumin
- ¼ teaspoon ground ginger
- 42 spring roll wrappers
  Oil for deep-fat frying
  Honey

1. In a small saucepan, bring water to a boil. Stir in couscous. Remove from heat; let stand, covered, 4-6 minutes or until the water is absorbed. Fluff with a fork.

2. Place the carrots, raisins, dates and spreadable fruit in a food processor; pulse until fruit is coarsely chopped. In a Dutch oven, heat the oil over medium heat. Add the onion; cook and stir 2-3 minutes or until tender. Add the garlic; cook 1 minute longer. Stir in vegetarian crumbles, carrot mixture and seasonings; heat through, stirring occasionally. Remove from heat; stir in couscous.

3. With one side of a wrapper facing you, place 3 tablespoons filling just below the center of wrapper. (Cover the remaining wrappers with a damp paper towel until ready to use.) Fold the bottom side over filling; moisten remaining wrapper edges with water. Fold sides toward center over filling. Roll up tightly, pressing edge to seal.

4. In an electric skillet or deep-fat fryer, heat oil to 375°. Fry the rolls, a few at a time, 3-4 minutes or until golden brown, turning frequently. Drain on paper towels. Serve with honey for dipping.

FREEZE OPTION *Cover and freeze unfried rolls on waxed paper-lined baking sheets until firm. Transfer to resealable plastic freezer bags; return to freezer. To use, fry and serve rolls as recipe directs, increasing cooking time to 4-5 minutes.*

NOTE *Vegetarian meat crumbles are a nutritious protein source made from soy. Look for them in the natural foods freezer section of your grocery store.*

Bacon & Sun-Dried Tomato Phyllo Tarts

PREP: 40 MIN. • **BAKE:** 10 MIN.
MAKES: 45 TARTLETS

- 2 teaspoons olive oil
- ¾ cup chopped onion (about 1 medium)
- ¾ cup chopped green pepper (about 1 small)
- ¾ cup chopped sweet red pepper (about 1 small)
- 1 garlic clove, minced
  Dash dried oregano
- 3 packages (1.9 ounces each) frozen miniature phyllo tart shells
- 1 package (8 ounces) cream cheese, softened
- 1½ teaspoons lemon juice
- ⅛ teaspoon salt
- 1 egg, lightly beaten
- ½ cup oil-packed sun-dried tomatoes, chopped and patted dry
- 2 bacon strips, cooked and crumbled
- 1 tablespoon minced fresh basil or 1 teaspoon dried basil
- ½ cup crushed butter-flavored crackers
- ½ cup shredded cheddar cheese

1. Preheat oven to 350°. In a large skillet, heat oil over medium-high heat. Add onion and peppers; cook and stir 6-8 minutes or until tender. Add garlic and oregano; cook 1 minute longer. Cool completely.

2. Place phyllo tart shells on ungreased baking sheets. In a large bowl, beat the cream cheese, lemon juice and salt until smooth. Add egg; beat on low speed just until blended. Stir in tomatoes, bacon, basil and onion mixture.

3. Spoon 2 teaspoons filling into each tart shell. Top each with ½ teaspoon crushed crackers and ½ teaspoon cheddar cheese.

4. Bake 10-12 minutes or until set. Serve warm.

FREEZE OPTION *Freeze the cooled baked pastries in freezer containers. To use, reheat pastries on a baking sheet in a preheated 350° oven 15-18 minutes or until heated through.*

"Frozen mini phyllo tart shells are so convenient and easy to use. Simply add a savory filling featuring sun-dried tomatoes and bacon, then pop them in the oven."

—PATRICIA QUINN OMAHA, NE

Artichoke-Walnut Cheese Ball

I like to pair this rich, flavorful spread with a variety of crackers, fresh vegetables or sliced apples. But my best friend thinks it tastes best on slices of garlic bread. Give the cheese ball extra color and appeal for parties with a sprinkling of minced parsley and more of the toasted nuts.

—AYSHA SCHURMAN AMMON, ID

PREP: 20 MIN. + CHILLING • **MAKES:** 1½ CUPS

- 1 package (8 ounces) cream cheese, softened
- 1 jar (6 ounces) marinated quartered artichoke hearts, drained and finely chopped
- 6 tablespoons chopped toasted walnuts, divided
- ¼ cup crumbled feta cheese
- 2 tablespoons grated Romano cheese
- 1 green onion, finely chopped
- 1 tablespoon minced roasted garlic
- ½ teaspoon pepper
- 1 tablespoon minced fresh parsley
  Assorted crackers, fresh vegetables or sliced apples

1. In a large bowl, beat cream cheese until smooth. Beat in artichokes, 4 tablespoons nuts, remaining cheeses, onion, garlic and pepper until blended. Refrigerate mixture, covered, 1 hour or until firm enough to shape.

2. Shape cheese mixture into a ball; place on a serving plate. Sprinkle with parsley and remaining walnuts. Serve with crackers.

NOTE *To make your own roasted garlic, remove the papery outer skin from three garlic bulbs, but do not peel or separate cloves. Cut off the top of garlic bulbs, exposing the individual cloves. Drizzle cut cloves with 2-3 teaspoons olive oil. Wrap the bulbs individually in heavy-duty foil. Bake in a preheated 425° oven for 30-35 minutes or until cloves are very soft. Unwrap and cool 10 minutes. Squeeze garlic from skins. Mash with a fork. Refrigerate leftover roasted garlic in an airtight container for up to 1 week.*

Cashew & Olive Feta Cheese Dip

My bold cheese dip goes well with mellow baked pita chips. For guests who have milder tastes, I reduce the amount of red pepper.
—**SONYA LABBE** WEST HOLLYWOOD, CA

START TO FINISH: 15 MIN. • **MAKES:** 1½ CUPS

- 1½ cups (6 ounces) crumbled feta cheese
- ½ cup lightly salted cashews
- ¼ cup 2% milk
- 1 tablespoon lemon juice
- 1 teaspoon dried oregano
- ¼ teaspoon crushed red pepper flakes
- ¼ teaspoon pepper
- 3 tablespoons chopped pitted green olives, divided
- 3 tablespoons chopped pitted kalamata olives, divided
  Baked pita chips

1. Place the first seven ingredients in a food processor; process until smooth. Add 2 tablespoons green olives and 2 tablespoons kalamata olives; pulse just until combined.
2. Transfer to a serving dish; sprinkle with remaining olives. Serve with pita chips. Refrigerate leftovers.

Baked Baby Potatoes with Olive Pesto

These little cuties pack all the appeal of a dinner-sized baked potato into the perfect one-bite appetizer. I top off each spud with homemade pesto, sour cream and coarsely ground pepper.
—**SARAH SHAIKH** MUMBAI, INDIA

PREP: 35 MIN. • **BAKE:** 30 MIN. • **MAKES:** ABOUT 3 DOZEN

- 3 pounds baby red potatoes (1¾ inch wide, about 36)
- 6 tablespoons olive oil, divided
- 2 teaspoons salt
- 1½ cups pimiento-stuffed olives
- ½ cup chopped onion
- ¼ cup pine nuts, toasted
- 2 garlic cloves, minced
- ½ cup sour cream
  Coarsely ground pepper, optional

1. Preheat oven to 400°. Place potatoes in a large bowl. Add 2 tablespoons oil and salt; toss to coat. Transfer to a greased 15x10x1-in. baking pan. Bake 30-35 minutes or until tender.
2. Meanwhile, place the olives, onion, pine nuts and garlic in a food processor; pulse until chopped. Gradually add the remaining oil; process to reach desired consistency.
3. When potatoes are cool enough to handle, cut thin slices off bottoms to allow potatoes to sit upright. Cut an X in the top of each potato; squeeze sides to open tops slightly. Place on a serving platter.
4. Spoon the olive pesto onto potatoes; top with sour cream. If desired, sprinkle with pepper. Serve warm.
NOTE *To toast nuts, spread in a 15x10x1-in. baking pan. Bake at 350° for 5-10 minutes or until lightly browned, stirring occasionally. Or, spread in a dry nonstick skillet and heat over low heat until lightly browned, stirring occasionally.*

Arranging a Cork Centerpiece

Make a splash at a wine-tasting party with this elegant table accent. Just place a small square vase inside a larger one, filling the space in between with corks. Pine sprigs in the center add the finishing touch.

Apple, Pecan & Goat Cheese Pastries

Party-goers will think you spent hours in the kitchen preparing gourmet pastries. Only you will know this recipe requires just 20 minutes of prep time, 15 minutes of baking and five simple ingredients!
—**HEATHER FOKY** HOWLAND, OH

PREP: 20 MIN. • **BAKE:** 15 MIN.
MAKES: 1½ DOZEN

- 1 large apple, peeled and finely chopped
- 1 log (4 ounces) honey-flavored fresh goat cheese
- ½ cup finely chopped pecans
- 1 package (17.3 ounces) frozen puff pastry, thawed
- ¼ teaspoon ground cinnamon

1. Preheat oven to 400°. In a small bowl, mix the apple, goat cheese and the pecans.
2. Unfold the puff pastry sheets. Cut each sheet into nine 3-in. squares; separate the squares slightly. Place 4 teaspoons apple mixture in the center of each square. Lightly brush the edges of pastry with water. Bring together the four corners of pastry over filling; pinch corners and seams to seal. Sprinkle tops with cinnamon.
3. Place pastries on greased baking sheets. Bake 15-18 minutes or until golden brown. Serve warm. Refrigerate leftovers.

Holiday Helper

Before handling puff pastry, thaw it at room temperature for about 20 minutes. When preparing a recipe, handle the pastry as little as possible to avoid stretching and tearing. Cut it with a sharp knife or cutter for a clean edge.

Southern-Style Egg Rolls

Sausage, black-eyed peas and turnip greens give these distinctive egg rolls a decidedly Southern accent. When I bring a batch of them to a party, I always come home with an empty plate.
—HOLLY JONES KENNESAW, GA

PREP: 40 MIN. • **COOK:** 5 MIN./BATCH
MAKES: 2 DOZEN (2⅓ CUPS SAUCE)

SAUCE
- 1 cup mayonnaise
- ½ cup sour cream
- ½ cup Dijon mustard
- ¼ cup honey
- 1 tablespoon prepared horseradish
- 1 teaspoon garlic powder
- 1 teaspoon Worcestershire sauce

EGG ROLLS
- 1 pound bulk pork sausage
- 1 package (8 ounces) cream cheese, softened
- 2 green onions, chopped
- 1 teaspoon reduced-sodium soy sauce
- ½ teaspoon garlic powder
- 1 package (16 ounces) frozen turnip greens, thawed and squeezed dry
- 2 cups (8 ounces) shredded pepper jack cheese
- 1 cup canned black-eyed peas
- 24 egg roll wrappers
  Oil for deep-fat frying

1. In a small bowl, mix the sauce ingredients until blended. Refrigerate, covered, until serving.

2. For egg rolls, in a large skillet, cook sausage over medium heat 6-8 minutes or until no longer pink, breaking into crumbles; drain. Cool slightly.

3. In a large bowl, beat the cream cheese, green onions, soy sauce and garlic powder until blended; stir in the turnip greens, pepper jack cheese, black-eyed peas and sausage.

4. With one corner of an egg roll wrapper facing you, place 3 tablespoons filling just below the center of wrapper. (Cover remaining wrappers with a damp paper towel until ready to use.) Fold bottom corner over filling; moisten the remaining wrapper edges with water. Fold side corners toward center over filling. Roll egg roll up tightly, pressing at the tip to seal. Repeat.

5. In an electric skillet or deep-fat fryer, heat oil to 375°. Fry rolls, a few at a time, 3-4 minutes or until golden brown, turning occasionally. Drain on paper towels. Serve with sauce.

Smoked-Almond Cheese Toasts

I created my recipe for appetizer toasts while planning the menu for a friend's bridal luncheon. Smoked almonds add a special touch to the chunky cheese spread.
—LAURA MURPHY COLUMBUS, MS

START TO FINISH: 30 MIN.
MAKES: ABOUT 3 DOZEN

- ¾ cup whipped cream cheese, softened
- 2 tablespoons 2% milk
- 1 cup (4 ounces) shredded sharp cheddar cheese
- 1 cup (4 ounces) shredded Swiss cheese
- ¾ cup chopped smoked almonds
- ½ cup soft sun-dried tomato halves (not packed in oil), chopped
- ⅛ teaspoon pepper
- 1 French bread baguette (10½ ounces), cut into ¼-inch slices

1. Preheat oven to 350°. In a large bowl, beat the cream cheese and milk until smooth. Stir in cheeses, almonds, sun-dried tomato and pepper; spread over bread slices.

2. Place on ungreased baking sheets. Bake 10-12 minutes or until the cheese is melted.

NOTE *This recipe was tested with sun-dried tomatoes that are ready to use without soaking. When using other sun-dried tomatoes that are not oil-packed, cover them with boiling water and let them stand until soft. Drain before using.*

christmas
FEASTS

Blue Cheese-Mushroom Stuffed Tenderloin

Here's my go-to entree for just about any special occasion. Loaded with a savory stuffing, the sliced beef looks and tastes like a dish from an upscale restaurant.

—**JOYCE CONWAY** WESTERVILLE, OH

PREP: 25 MIN. • **BAKE:** 40 MIN. + STANDING
MAKES: 8 SERVINGS

- 2 **tablespoons butter**
- ½ **pound sliced baby portobello mushrooms**
- 1 **tablespoon Worcestershire sauce**
- 3 **tablespoons horseradish mustard or spicy brown mustard**
- 1 **tablespoon coarsely ground pepper**
- 1 **tablespoon olive oil**
- 1 **teaspoon salt**
- 1 **beef tenderloin roast (4 pounds)**
- ¾ **cup crumbled blue cheese, divided**
- 1½ **cups French-fried onions**
    Additional French-fried onions, optional

1. Preheat oven to 425°. In a small skillet, heat butter over medium-high heat. Add portobello mushrooms and Worcestershire sauce; cook and stir 6-8 minutes or until mushrooms are tender. In a small bowl, mix mustard, pepper, oil and salt.

2. Cut lengthwise through the center of the roast to within ½ in. of bottom. Open the roast flat; cover with plastic wrap. Pound with a meat mallet to ¾-in. thickness.

3. Remove plastic. Spread mushrooms down center of roast to within ½ in. of ends; top with ½ cup blue cheese and the onions. Close roast; tie at 1½-in. intervals with kitchen string. Secure ends with toothpicks.

4. Place roast on a rack in a shallow roasting pan; spread with the mustard mixture. Roast 40-50 minutes or until the meat reaches desired doneness (for medium-rare, a thermometer should read 145°; medium, 160°; well-done, 170°).

5. Remove roast from oven; tent with foil. Let stand 15 minutes before slicing. Remove string and toothpicks. Top servings with remaining cheese. If desired, warm additional onions in microwave and sprinkle over tops.

Mixed Greens with Olives & Red Pepper

When it comes to Christmas dinner, an ordinary salad just won't do. Plain greens become festive when you toss in colorful ingredients. I like to add vibrant sun-dried tomatoes, sweet red pepper, red onion, ripe olives and croutons. Top it all off with your favorite Italian dressing.

—**NADINE MESCH** MOUNT HEALTHY, OH

START TO FINISH: 10 MIN.
MAKES: 6 SERVINGS

- 6 **cups torn mixed salad greens**
- 1 **cup garlic salad croutons**
- ½ **cup sliced ripe olives**
- ¼ **cup thinly sliced red onion**
- ¼ **cup thinly sliced sweet red pepper**
- ¼ **cup julienned oil-packed sun-dried tomatoes**
- ¼ **cup Italian salad dressing**

In a large bowl, combine the salad greens, croutons, olives, onion, pepper and tomatoes. Drizzle with Italian dressing; toss to coat.

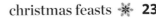

Stilton, Bacon & Garlic Smashed Potatoes

The bold flavors of Stilton cheese, bacon and garlic take mashed potatoes to a whole new level. They're so rich and satisfying, you could eat them as an entree!

—JAMIE BROWN-MILLER NAPA, CA

PREP: 25 MIN. • **BAKE:** 35 MIN. + COOLING
MAKES: 8 SERVINGS

- 6 **garlic cloves**
- 1 **teaspoon olive oil**
- 2 **pounds small red potatoes**
- ½ **cup butter, softened**
- ½ **cup cream cheese, softened**
- ¼ **to ⅓ cup 2% milk**
- ½ **cup (2 ounces) Stilton cheese**
- 6 **bacon strips, cooked and crumbled**
- 3 **tablespoons minced fresh parsley, divided**
- 1 **teaspoon coarsely ground pepper**
- ½ **teaspoon salt**

1. Preheat oven to 400°. Cut the stem ends off unpeeled garlic cloves. Place cloves on a piece of foil. Drizzle with oil; wrap in foil. Bake 35 minutes or until cloves are soft.

2. Meanwhile, place the potatoes in a Dutch oven; add water to cover. Bring to a boil. Reduce heat; cook, uncovered, 15-20 minutes or until tender.

3. Unwrap the garlic cloves; cool 10 minutes. Squeeze the garlic from skins. Mash with a fork.

4. Drain the potatoes; return to the pan. Coarsely mash the potatoes, gradually adding the butter, cream cheese and enough milk to reach the desired consistency. Stir in the Stilton cheese, bacon, 2 tablespoons parsley, pepper and salt. Sprinkle with the remaining parsley.

Fennel Carrot Soup

This smooth, golden soup can make a wonderful first course for your Christmas feast...or a comforting side for a sandwich anytime. The vegetables and apple are accented with fennel seed and curry.

—MARLENE BURSEY WAVERLY, NS

PREP: 10 MIN. • **COOK:** 45 MIN.
MAKES: 8 SERVINGS

- 1 tablespoon butter
- ½ teaspoon fennel seed
- 1½ pounds carrots, sliced
- 1 medium sweet potato, peeled and cubed
- 1 medium apple, peeled and cubed
- 3 cans (14½ ounces each) vegetable broth
- 2 tablespoons uncooked long grain rice
- 1 bay leaf
- ¼ teaspoon curry powder
- 1 tablespoon lemon juice
- 1 teaspoon salt
- ¼ teaspoon white pepper
- 2 tablespoons minced fresh parsley

1. In a large saucepan, melt butter over medium-high heat. Add fennel; cook and stir 2-3 minutes or until lightly toasted. Add carrots, sweet potato and apple; cook and stir 5 minutes longer.

2. Stir in the vegetable broth, rice, bay leaf and curry powder; bring to a boil. Reduce the heat; simmer, covered, 30 minutes or until the vegetables and rice are soft.

3. Remove from heat; cool slightly. Discard the bay leaf. Process in batches in a blender until smooth; return to the pan. Stir in the lemon juice, salt and white pepper. Cook over medium heat 5 minutes or until heated through, stirring occasionally. Sprinkle with minced parsley.

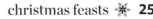

Raspberry & Cream Cheese Pastries

I wanted to surprise my grown daughter with a different dessert for her birthday. The puff pastry tarts I dressed up have a chocolaty center and a splash of amaretto.

—JENNIFER ZUK BURNABY, BC

PREP: 15 MIN. + COOLING
BAKE: 20 MIN. + COOLING
MAKES: 1 DOZEN

- 2 **packages (10 ounces each) frozen puff pastry shells**
- 2 **tablespoons sugar**
- 5 **tablespoons amaretto, divided**
- ½ **cup sliced almonds**
- ½ **cup seedless raspberry jam**
- 1 **package (8 ounces) cream cheese, softened**
- 6 **ounces white baking chocolate, melted and cooled**
- 1 **ounce semisweet chocolate, chopped**
- 1 **teaspoon canola oil**
- 12 **fresh raspberries**

1. Bake puff pastry shells according to package directions. Cool completely.
2. Meanwhile, in a heavy skillet, combine the sugar and 1 tablespoon amaretto. Cook and stir over medium heat 3-4 minutes or until the sugar is dissolved. Add almonds; cook and stir until golden brown, about 2-3 minutes. Spread on foil to cool completely.
3. In a small bowl, whisk the jam and 2 tablespoons amaretto until blended. Spoon into pastry shells.
4. In a large bowl, beat the cream cheese and remaining amaretto until smooth; gradually beat in the cooled white chocolate. Spoon over the jam mixture. Sprinkle with the candied almonds.
5. In a microwave, melt semisweet chocolate with oil; stir until smooth. Drizzle over tarts; top with raspberries. Refrigerate until serving.

Spiced Mulled Wine

PREP: 5 MIN. **COOK:** 30 MIN.
MAKES: 6 SERVINGS

- 1 bottle (750 ml) ruby port
- 1 bottle (750 ml) merlot
- ½ cup sugar
- 4 orange peel strips (1 to 3 inches)
- 2 cinnamon sticks (3 inches)
- 8 whole allspice
- 6 whole cloves

In a large saucepan, combine all ingredients; bring just to a simmer (do not boil). Reduce heat; simmer gently, uncovered, 30 minutes or until flavors are blended, stirring to dissolve sugar. Strain. Serve warm.

Pear Place Card

From light green to vibrant red, pears add beautiful natural color to holiday tables. Try this idea: Cut out circles and leaf shapes from coordinating card stock and write a guest's name on each leaf. Align the outer edges of each leaf with a circle and punch a hole through both pieces. Then simply thread a cord through the hole and tie the pieces to the stem of a small pear.

"Warm up friends and family on those chilly winter evenings with this classic yuletide beverage. As it simmers, your home will fill with the Christmasy scent of citrus and spice."

—LANA GRYGA GLEN FLORA, WI

Buttery Lemon Turkey

A simple seasoned butter featuring a dash of hot sauce and a splash of lemon adds all the flavor you could want to a Christmas turkey. Even cooks who have never made one will find the recipe easy.

—SHARON TIPTON WINTER GARDEN, FL

PREP: 15 MIN.
BAKE: 2½ HOURS + STANDING
MAKES: 12 SERVINGS

- ¾ **cup butter, melted**
- ½ **cup lemon juice**
- 2 **teaspoons paprika**
- 1 **teaspoon sugar**
- 1 **teaspoon salt**
- ½ **teaspoon pepper**
- ¼ **teaspoon ground mustard**
- ⅛ **teaspoon hot pepper sauce**
- 1 **turkey (10 to 12 pounds)**

1. Preheat oven to 325°. In a small bowl, whisk the first eight ingredients until blended; reserve ¼ cup mixture for brushing turkey after roasting.
2. Place turkey on a rack in a shallow roasting pan, breast side up. Tuck wings under turkey; tie drumsticks together. Roast, uncovered, 2 hours, basting occasionally with remaining butter mixture.
3. Roast 30-60 minutes longer or until a thermometer inserted in thigh reads 180°. Baste occasionally with the pan drippings.
4. Remove turkey from oven. Warm reserved butter mixture to melt butter; brush over turkey. Tent with foil. Let stand 20 minutes before carving.

Carving a Whole Turkey

The last step before serving delicious Buttery Lemon Turkey (recipe at left) is carving. To get that mouthwatering meat on your holiday table without delay, sharpen up your knife and refer to the simple step-by-step photos here. You'll soon be carving like a pro!

1. Place the turkey on a carving board (remove stuffing if added). Holding the end of the drumstick, pull the leg away from the body and cut between the thigh joint and body to remove the entire leg. Repeat with the other leg.

2. To separate the drumstick and thigh, cut through the connecting joint.

3. Hold the drumstick by the end and slice the meat into ¼-in. slices. Cut the thigh meat parallel to the bone into ¼-in. slices.

4. Holding the turkey with a meat fork, make a deep cut in the breast meat just above the wing area.

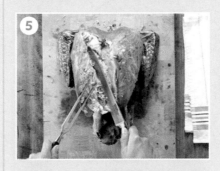

5. Slice down from the top of the breast into the cut made in Step 4. Slice the meat ¼ in. thick. Repeat Steps 4-5 on the other side.

6. To remove the turkey wings, cut through the connecting joints by the wing bones and backbone.

Savory Roasted Carrots with Mushrooms

You'll need only 10 minutes to get these flavorful veggies ready for the oven. Then just stir them a few times during roasting.

—**PAM CORDER** MONROE, LA

PREP: 10 MIN. • **BAKE:** 45 MIN.
MAKES: 4 SERVINGS

- 1 **pound fresh baby carrots**
- 1 **medium onion, cut into small wedges**
- ½ **pound small fresh mushrooms**
- ¼ **cup butter, melted**
- 2 **tablespoons Worcestershire sauce**
- 2 **garlic cloves, minced**
- ¼ to ½ **teaspoon salt**
- ¼ **teaspoon pepper**

1. Preheat oven to 425°. Place the baby carrots, onion wedges and mushrooms in a greased 15x10x1-in. baking pan.

2. In a small bowl, mix the remaining ingredients; drizzle over the vegetables and toss to coat. Roast 45-55 minutes or until the carrots are tender, stirring occasionally.

Surprise Herb Rolls

My mother and I came up with a new roll recipe one year for holiday guests, and we got lots of compliments. The basil, thyme, oregano and other herbs make frozen dough taste like a homemade treat.

—**HANNAH HEINRITZ** MENOMONEE FALLS, WI

PREP: 20 MIN. + RISING • **BAKE:** 20 MIN.
MAKES: 1 DOZEN

- ½ **cup sour cream**
- ⅛ **teaspoon dried basil**
- ⅛ **teaspoon dried marjoram**
- ⅛ **teaspoon dried oregano**
- ⅛ **teaspoon dried parsley flakes**
- ⅛ **teaspoon dried rosemary, crushed**
- ⅛ **teaspoon dried thyme**
  Dash rubbed sage
- 1 **loaf (1 pound) frozen bread dough, thawed**
- 2 **tablespoons butter, melted**
- 3 **tablespoons grated Parmesan cheese**

1. In a small bowl, mix the sour cream and herbs until blended. Divide the dough into 12 portions. On a lightly floured surface, roll each into a 4-in. circle. Top each with 2 teaspoons sour cream mixture; bring edges of dough up over filling and pinch to seal.
2. Place in greased muffin cups, seam side down. Cover with kitchen towels; let rise in a warm place until doubled, about 45 minutes. Preheat oven to 350°.
3. Brush the tops with melted butter; sprinkle with Parmesan cheese. Bake 18-20 minutes or until golden brown.

Holiday Helper

It's easy to serve molded pats of butter with rolls on a buffet—and they look so special! I purchase candy molds in seasonal shapes. Then I soften butter, press it into the molds and chill them in the fridge. There's very little fuss, and guests like the fun presentation.

—**ANNA R.** ALBUQUERQUE, NM

Parmesan-Baked Mashed Potatoes

This comforting side dish is a family favorite for Christmas dinner. Whether the main course is ham or turkey, everyone wants a big scoop of Parmesan mashed potatoes alongside.

—ROSEMARY JANZ CONCORD, NC

PREP: 20 MIN. • **BAKE:** 25 MIN. • **MAKES:** 4 SERVINGS

- 1¾ pounds red potatoes (about 6 medium), peeled and cubed
- ⅔ cup sour cream
- 2 egg whites, lightly beaten
- ¼ cup butter
- ¼ cup minced fresh parsley
- 2 green onions, thinly sliced
- ¾ teaspoon salt
- ¼ teaspoon pepper
  Dash ground nutmeg
- 3 tablespoons grated Parmesan cheese

1. Preheat oven to 400°. Place potatoes in a large saucepan; add water to cover. Bring to a boil. Reduce the heat; cook, uncovered, 10-15 minutes or until tender.

2. Drain; return to the pan. Mash potatoes, gradually adding sour cream, egg whites and butter. Stir in the parsley, green onions, salt, pepper and nutmeg.

3. Transfer to a greased 1½-qt. baking dish; sprinkle with cheese. Bake 25-30 minutes or until golden brown.

Layered Christmas Gelatin

My jewel-tone gelatin always makes an appearance on our yuletide table. Filled with cranberry sauce, pineapple and cream cheese, the sweet-tart salad could even be served as a dessert.

—DIANE SCHEFELKER IRETON, IA

PREP: 30 MIN. + CHILLING • **MAKES:** 10 SERVINGS

- 1 package (3 ounces) lime gelatin
- 1 cup boiling water
- ⅓ cup unsweetened pineapple juice
- 1 cup crushed pineapple, drained

CREAM CHEESE LAYER
- 1 teaspoon unflavored gelatin
- 2 tablespoons cold water
- 1 package (8 ounces) cream cheese, softened
- ⅓ cup milk

BERRY LAYER
- 2 packages (3 ounces each) strawberry gelatin
- 2 cups boiling water
- 1 can (14 ounces) whole-berry cranberry sauce
  Whipped topping, optional

1. Dissolve lime gelatin in boiling water; stir in pineapple juice. Stir in pineapple. Pour into an 11-in. x 7-in. dish; refrigerate until set.

2. In a small saucepan, sprinkle the unflavored gelatin over cold water; let stand for 1 minute. Heat over low heat, stirring until gelatin is completely dissolved. Transfer to a small bowl. Beat in cream cheese and milk until smooth. Spread over lime layer; refrigerate until set.

3. Dissolve the strawberry gelatin in boiling water; stir in cranberry sauce. Cool for 10 minutes. Carefully spoon over cream cheese layer. Refrigerate until set.

4. Cut into squares. Garnish with whipped topping if desired.

Citrus-Kissed
Sweet Potato Layer Cake

Here's a yummy way to use up extra sweet potatoes! I prevent them from becoming discolored after grating by keeping them loosely covered with a damp paper towel.
—**DEBORAH BIGGS** OMAHA, NE

PREP: 35 MIN. • **BAKE:** 45 MIN. + COOLING
MAKES: 12 SERVINGS

- 2 **cups sugar**
- 1½ **cups canola oil**
- 4 **eggs**
- 1 **tablespoon grated orange peel**
- 2½ **cups all-purpose flour**
- 2 **teaspoons baking soda**
- 1¾ **teaspoons pumpkin pie spice**
- ¾ **teaspoon salt**

- 3 **cups shredded peeled sweet potatoes (about 9 ounces)**

FROSTING
- 1 **package (8 ounces) cream cheese, softened**
- ½ **cup butter, softened**
- 3½ **cups confectioners' sugar**
- 1½ **teaspoons grated orange or lemon peel**
- 1½ **teaspoons lemon juice**
- ⅛ **teaspoon orange or lemon extract**
  Orange peel strips

1. Preheat oven to 325°. Line bottoms of two greased 9-in. round baking pans with parchment paper; grease paper.
2. In a large bowl, beat the sugar, oil, eggs and orange peel until well blended. In another bowl, whisk the flour, baking soda, pumpkin pie spice and salt; gradually beat into the sugar mixture. Stir in sweet potatoes.
3. Transfer to prepared pans. Bake 45-50 minutes or until a toothpick inserted in center comes out clean. Cool in the pans 10 minutes before removing to wire racks; remove paper. Cool completely.
4. For the frosting, in a large bowl, beat cream cheese and butter until blended. Gradually beat in confectioners' sugar, orange peel, lemon juice and extract until smooth. Spread frosting between the layers and over the top and sides of the cake. Decorate with orange peel. Refrigerate leftovers.

Holiday Baked Ham

One of the best things about the yuletide season is the aroma of a baking ham—and the anticipation it creates of the feast to come! The simple but tasty glaze in this recipe is sure to please guests.

—**STACY DUFFY** CHICAGO, IL

PREP: 10 MIN. • **BAKE:** 1¾ HOURS
MAKES: 16 SERVINGS

- 1 **fully cooked smoked half ham (6 to 7 pounds)**
- 1 **tablespoon whole cloves**
- ¼ **cup apricot preserves**
- 1 **tablespoon butter**
- 2 **teaspoons Dijon mustard**

1. Preheat oven to 325°. Place the ham on a rack in a shallow roasting pan. Using a sharp knife, score the surface of the ham with ¼-in.-deep cuts in a diamond pattern; insert a whole clove in each diamond. Bake, uncovered, 1¼ hours.

2. Meanwhile, in a small saucepan, combine the apricot preserves, butter and Dijon mustard; heat through. Remove the ham from the oven. Spoon the preserves mixture over ham. Bake, uncovered, 30-40 minutes longer or until a thermometer reads 140°.

Holiday Helper

When I have extra ham from a Christmas meal or other holiday, I cube the leftovers, place them in a freezer bag and store them in the freezer. The ham makes a tasty addition to so many dishes, from scrambled eggs and potato soup to macaroni and cheese.

—**RUBY W.** BOGALUSA, LA

"Chunks of apples and sausage bring a delicious, sweet-and-savory contrast to a side dish of rice. My husband really loves it, and the prep work takes only 15 minutes."

—**REBECCA MCINTIRE** MANITOU SPRINGS, CO

Apple & Sausage Wild Rice

PREP: 15 MIN. • **COOK:** 1 HOUR
MAKES: 4 SERVINGS

- 2 **tablespoons olive oil**
- 5 **ounces summer sausage, cut into ¼-inch cubes**
- 2 **celery ribs, chopped**
- 1 **small onion, finely chopped**
- ½ **cup uncooked long grain brown rice**
- ½ **cup uncooked wild rice**
- 2 **medium apples, coarsely chopped**
- 2 **garlic cloves, minced**
- 1½ **cups apple cider or juice**
- 1 **cup beef broth**
- ⅛ **teaspoon pepper**

1. In a large saucepan, heat oil over medium-high heat. Add sausage, celery and onion; cook and stir 4-6 minutes or until tender.

2. Add the brown and wild rice, apples and garlic; cook and stir 1-2 minutes or until the rice is lightly browned. Add the apple cider, beef broth and pepper; bring to a boil. Reduce heat; simmer, covered, 1 to 1¼ hours or until the liquid is absorbed and the rice is tender. Fluff with a fork.

Pomegranate-Glazed Green Beans

Fresh green beans are always a popular vegetable in our house, no matter what the season or occasion may be. They get a nice zing from this simple but special recipe. The slightly tangy glaze features fruit juices, vinegar, maple syrup and seasonings.

—GERALDINE SAUCIER ALBUQUERQUE, NM

PREP: 15 MIN. • **COOK:** 20 MIN.
MAKES: 6 SERVINGS

1½ pounds fresh green beans, trimmed
⅓ cup orange juice
¼ cup pomegranate juice
3 tablespoons butter
2 tablespoons white balsamic vinegar
1 tablespoon maple syrup
2 teaspoons grated orange peel
1 teaspoon onion powder
½ teaspoon salt
¼ teaspoon pepper
¼ cup dried cranberries

1. In a Dutch oven, place steamer basket over 1 in. of water. Place green beans in basket. Bring water to a boil. Reduce heat to maintain a simmer; steam, covered, 8-10 minutes or until crisp-tender.

2. In a large skillet, combine orange juice, pomegranate juice, butter, vinegar, syrup, peel and seasonings. Bring to a boil; cook until liquid is reduced by half. Stir in cranberries. Add beans and toss to coat.

circle into 12 wedges. Roll up wedges from the wide ends. Place 2 in. apart on greased baking sheets, point side down; curve to form crescents.

4. Cover with a kitchen towel; let rise in a warm place until doubled, about 30 minutes. Preheat oven to 400°. Bake 8-12 minutes or until golden brown. Brush with melted butter; remove to wire racks.

Apple Cider Sipper

When I had some apple schnapps, I decided to try mixing it with chilled cider. Tinting the drink green and dipping the rim of the glass in red sugar creates a fun cocktail for Christmas.

—CRYSTAL SCHLUETER NORTHGLENN, CO

START TO FINISH: 5 MIN. • **MAKES:** 1 SERVING

    Red-colored sugar
    Grenadine syrup
4 ounces chilled apple cider or juice
2 ounces apple schnapps liqueur
2 drops green food coloring

Sprinkle a thin layer of sugar on a plate. Moisten the rim of a martini glass with grenadine syrup; hold glass upside down and dip rim into sugar. Add apple juice to glass; gently stir in liqueur and food coloring.

Onion Crescents

I frequently bake my homemade crescents for family dinners on holidays. Everyone likes the addition of minced onion, which lends extra flavor without being overpowering.

—MARY MAXEINER LAKEWOOD, CO

PREP: 30 MIN. + RISING • **BAKE:** 10 MIN. • **MAKES:** 2 DOZEN

1 package (¼ ounce) active dry yeast
1 cup warm milk (110° to 115°)
½ cup butter, softened
½ cup sugar
2 eggs
½ cup dried minced onion
½ teaspoon salt
3½ to 4½ cups all-purpose flour
2 tablespoons butter, melted

1. In a small bowl, dissolve yeast in warm milk. In a large bowl, cream butter and sugar. Beat in eggs. Add onion, salt, yeast mixture and 2 cups flour; beat until blended. Stir in enough remaining flour to form a soft dough.
2. Turn dough onto a floured surface; knead until smooth and elastic, about 6-8 minutes. Place in a greased bowl, turning once to grease the top. Cover with plastic wrap and let rise in a warm place until doubled, about 1 hour.
3. Punch dough down. Turn onto a lightly floured surface; divide in half. Roll each portion into a 12-in. circle; cut each

Making Pastry for a Single-Crust Pie

The Molasses-Bourbon Pecan Pie recipe (at right) calls for making the pie pastry from scratch. If you're a beginner or just want a refresher course in making pastry, look here. These easy directions and photos will guide you through every step of the process, from combining the ingredients for the pastry dough to rolling out the crust and expertly draping it over the plate.

1. Combine the flour and salt in a bowl. With a pastry blender or two knives, cut in the shortening until the dough is crumbly (about the size of small peas).

2. Sprinkle 1 tablespoon ice-cold water over the mixture and toss gently with a fork. Repeat until the dry ingredients are moist and the mixture forms a ball.

3. On a floured surface, shape the dough into a ball for making the single crust called for in Molasses-Bourbon Pecan Pie. Flatten the ball into a circle, pressing together any cracks or breaks. Wrap the dough circle in plastic wrap and refrigerate it for 1 to 1½ hours for easier handling.

4. Using a rolling pin and working on a lightly floured surface, roll the chilled dough circle into a larger circle, rolling from the center of the pastry to the edges. Shape it 2 in. larger than the pie plate and about ⅛ in. thick.

5. Roll the finished pastry loosely around the rolling pin. Position the dough over the edge of the pie plate and unroll it. Allow the pastry to gently ease into the pie plate—do not stretch the pastry to fit. With kitchen shears, trim the pastry ½ in. beyond the edge of the plate and flute the edges.

Molasses-Bourbon Pecan Pie

A splash of bourbon in the rich molasses filling gives this made-from-scratch pecan pie extra flair for the Christmas season.
—**CHARLENE CHAMBERS** ORMOND BEACH, FL

PREP: 35 MIN. + CHILLING
BAKE: 55 MIN. + COOLING
MAKES: 8 SERVINGS

- 1½ cups all-purpose flour
- ¾ teaspoon salt
- 6 tablespoons shortening
- 5 to 6 tablespoons ice water

FILLING
- ¾ cup packed brown sugar
- ¾ cup corn syrup
- ½ cup molasses
- 3 tablespoons butter
- ½ teaspoon salt
- 3 eggs, beaten
- 2 tablespoons bourbon
- 2 teaspoons vanilla extract
- 2 cups pecan halves
- Whipped cream

1. In a large bowl, combine flour and salt; cut in shortening until crumbly. Gradually add the ice water, tossing with a fork until dough forms a ball. Wrap in plastic wrap. Refrigerate for 1 to 1½ hours or until easy to handle.
2. Roll out the pastry to fit a 9-in. pie plate. Transfer pastry to pie plate. Trim pastry to ½ in. beyond the edge of the plate; flute edges. Refrigerate.
3. Meanwhile, in a large saucepan, combine the brown sugar, corn syrup, molasses, butter and salt; bring to a simmer over medium heat. Cover and stir for 2-3 minutes or until sugar is dissolved. Remove from the heat and cool to room temperature. (Mixture will be thick when cooled.)
4. Stir in the eggs, bourbon and vanilla. Stir in pecans. Pour into pastry shell. Bake at 350° for 55-60 minutes or until a knife inserted near the center comes out clean. Cover the edges with foil during the last 30 minutes to prevent overbrowning if necessary.
5. Cool on a wire rack. Serve with whipped cream. Refrigerate leftovers.

More Choices for Christmas Menus

If you like the three holiday menus featured in this chapter but want even more options for entrees, sides and desserts, page through this extra-special section. You'll find bonus recipes that can make wonderful substitutions in any of the previous dinners.

Cheesy Lasagna

During the holidays, I like to host friends and family for a casual but hearty meal of homemade lasagna. Italian sausage and three kinds of cheese make it incredibly rich and delicious.

—**GAY BARKER** CHANUTE, KS

PREP: 1½ HOURS • **BAKE:** 55 MIN. + STANDING • **MAKES:** 12 SERVINGS

- 1 **pound bulk Italian sausage**
- 2 **medium onions, chopped**
- 3 **to 4 garlic cloves, minced**
- 2 **cans (one 28 ounces, one 15 ounces) crushed tomatoes**
- 1 **can (6 ounces) tomato paste**
- 1 **celery rib, chopped**
- ¼ **cup minced fresh parsley**
- 1 **bay leaf**
- 1 **tablespoon brown sugar**
- 2 **teaspoons dried oregano**
- 1½ **teaspoons salt**
- ½ **teaspoon dried thyme**
- 6 **lasagna noodles, cooked and drained**
- 1 **carton (15 ounces) ricotta cheese**
- 1 **pound sliced part-skim mozzarella cheese**
- ½ **pound sliced provolone cheese**

1. Preheat oven to 350°. In a Dutch oven, cook sausage over medium heat 6-8 minutes or until no longer pink, breaking into crumbles. Remove with a slotted spoon. Discard the drippings in pan.

2. Add the onions to same pan; cook and stir over medium heat until tender. Add the garlic; cook 1 minute longer. Stir in the tomatoes, tomato paste, celery, parsley, bay leaf, brown sugar, oregano, salt and thyme. Bring to a boil. Reduce heat; simmer, uncovered, 1 hour, stirring occasionally. Remove the bay leaf.

3. Remove 1 cup sauce from pan. Stir cooked sausage into the remaining sauce. Spread reserved sauce into a greased 13x9-in. baking dish. Layer with three noodles and half of each of the following: sausage mixture, ricotta, mozzarella and provolone. Repeat layers (dish will be full).

4. Bake, covered, 55-65 minutes or until cheese is melted. Let stand 10 minutes before serving.

Almond Beef Roast with Wild Rice

This tender, saucy beef roast with wild rice has been one of my daughter's favorite dinners for years. She now lives in Georgia, and I often serve it when she comes to visit.

—**GLORIA MCKENZIE** PANAMA CITY, FL

PREP: 15 MIN. • **BAKE:** 2¾ HOURS • **MAKES:** 8 SERVINGS

- 1 **beef sirloin tip roast (about 3 pounds)**
- 2 **tablespoons all-purpose flour**
- ¼ **teaspoon pepper**
- 2 **tablespoons canola oil**
- 1 **can (10¾ ounces) condensed cream of chicken soup, undiluted**

- ½ **cup apple cider or juice**
- 1 **envelope onion soup mix**
- 1½ **cups uncooked wild rice**
- ¼ **cup minced fresh parsley**
- 2 **tablespoons butter**
- ½ **cup slivered almonds**

1. Preheat oven to 325°. Sprinkle the roast with flour and pepper. In a Dutch oven, heat the oil over medium heat. Brown roast on all sides. Remove from heat.

2. In a small bowl, whisk the chicken soup and cider until blended; stir in soup mix. Pour over roast. Bake, covered, 2¾ to 3¼ hours or until meat is tender.

3. Meanwhile, cook the wild rice according to the package directions. Stir in parsley and butter.

4. Remove roast from pan. Stir almonds into sauce in pan. Serve roast with rice and sauce.

Four-Pepper Egg Casserole

My husband loves peppers, so he's a big fan of this breakfast. Cumin and cayenne add a little south-of-the-border spice.

—JOYCE MOYNIHAN LAKEVILLE, MN

PREP: 35 MIN. • **BAKE:** 35 MIN.
MAKES: 8 SERVINGS

- 2 tablespoons olive oil
- 2 large onions, sliced
- 1 each large green, sweet yellow, orange and red pepper, thinly sliced
- 3 garlic cloves, minced
- 2 teaspoons ground cumin
- 1 teaspoon salt
- 1 teaspoon ground coriander
- 1 teaspoon ground mustard
- ½ teaspoon pepper
- ¼ teaspoon cayenne pepper
- 2 tablespoons all-purpose flour
- 4 eggs
- 2 cups (16 ounces) sour cream
- ½ cup minced fresh cilantro
- 2 cups (8 ounces) shredded Monterey Jack cheese
- ¼ teaspoon paprika

1. Preheat oven to 350°. In a large skillet, heat the oil over medium-high heat. Add onions and peppers; cook and stir until tender. Add garlic and seasonings; cook 2 minutes longer. Remove from heat. Stir in the flour until smooth. Transfer to a greased 11x7-in. baking dish.

2. In a large bowl, whisk eggs, sour cream and cilantro. Pour over pepper mixture. Top with cheese; sprinkle with paprika. Bake, uncovered, 35-40 minutes or until center is set.

Holiday Helper

Like the spice of Mexican food? To make Four-Pepper Egg Casserole (recipe above) even more of a flavor fiesta, top it off with salsa. For a cool contrast, add a dollop of sour cream...or serve a side dish of fruit salad. If your family prefers food that's on the milder side, reduce or omit the cayenne.

Butternut Gratin with Parmesan-Sage Topping

This is a wonderful side dish for winter meals because it's seasonal, comforting and delicious. It's also surprisingly simple to prepare. The baked butternut squash and onions get extra flavor from a topping of panko bread crumbs, Parmesan cheese, fresh sage and seasonings.

—DEIRDRE COX KANSAS CITY, MO

PREP: 35 MIN. • **BAKE:** 30 MIN.
MAKES: 8 SERVINGS

- 2 **tablespoons butter**
- 1 **tablespoon olive oil**
- 2 **medium onions, halved and thinly sliced**

- 1 **small butternut squash (about 2½ pounds), peeled and cubed**
- 1 **teaspoon sugar**
- ½ **teaspoon salt**
- ½ **teaspoon pepper**
- ½ **teaspoon ground nutmeg**
- ¾ **cup chicken or vegetable stock**

TOPPING
- 1½ **cups panko (Japanese) bread crumbs**
- 1 **cup grated Parmesan cheese**
- 2 **tablespoons chopped fresh sage**
- ⅛ **teaspoon pepper**
  Dash salt

1. Preheat oven to 400°. In a large skillet, heat the butter and oil over medium-high heat. Add onions; cook and stir 6-8 minutes or until lightly browned. Add the butternut squash; cook 2 minutes longer. Sprinkle with the sugar, salt, pepper and nutmeg; cook and stir 3-4 minutes or until the squash is lightly browned.

2. Transfer to a greased 13x9-in. baking dish. Pour chicken stock over top. Bake, covered, 20-30 minutes or until squash is tender.

3. Meanwhile, in a bowl, toss the panko bread crumbs with Parmesan cheese and seasonings. Sprinkle over the vegetables. Bake, uncovered, 10-12 minutes longer or until the topping is golden brown.

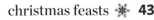

Plum-Glazed Roast Chicken

I adjusted a recipe for duck so I could use a chicken instead, and it's been a favorite holiday main course ever since. I've also substituted a small 9- to 11-pound turkey.
—**LILY JULOW** LAWRENCEVILLE, GA

PREP: 15 MIN. • **BAKE:** 2 HOURS + STANDING
MAKES: 8 SERVINGS

- 4 **medium oranges, halved and seeds removed**
- 1 **roasting chicken (6 to 7 pounds)**
- 1 **teaspoon garlic powder**
- 1 **teaspoon salt**
- 1 **can (15 ounces) plums**
- ¼ **cup butter, cubed**
- 1 **medium onion, chopped**
- ¾ **cup thawed lemonade concentrate**
- ⅓ **cup chili sauce**
- ¼ **cup reduced-sodium soy sauce**
- 2 **teaspoons Dijon mustard**
- 1 **teaspoon ground ginger**
- 1 **teaspoon Worcestershire sauce**
- 2 **drops hot pepper sauce, optional**

1. Preheat oven to 350°. Arrange oranges in a shallow roasting pan, cut sides down. Place chicken over oranges, breast side up. Mix garlic powder and salt; rub over the outside and inside of chicken. Tuck wings under chicken; tie drumsticks together.

2. Roast 1¼ hours. Meanwhile, drain plums, reserving the liquid. Remove pits from plums. Place plums in a food processor; process until pureed.

3. In a large skillet, heat the butter over medium-high heat. Add onion; cook and stir 3-4 minutes or until tender. Add the pureed plums and reserved plum liquid; stir in remaining ingredients.

4. Bring to a boil. Reduce the heat; simmer, uncovered, 10-15 minutes or until slightly thickened, stirring occasionally. Remove ¾ cup mixture for the glaze; reserve the remaining mixture for the sauce.

5. Remove the chicken from oven; brush the chicken with some of the glaze. Roast ¾ to 1¼ hours longer or until a thermometer inserted in thigh reads 180°, brushing occasionally with remaining glaze. (Cover loosely with foil if chicken browns too quickly.)

6. Remove chicken from oven; tent with foil. Let stand 15 minutes before carving. Reheat the reserved sauce. Serve chicken with sauce.

Herbed Seafood Casserole

When I wanted a seafood dish for my annual Christmas Eve buffet, my friend introduced me to this wonderful casserole. It's a rich, creamy entree loaded with shrimp, scallops and crab.
—**DONNA SCHMULAND** WETASKIWIN, AB

PREP: 40 MIN. • **BAKE:** 50 MIN. + STANDING • **MAKES:** 12 SERVINGS

- 1½ cups uncooked long grain rice
- 2 tablespoons butter
- 3 celery ribs, thinly sliced
- 1 medium onion, finely chopped
- 1 medium carrot, shredded
- 3 garlic cloves, minced
- ½ teaspoon salt
- ¼ teaspoon pepper
- 2 tablespoons minced fresh parsley
- 1½ teaspoons snipped fresh dill or ½ teaspoon dill weed

SEAFOOD
- 1 pound uncooked medium shrimp, peeled and deveined
- 1 pound bay scallops
- 1 can (16 ounces) crabmeat, drained, flaked and cartilage removed
- 5 tablespoons butter, cubed
- ¼ cup all-purpose flour
- 1½ cups half-and-half cream
- 1 package (8 ounces) cream cheese, cubed
- 1½ teaspoons snipped fresh dill or ½ teaspoon dill weed
- ½ teaspoon salt
- ¼ teaspoon pepper
- ¼ teaspoon dried thyme

TOPPING
- 1½ cups soft bread crumbs
- 2 tablespoons butter, melted

1. Preheat oven to 325°. Cook rice according to the package directions. Meanwhile, in a large skillet, heat the butter over medium-high heat. Add celery, onion and carrot; cook and stir until crisp-tender. Add the garlic, salt and pepper; cook 1 minute longer.

2. Add to cooked rice. Stir in parsley and dill. Transfer to a greased 13x9-in. baking dish.

3. Fill a large saucepan two-thirds full with water; bring to a boil. Reduce heat to medium. Add shrimp; simmer, uncovered, 30 seconds. Add scallops; simmer 2-3 minutes longer or just until shrimp turn pink and scallops are firm and opaque. Drain, reserving 1 cup cooking liquid. Place the seafood in a large bowl; stir in crab.

4. In a small saucepan, melt butter over medium heat. Stir in flour until blended; gradually stir in half-and-half cream and reserved cooking liquid. Bring to a boil; cook and stir 2 minutes or until thickened and bubbly. Reduce heat. Stir in the cream cheese, dill and seasonings until smooth. Stir into the seafood mixture.

5. Pour over rice mixture. Toss bread crumbs with melted butter; sprinkle over top. Bake, uncovered, 50-55 minutes or until golden brown. Let stand 10 minutes before serving.

Apple & Apricot Stuffing

A magazine gave me the idea for this fruit-filled stuffing. I tweaked it by leaving out the pork sausage, and everyone likes the meatless version that features apples and apricots.
—**JEANNE HORN** DULUTH, MN

PREP: 30 MIN. • **BAKE:** 45 MIN. • **MAKES:** 16 SERVINGS (¾ CUP EACH)

- 5 cups cubed Italian bread
- 5 cups cubed whole wheat bread
- 1 tablespoon butter
- 2 celery ribs, chopped
- 1 large onion, chopped
- 2 small apples, chopped
- 1 cup chopped dried apricots
- ½ cup minced fresh parsley
- 1 cup chicken broth
- ⅓ cup butter, melted

1. Preheat oven to 350°. Place the bread cubes on ungreased baking sheets. Bake 18-20 minutes or until toasted. Cool on baking sheets.

2. In a Dutch oven, heat the butter over medium-high heat. Add celery and onion; cook and stir until tender. Add apples, apricots, parsley and bread cubes. Stir in broth and melted butter. Transfer to a greased 13x9-in. baking dish.

3. Bake, covered, 35 minutes. Uncover; bake 10-15 minutes longer or until lightly browned.

Orange Marmalade Vinaigrette

I rely on my tangy vinaigrette when I want a special dressing for guests. With orange marmalade and Dijon mustard, it turns ordinary salad greens into a treat.

—**RITA HEIKENFELD** BATAVIA, OH

START TO FINISH: 10 MIN. • **MAKES:** 2 CUPS

- ¾ cup orange marmalade
- 6 tablespoons white wine vinegar
- 1 tablespoon finely chopped red onion
- 1 tablespoon Dijon mustard
- 1 teaspoon sugar
- ½ teaspoon salt
- ⅛ teaspoon pepper
- 1 cup canola oil

In a small bowl, whisk the first seven ingredients. Gradually whisk in oil until blended. Refrigerate, covered, until serving. Whisk again just before serving.

Baked Pearl Onions

Tender and buttery, these little baked onions will enhance just about any dinner menu. I perk them up with plenty of fresh herbs—garlic, rosemary, tarragon and parsley—then pop them into the oven.

—**MARILEE CARDINAL** BURLINGTON, NJ

PREP: 15 MIN. • **BAKE:** 50 MIN.
MAKES: 2 CUPS

- 1 package (14.4 ounces) frozen pearl onions, thawed and patted dry
- 10 garlic cloves, peeled
- ¼ cup butter, melted
- ½ teaspoon minced fresh rosemary
- ¼ teaspoon salt
  Dash pepper
- ¼ teaspoon minced fresh tarragon
  Minced fresh parsley

1. Preheat oven to 350°. In a bowl, combine the pearl onions and garlic cloves. Add the butter, rosemary, salt and pepper; toss to combine. Transfer to a greased 15x10x1-in. baking pan. Bake 50-60 minutes or until pearl onions are golden brown, stirring occasionally.
2. If desired, discard the garlic before serving. Sprinkle tarragon and parsley over onions before serving.

Personal Pear Pot Pies

Talk about cutie pies! These mini desserts made in ramekins are yummy and easy to prepare using frozen puff pastry. Top each warm dessert with a scoop of ice cream.

—**BEE ENGELHART** BLOOMFIELD TOWNSHIP, MI

PREP: 30 MIN. • **BAKE:** 25 MIN.
MAKES: 4 SERVINGS

- 2 tablespoons butter, divided
- 2 tablespoons sugar
- 1 tablespoon cornflake crumbs
- 1 tablespoon brown sugar
- ¼ teaspoon ground ginger
- 2 cups finely chopped peeled Anjou pears
- 2 cups finely chopped peeled Bartlett pears
- 1 tablespoon orange juice
- ½ sheet frozen puff pastry, thawed
- 1 egg, lightly beaten
  Vanilla ice cream

1. Preheat oven to 400°. Grease the bottoms and sides of four 8-oz. ramekins with 1 tablespoon butter (do not butter the rims of ramekins). Place on a baking sheet.
2. In a small bowl, mix sugar, cornflake crumbs, brown sugar and ginger. In a large bowl, toss the pears with orange juice. Add the crumb mixture and toss to combine. Divide the mixture among ramekins; dot with remaining butter.
3. Without unfolding, cut the pastry crosswise into fourteen ¼-in. strips. Carefully unfold strips. Cut eight strips in half; cut remaining strips into thirds. Place over ramekins in a lattice pattern, using four long strips and four short strips for each. Gently press ends onto ramekin rims. Brush lattices with egg.
4. Bake 25-30 minutes or until filling is bubbly and pastry is golden brown. Serve warm with ice cream.

heartwarming BREADS

Caramelized Onion & Date Flatbread

Here's a deliciously different appetizer for a holiday party. I smother a prebaked pizza crust with unusual but tasty toppings—caramelized onions, two kinds of cheese, orange chunks, dates and seasoning.

—MARY TAMAKI CALGARY, AB

PREP: 40 MIN. • **BROIL:** 5 MIN.
MAKES: 1 FLATBREAD (8 SLICES)

- 2 **teaspoons olive oil**
- 1 **medium red onion, thinly sliced**
- ⅛ **teaspoon salt**
- 1 **prebaked 12-inch thin pizza crust**
- 1 **cup (4 ounces) shredded part-skim mozzarella cheese**
- ¼ **teaspoon Italian seasoning**
- 1 **large navel orange, peeled, sectioned and cut into ½-inch pieces**
- ½ **cup pitted dates, chopped**
- ¼ **cup crumbled feta cheese**

1. Preheat broiler. In a large skillet, heat oil over medium heat. Add onion and salt; cook and stir 6-8 minutes or until onion is softened. Reduce heat to medium-low; cook 20-25 minutes or until deep golden brown, stirring occasionally.

2. Place crust on an ungreased baking sheet; sprinkle with mozzarella cheese. Broil 3-4 in. from heat 1-2 minutes or until cheese is melted.

3. Top with Italian seasoning, onion, orange and dates. Sprinkle with feta cheese. Broil 2-3 minutes longer or until heated through.

Brown Sugar Glazed Coffee Ring

In our family, Christmas is even more special because it's also my daughter's birthday. We've always started off the morning with this delightful coffee ring and a bowl of fresh fruit.

—DONNA CONDA NORTH CANTON, OH

PREP: 15 MIN. • **BAKE:** 30 MIN. + COOLING • **MAKES:** 8 SERVINGS

- 2 cups all-purpose flour
- ¾ cup sugar
- 2½ teaspoons baking powder
- ½ teaspoon salt
- ⅓ cup cold butter, cubed
- ¾ cup prepared mincemeat
- ½ cup 2% milk
- 1 egg

GLAZE
- ¾ cup packed brown sugar
- 2 tablespoons water
- 1 tablespoon light corn syrup
- 1 cup confectioners' sugar

1. Preheat oven to 375°. In a large bowl, whisk the flour, sugar, baking powder and salt; cut in butter until mixture resembles coarse crumbs. In another bowl, mix mincemeat, milk and egg; stir into flour mixture just until moistened.

2. Transfer to a greased and floured 8-in. fluted tube pan. Bake 30-35 minutes or until a toothpick inserted in center comes out clean. Cool 10 minutes before removing from pan to a wire rack.

3. For the glaze, in a small saucepan, combine the brown sugar, water and corn syrup; bring to a boil over medium heat, stirring constantly. Remove from heat; whisk in the confectioners' sugar just until blended. Immediately pour over warm coffee ring.

Autumn Sweet Rolls with Cider Glaze

I love cooking with pumpkin. That ingredient, bits of apple and a splash of cider give these sweet rolls their autumn appeal.

—JENNIFER CODUTO KENT, OH

PREP: 30 MIN. + RISING • **BAKE:** 25 MIN. • **MAKES:** 1 DOZEN

- 2 teaspoons active dry yeast
- ⅓ cup warm water (110° to 115°)
- 1 tablespoon honey
- ¾ cup canned pumpkin
- 2 eggs
- ¼ cup packed brown sugar
- 2 tablespoons butter, softened
- 1½ teaspoons pumpkin pie spice
- ½ teaspoon salt
- 4 to 4½ cups all-purpose flour

FILLING
- ¼ cup sugar
- 1 teaspoon ground cinnamon
- 2 tablespoons butter, melted
- 1 small apple, peeled and finely chopped (about 1 cup)

GLAZE
- 1 cup confectioners' sugar
- 3 tablespoons apple cider or juice
- ¼ cup finely chopped walnuts, toasted

1. In a small bowl, dissolve the yeast in warm water and honey. In a large bowl, combine the pumpkin, eggs, brown sugar, butter, pumpkin pie spice, salt, yeast mixture and 1½ cups flour; beat on medium speed until smooth. Stir in enough remaining flour to form a soft dough (the dough will be sticky).

2. Turn dough onto a floured surface; knead until smooth and elastic, about 6-8 minutes. Place in a greased bowl, turning once to grease the top. Cover with plastic wrap and let rise in a warm place until doubled, about 1 hour.

3. For the filling, mix the sugar and cinnamon. Punch down dough. Turn onto a lightly floured surface. Press dough into a 14x12-in. rectangle. Brush with melted butter to within ½ in. of edges. Sprinkle with cinnamon-sugar and apple. Roll up jelly-roll style, starting with a long side; pinch seam to seal. Cut into 12 slices.

4. Place in a greased 13x9-in. baking pan, cut side down. Cover with a kitchen towel; let rise in a warm place until doubled, about 30 minutes.

5. Preheat oven to 350°. Bake 25-30 minutes or until golden brown. In a small bowl, mix confectioners' sugar and apple cider; drizzle over warm rolls. Sprinkle with walnuts.

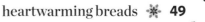

Italian Cheese Beer Bread

After using a store-bought mix to bake a cheesy beer loaf, I realized I could create a better one from scratch. We serve hefty slices appetizer-style with a bowl of warm marinara sauce for dipping.

—**KELLY MAXWELL** PLAINFIELD, IL

PREP: 10 MIN. • **BAKE:** 40 MIN. + COOLING
MAKES: 1 LOAF (12 SLICES)

- 3 cups all-purpose flour
- 1 tablespoon sugar
- 3 teaspoons baking powder
- 1½ teaspoons salt
- 1 garlic clove, minced
- ½ teaspoon dried basil
- ¼ teaspoon dried oregano
- 1 cup (4 ounces) shredded Italian cheese blend
- 1 bottle (12 ounces) beer
- ¼ cup butter, melted

1. Preheat oven to 375°. In a large bowl, whisk the first seven ingredients; stir in cheese. Stir in beer just until moistened (batter will be thick).
2. Transfer the batter to a greased 8x4-in. loaf pan; pour butter over the top. Bake 40-45 minutes or until a toothpick inserted in center comes out clean. Cool in pan 10 minutes before removing to a wire rack to cool.

Maple Nut Banana Bread

Banana bread rises to a whole new level when you add maple syrup, sour cream, pecans and a cinnamon-spiced streusel on top. It's a comforting, home-style treat for breakfast or any time of day.

—**DAVID DAHLMAN** CHATSWORTH, CA

PREP: 40 MIN. • **BAKE:** 55 MIN. + COOLING
MAKES: 1 LOAF (12 SLICES)

- ½ cup butter, softened
- ½ cup packed brown sugar
- 2 eggs
- 1 cup mashed ripe bananas (about 2 medium)
- ½ cup sour cream
- ⅓ cup maple syrup
- 1 teaspoon vanilla extract
- 2 cups all-purpose flour
- 1 teaspoon baking powder
- 1 teaspoon baking soda
- 1 teaspoon salt
- 1 cup chopped pecans

STREUSEL

- 2 tablespoons all-purpose flour
- 2 tablespoons sugar
- 1 tablespoon packed brown sugar
- 1 tablespoon butter, softened
- ⅛ teaspoon ground cinnamon
- 2 tablespoons finely chopped pecans

1. Preheat oven to 350°. In a large bowl, cream butter and brown sugar until light and fluffy. Add eggs, one at a time, beating well after each addition. In a small bowl, mix the bananas, sour cream, maple syrup and vanilla. In another bowl, whisk the flour, baking powder, baking soda and salt; add to the creamed mixture alternately with the banana mixture, beating well after each addition. Fold in pecans.

2. Transfer to a greased 9x5-in. loaf pan. For streusel, in a small bowl, mix the flour, sugars, butter and cinnamon until blended. Stir in pecans; sprinkle over batter.
3. Bake 55-60 minutes or until a toothpick inserted in center comes out clean. Cool in pan 10 minutes before removing to a wire rack to cool.

Holiday Helper

Want banana muffins instead of a loaf? Use 16 greased or paper-lined muffin cups and bake at 350° for 18-22 minutes or until a toothpick comes out clean.

John's Pineapple-Cream Cheese Muffins

When I got married, my mother-in-law gave me her recipe for pineapple muffins so I could make them for my husband, John. They're his all-time favorites—and now they're mine, too!

—DIANE TURNER BRUNSWICK, OH

PREP: 25 MIN. • **BAKE:** 20 MIN.
MAKES: 1½ DOZEN

- 1 can (20 ounces) crushed pineapple
- 1 package (3 ounces) cream cheese, softened
- 1 cup sugar
- 1 egg
- 2 teaspoons vanilla extract
- 2 cups all-purpose flour
- 1 teaspoon baking soda
- 1 teaspoon salt
- ½ cup sour cream
- ½ cup confectioners' sugar
- 1½ teaspoons butter, softened

1. Preheat oven to 350°. Drain the pineapple, reserving 1-2 tablespoons pineapple syrup.

2. In a large bowl, beat cream cheese and sugar until blended. Add egg and vanilla; beat well. In another bowl, whisk flour, baking soda and salt. Add to cream cheese mixture alternately with sour cream, beating well after each addition. Fold in pineapple.

3. Fill greased or paper-lined muffin cups two-thirds full. Bake 20-25 minutes or until a toothpick inserted in the center comes out clean. Cool 5 minutes before removing from pans to wire racks.

4. In a small bowl, mix confectioners' sugar, butter and enough reserved syrup to reach a drizzling consistency. Drizzle over warm muffins.

Apricot-Glazed Bacon Spirals

Here's a guaranteed crowd-pleaser for an appetizer table or brunch buffet. Each spiral boasts a whole piece of crispy bacon, which contrasts with the apricot preserves for a sweet-and-salty treat.

—KELLIE MULLEAVY LAMBERTVILLE, MI

START TO FINISH: 25 MIN.
MAKES: 15 SERVINGS

- 1 **tablespoon butter**
- ½ **cup finely chopped onion**
- 3 **tablespoons apricot preserves**
- 1 **tube (8 ounces) refrigerated crescent rolls**
- 1 **package (2.1 ounces) ready-to-serve fully cooked bacon**

1. Preheat oven to 375°. In a small skillet, heat butter over medium heat. Add onion; cook and stir 3-5 minutes or until tender. Reduce heat to low; add preserves. Cook and stir until melted.
2. Unroll crescent dough into one long rectangle. Roll into a 15x9-in. rectangle, sealing seams and perforations. Cut crosswise into fifteen 1-in. strips; top each with one piece of bacon. Roll up jelly-roll style, starting with a short side; pinch seam to seal. Place on an ungreased baking sheet, cut side down.
3. Spoon apricot mixture over each spiral. Bake 12-15 minutes or until golden brown. Let stand 5 minutes before serving. Refrigerate leftovers.

Almond-Filled Stollen

I've been making this during the holiday season for nearly 50 years. When we flew to my daughter's home in Alaska one Christmas, I took my stollen on the plane!

—RACHEL SEEL ABBOTSFORD, BC

PREP: 1 HOUR + RISING
BAKE: 30 MIN. + COOLING
MAKES: 3 LOAVES (12 SLICES EACH)

- 1¾ **cups chopped mixed candied fruit**
- ½ **cup plus 2 tablespoons rum, divided**
- 2 **packages (¼ ounce each) active dry yeast**
- ½ **cup warm water (110° to 115°)**
- 1½ **cups warm 2% milk (110° to 115°)**
- 1¼ **cups butter, softened**
- ⅔ **cup sugar**
- 2½ **teaspoons salt**

- 2 **teaspoons grated lemon peel**
- 1 **teaspoon almond extract**
- 7 **to 8 cups all-purpose flour**
- 4 **eggs**
- ⅓ **cup slivered almonds**
- 1 **can (8 ounces) almond paste**
- 1 **egg yolk**
- 2 **teaspoons water**
- 2 **to 2¼ cups confectioners' sugar**

1. In a small bowl, combine candied fruit and ½ cup rum; let stand, covered, 1 hour.
2. In a small bowl, dissolve yeast in warm water. In a large bowl, combine milk, butter, sugar, salt, lemon peel, almond extract, remaining rum, yeast mixture and 4 cups flour; beat on medium speed until smooth. Cover with plastic wrap and let stand in a warm place, about 30 minutes.
3. Beat in the eggs. Stir in enough remaining flour to form a soft dough (dough will be sticky). Drain candied fruit, reserving rum for glaze. Reserve ½ cup fruit for topping. Stir almonds and remaining fruit into dough.

4. Turn dough onto a floured surface; knead until smooth and elastic, about 6-8 minutes. Place in a greased bowl, turning once to grease the top. Cover with plastic wrap and let rise in a warm place until doubled, about 1 hour.
5. Punch down dough; divide into three portions. On a greased baking sheet, roll each portion into a 12-in. circle. Crumble one-third of almond paste over one-half of each circle. Fold dough partially in half, covering filling and placing the top layer within 1 in. of the bottom edge. Cover with kitchen towels and let rise in a warm place until doubled in size, about 1 hour. Preheat oven to 375°.
6. In a small bowl, whisk egg yolk and water; brush over loaves. Bake 30-35 minutes or until golden brown. Cover loosely with foil if the tops brown too quickly. Remove from pans to wire racks to cool completely.
7. In a small bowl, mix reserved rum with enough confectioner's sugar to make a thin glaze. Drizzle over stollen. Sprinkle with reserved candied fruit.

Whole Wheat Knot Rolls

I found a magazine recipe for whole wheat rolls and changed it a bit to suit my family's tastes. The little knots disappear quickly when I bring them to potlucks.

—DEBRA TROESTER HAMPTON, NE

PREP: 45 MIN. + RISING • **BAKE:** 15 MIN.
MAKES: 3 DOZEN

- 2 **packages (¼ ounce each) active dry yeast**
- 2 **tablespoons plus ⅔ cup sugar, divided**
- 1½ **cups warm water (110° to 115°)**
- 1 **cup warm 2% milk (110° to 115°)**
- ½ **cup plus ¼ cup butter, melted, divided**
- 2 **eggs**
- 2 **teaspoons salt**
- 5½ **to 6 cups all-purpose flour**
- 2 **cups whole wheat flour**

1. In a small bowl, dissolve the yeast and 2 tablespoons sugar in the warm water. In a large bowl, combine the milk, ½ cup melted butter, eggs, salt, remaining sugar, yeast mixture and 4 cups all-purpose flour. Beat until smooth. Stir in whole wheat flour and enough remaining all-purpose flour to form a stiff dough.

2. Turn dough onto a floured surface; knead until smooth and elastic, about 6-8 minutes. Place in a greased bowl, turning once to grease the top. Cover with plastic wrap and let rise in a warm place until doubled, about 1 hour.

3. Punch down dough. Turn onto a lightly floured surface; divide and shape into 36 balls. Roll each into a 10-in. rope; tie into a loose knot. Tuck ends under. Place 2 in. apart on greased baking sheets. Cover with kitchen towels; let rise in a warm place until doubled, about 30 minutes. Preheat oven to 350°.

4. Bake 12-15 minutes or until golden brown. Brush the warm rolls with the remaining melted butter. Remove from the pans to wire racks.

Sun-Dried Tomato & Olive Loaf

It's virtually impossible to resist this beautiful, richly flavored loaf that starts in the bread machine and finishes in the oven. My mouth starts watering when I think of tearing off big chunks and dipping them into extra virgin olive oil. Delicious!

—CAROLE HOLT MENDOTA HEIGHTS, MN

PREP: 20 MIN. + RISING • **BAKE:** 20 MIN.
MAKES: 1 LOAF (16 SLICES)

- 1 **cup warm tomato juice (70° to 80°)**
- 2 **tablespoons olive oil, divided**
- ½ **teaspoon salt**
- 2 **teaspoons brown sugar**
- 1 **tablespoon minced fresh rosemary or 1 teaspoon dried rosemary, crushed**
- 2¾ **cups bread flour**
- 1 **package (¼ ounce) quick-rise yeast**
- ½ **cup chopped oil-packed sun-dried tomatoes, well-drained**
- ½ **cup chopped pitted Greek olives, well-drained**

1. In bread machine pan, place tomato juice, 1 tablespoon oil, salt, brown sugar, rosemary, flour and yeast in order suggested by manufacturer. Select dough setting. Check dough after 5 minutes of mixing; add 1-2 tablespoons water or flour if needed. Just before the final kneading (your machine may audibly signal this), add tomatoes and olives.

2. When cycle is completed, turn dough onto a lightly floured surface. Roll into a 15x10-in. oval. Roll up jelly-roll style, starting with a long side; pinch the seam to seal and tuck ends under. Place on a greased baking sheet, seam side down. Cover with a kitchen towel; let rise in a warm place until doubled, about 45 minutes. Preheat oven to 400°.

3. Brush loaf with remaining oil. With a sharp knife, make five deep slashes across top of loaf. Bake 20-25 minutes or until golden brown. Remove from pan to a wire rack to cool.

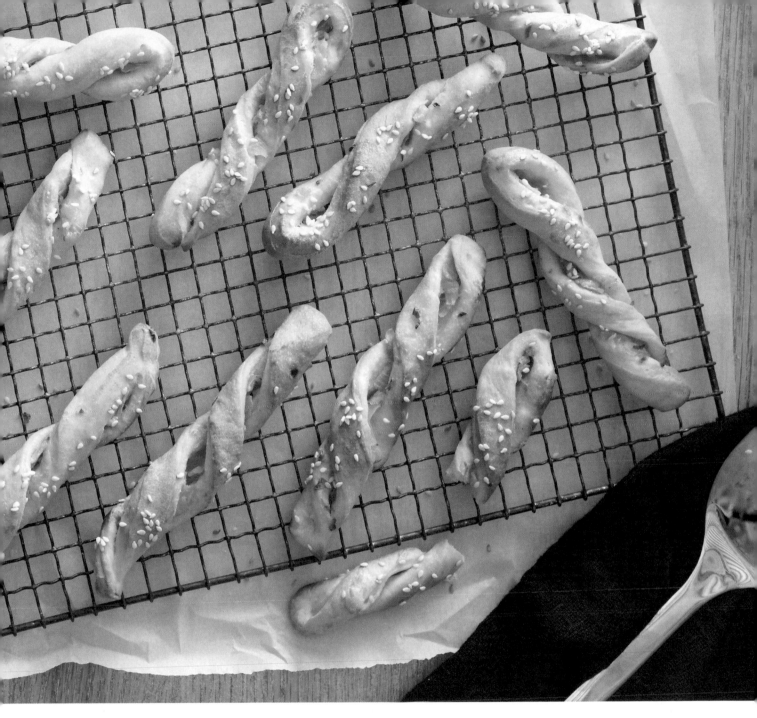

Sesame Onion Breadsticks

We've enjoyed these treats at countless get-togethers. The sesame-sprinkled sticks are easy to make using frozen dough and just five other ingredients.

—MARY RELYEA CANASTOTA, NY

PREP: 30 MIN. + RISING • **BAKE:** 15 MIN.
MAKES: 32 BREADSTICKS

- 2 **tablespoons butter**
- 1½ **cups finely chopped onions (about 2 medium)**
- ¼ **teaspoon paprika**
- 1 **loaf (1 pound) frozen bread dough, thawed**
- 1 **egg, lightly beaten**
- 1 **tablespoon sesame seeds**

1. In a large skillet, heat butter over medium heat. Add onions; cook and stir until tender. Stir in paprika; cool completely.

2. On a lightly floured surface, roll the dough to a 16x14-in. rectangle. Spread the onion mixture down one half of the rectangle. Fold the dough lengthwise in half over the onion mixture, forming a 16x7-in. rectangle; seal the edges.

3. Cut rectangle of dough lengthwise into thirty-two ½-in.-thick strips. Twist each strip two or three times. Place 2 in. apart on greased baking sheets. Cover with kitchen towels; let rise in a warm place until almost doubled, about 45 minutes. Preheat oven to 375°.

4. Brush the breadsticks with the beaten egg; sprinkle with sesame seeds. Bake 13-16 minutes or until golden brown. Remove from the pans to wire racks to cool.

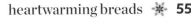

Orange-Fig Pull-Aparts

For breakfast on Thanksgiving, my mom requested an orange-flavored pull-apart bread. I tried making one by dressing up tubes of refrigerated rolls. She loved it!

—SHELLY BEVINGTON HERMISTON, OR

PREP: 25 MIN. • **BAKE:** 30 MIN.
MAKES: 20 SERVINGS

- ½ cup unsalted butter, melted, divided
- 1 package (3.4 ounces) instant vanilla pudding mix
- 30 dried figs, quartered
- ½ cup chopped walnuts
- 3 teaspoons grated orange peel
- 2 tubes (13.9 ounces each) refrigerated orange sweet rolls with icing

1. Preheat oven to 350°. Grease a 10-in. fluted tube pan with 1 tablespoon butter.

2. Place the pudding mix in a shallow bowl. In a small bowl, toss the figs and walnuts with orange peel. Reserve the icing from sweet rolls. Separate rolls and cut each in half. Roll each piece in pudding mix. Arrange half of the pieces in prepared pan, cut side facing center of pan. Top with half of the fig mixture; repeat layers.

3. Add the remaining melted butter to the remaining pudding mix; stir until smooth. Drizzle over top.

4. Bake, uncovered, 30-35 minutes or until golden brown. Immediately invert onto a serving plater. Spread with reserved icing; serve warm.

Golden Caraway Puffs

Here's a wonderful accompaniment for piping-hot bowls of soup, chili or stew. Dotted with caraway seeds and bits of onion, the savory little puffs conveniently bake in a standard muffin pan.

—**JOAN ANTONEN** ARLINGTON, SD

PREP: 20 MIN. + RISING • **BAKE:** 15 MIN.
MAKES: 1 DOZEN

- 1 package (¼ ounce) active dry yeast
- ¼ cup warm water (110° to 115°)
- 1 cup (8 ounces) 4% cottage cheese, warmed (110° to 115°)
- 1 egg
- 2 tablespoons sugar
- 1 tablespoon butter, softened
- 2 teaspoons grated onion
- 2 teaspoons caraway seeds
- 1 teaspoon salt
- ¼ teaspoon baking soda
- 2⅓ cups all-purpose flour

1. In a small bowl, dissolve yeast in warm water. In a large bowl, combine cottage cheese, egg, sugar, butter, onion, caraway seeds, salt, baking soda, yeast mixture and 1⅓ cups flour; beat on low speed 30 seconds. Beat on high 4 minutes. Stir in remaining flour. Do not knead. Cover with plastic wrap and let rise in a warm place until doubled, about 45 minutes.

2. Stir down the batter. Spoon into 12 greased muffin cups. Cover with a kitchen towel; let rise in a warm place until almost doubled, about 40 minutes. Preheat oven to 375°.

3. Bake 12-15 minutes or until golden brown. Cool in pan 1 minute before removing to a wire rack; serve warm.

Glazed Citrus Loaf

I always have the ingredients on hand for this cakelike treat bursting with tangy lemon and lime. The simple citrus glaze is a must—it creates a wonderful sweet-tart coating on the warm loaf. Enjoy a slice with your morning or afternoon tea.

—**JOYCE MOYNIHAN** LAKEVILLE, MN

PREP: 25 MIN. • **BAKE:** 1 HOUR + COOLING
MAKES: 1 LOAF (16 SLICES)

- 1 cup unsalted butter, softened
- 1½ cups sugar
- 4 eggs
- 3 teaspoons grated lemon peel
- 3 teaspoons grated lime peel
- 2 cups all-purpose flour
- 2 teaspoons baking powder
- ½ teaspoon salt

GLAZE
- ½ cup sugar
- 2 tablespoons lemon juice
- 1 tablespoon lime juice
- 1 teaspoon grated lime peel

1. Preheat oven to 325°. Grease and flour a 9x5-in. loaf pan. In a large bowl, cream the butter and sugar until light and fluffy. Add the eggs, one at a time, beating well after each addition. Beat in the lemon and lime peels. In another bowl, whisk the flour, baking powder and salt; gradually add to the creamed mixture (batter will be thick).

2. Transfer the batter to the prepared pan. Bake 60-70 minutes or until a toothpick inserted in the center comes out clean. Cool in the pan 10 minutes before removing to a wire rack; cool 10 minutes longer.

3. In a small saucepan, combine the glaze ingredients; cook and stir over medium heat until sugar is dissolved. Gradually brush onto the warm loaf, allowing glaze to soak into loaf before adding more. Cool completely.

Easy Cranberry-Pecan Sticky Buns

These ooey-gooey breakfast buns will have your whole family happily licking their fingers! The recipe is easy to prepare using refrigerated crescent roll dough, dried cranberries, pecans and kitchen staples.

—BARB MILLER OAKDALE, MN

PREP: 20 MIN. • **BAKE:** 20 MIN.
MAKES: 1 DOZEN

⅓ **cup packed brown sugar**
¼ **cup butter, melted**
2 **tablespoons maple syrup**
1 **tablespoon grated orange peel**
⅓ **cup dried cranberries or golden raisins**
¼ **cup chopped pecans**
2 **tablespoons sugar**
½ **teaspoon ground cinnamon**
1 **tube (8 ounces) refrigerated crescent rolls**

1. Preheat oven to 375°. In a small bowl, mix brown sugar, butter, maple syrup and orange peel. Spread onto the bottom of a greased 8-in. round baking pan. Sprinkle with cranberries and pecans.

2. In another bowl, mix the sugar and cinnamon. Remove the crescent roll dough from the can but do not unroll; cut crosswise into 12 slices, about ½-in. thick. Dip both sides in the cinnamon-sugar; place in baking pan, cut side down. Sprinkle any remaining cinnamon-sugar over tops.

3. Bake, uncovered, 18-22 minutes or until golden brown. Immediately invert onto a serving plate. Serve warm.

Bacon Walnut Bread with Honey Butter

My savory loaf loaded with bacon bits, chopped walnuts and blue cheese dressing is complemented by the creamy sweetness of honey-flavored butter. Slather that spread on a thick slice and enjoy!

—**PAM IVBULS** OMAHA, NE

PREP: 25 MIN. • **BAKE:** 40 MIN. + COOLING
MAKES: 1 LOAF (16 SLICES) AND ¾ CUP HONEY BUTTER

- 2 **cups all-purpose flour**
- 2 **teaspoons baking powder**
- ½ **teaspoon baking soda**
- ¼ **teaspoon salt**
- ¼ **teaspoon coarsely ground pepper**
- 1 **cup half-and-half cream**
- ¾ **cup refrigerated blue cheese salad dressing**
- 2 **eggs**
- 1 **tablespoon honey**
- ⅔ **cup coarsely chopped walnuts**
- ½ **cup bacon bits**

HONEY BUTTER
- ¾ **cup butter, softened**
- 2 **tablespoons honey**

1. Preheat oven to 325°. In a large bowl, whisk the first five ingredients. In another bowl, whisk half-and-half cream, salad dressing, eggs and honey until blended. Add to flour mixture; stir just until moistened. Fold in walnuts and bacon bits.

2. Transfer to a greased and floured 9x5-in. loaf pan. Bake 40-50 minutes or until a toothpick inserted in the center comes out clean. Cool in pan 10 minutes before removing to wire rack to cool completely.

3. In a small bowl, beat honey butter ingredients. Serve with bread.

Quick & Easy Pumpkin Crescents

These homemade goodies are simple enough for my children to help with. Sprinkled with cinnamon-sugar, the yummy crescents are perfect with hot cocoa on a chilly winter's day.

—**MINDEE ERICKSON** ST. GEORGE, UT

START TO FINISH: 25 MIN. • **MAKES:** 16 ROLLS

- 1¾ cups all-purpose flour
- 2 teaspoons baking powder
- ¼ teaspoon baking soda
- ¼ teaspoon ground nutmeg
- ⅛ teaspoon salt
- ⅛ teaspoon ground ginger
- 1½ teaspoons ground cinnamon, divided
- ¾ cup canned pumpkin
- 3 tablespoons canola oil
- 2 tablespoons brown sugar
- 2 tablespoons sugar
- 4 tablespoons butter, melted, divided

1. Preheat oven to 400°. In a large bowl, whisk the first six ingredients; stir in ½ teaspoon cinnamon. In another bowl, whisk pumpkin, oil and brown sugar; stir into flour mixture just until moistened.

2. In a small bowl, mix the sugar and remaining cinnamon; reserve 2 teaspoons cinnamon-sugar for the topping. Turn dough onto a lightly floured surface; knead gently 10 times. Divide in half; roll each portion into a 10-in. circle. Brush each circle with 1 tablespoon melted butter; sprinkle with 2 teaspoons cinnamon-sugar. Cut each into eight wedges. Roll up the wedges from the wide ends. Place 1 in. apart on a greased baking sheet, point side down; curve to form crescents. Brush the tops with remaining butter; sprinkle with reserved cinnamon-sugar.

3. Bake 9-11 minutes or until golden brown. Remove from pan to a wire rack; serve warm.

Ginger Buttermilk Biscuits

After we sampled spiced biscuits at a restaurant, I came up with my own version at home. I keep crystallized ginger handy so I can whip up a batch at a moment's notice!

—**REBECCA LITTLEJOHN** MEADOW VISTA, CA

START TO FINISH: 25 MIN. • **MAKES:** 20 BISCUITS

- 2 cups all-purpose flour
- 2 tablespoons brown sugar
- 2 teaspoons baking powder
- 1 teaspoon ground ginger
- ½ teaspoon salt
- ½ teaspoon baking soda
- ½ teaspoon ground cinnamon
- ⅓ cup shortening
- ½ cup finely chopped crystallized ginger
- ¾ cup buttermilk
- 2 tablespoons butter, melted
  Coarse sugar, optional

1. Preheat oven to 425°. In a large bowl, whisk the first seven ingredients. Cut in the shortening until the mixture resembles coarse crumbs. Stir in the crystallized ginger. Add buttermilk; stir just until moistened.

2. Turn dough onto a lightly floured surface; knead gently 8-10 times. Pat or roll dough to ½-in. thickness; cut with a floured 2-in. biscuit cutter. Place 1 in. apart on a parchment paper-lined baking sheet. Brush tops with butter. If desired, sprinkle with coarse sugar. Bake 7-8 minutes or until the bottoms are golden brown. Serve warm.

Overnight Cranberry-Eggnog Coffee Cake

To use up leftover eggnog, cranberries and pecans from the holiday season, I added them to a classic coffee cake recipe. It goes together the day before, chills overnight and bakes in the morning.

—LISA VARNER EL PASO, TX

PREP: 25 MIN. + CHILLING
BAKE: 35 MIN. + COOLING
MAKES: 15 SERVINGS

- ½ cup butter, softened
- 1 cup sugar
- 2 eggs
- 1 cup eggnog
- 1 cup (8 ounces) sour cream
- 1 teaspoon vanilla extract
- 2½ cups all-purpose flour
- 1½ teaspoons baking powder
- 1 teaspoon grated orange peel
- ½ teaspoon baking soda
- ½ teaspoon salt
- ½ cup dried cranberries

STREUSEL
- ⅔ cup sugar
- 2 tablespoons all-purpose flour
- 2 tablespoons butter, softened
- ½ teaspoon ground cinnamon
- ½ cup chopped pecans

GLAZE
- ½ cup confectioners' sugar
- 1 tablespoon eggnog

1. In a large bowl, cream butter and sugar until blended. Add eggs, one at a time, beating well after each addition. In a small bowl, whisk eggnog, sour cream and vanilla. In another bowl, whisk flour, baking powder, orange peel, baking soda and salt; add to the creamed mixture alternately with eggnog mixture, beating well after each addition. Stir in cranberries.

2. Transfer to a greased 13x9-in. baking pan. For streusel, in a small bowl, mix the sugar, flour, butter and cinnamon until blended. Stir in pecans; sprinkle over the batter. Refrigerate, covered, at least 8 hours or overnight.

3. Preheat oven to 350°. Remove pan from the refrigerator while the oven heats. Bake 35-40 minutes or until a toothpick inserted in center comes out clean. Cool on a wire rack 20 minutes.

4. For glaze, in a small bowl, mix the confectioners' sugar and eggnog until smooth; drizzle over cake. Serve warm.

NOTE *This recipe was tested with commercially prepared eggnog.*

Cranberry Whole Wheat Bagels

The bagel recipes I spotted in a magazine inspired me to try making my own. I've been baking them like crazy ever since! My whole wheat version dotted with dried cranberries is a favorite at Christmastime.

—TAMI KUEHL LOUP CITY, NE

PREP: 30 MIN. + RISING
BAKE: 15 MIN. + COOLING
MAKES: 1 DOZEN

- 1¼ cups water (70° to 80°)
- ⅓ cup honey
- 2 tablespoons butter, softened
- 1½ teaspoons salt
- 1 teaspoon dried orange peel
- ¼ teaspoon ground mace
- 2 cups all-purpose flour
- 1¼ cups whole wheat flour
- 2¾ teaspoons active dry yeast
- ½ cup dried cranberries
- 1 egg white
- 1 tablespoon water

1. In bread machine pan, place the first nine ingredients in the order suggested by the manufacturer. Select the dough setting. Check the dough after 5 minutes of mixing; add 1-2 tablespoons water or flour if needed. Just before the final kneading (your machine may audibly signal this), add the cranberries.

2. Preheat oven to 400°. When the cycle is completed, turn the dough onto a lightly floured surface. Divide and shape dough into 12 balls. Push your thumb through the center of each, stretching and shaping to form an even ring with a 1½-in. hole. Place on a floured surface. Cover with kitchen towels; let rest 10 minutes. Flatten bagels slightly.

3. Fill a Dutch oven two-thirds full with water; bring to a boil. Drop bagels, two at a time, into boiling water. Cook 45 seconds; turn and cook 45 seconds longer. Remove with a slotted spoon; drain well on paper towels.

4. Place the bagels 2 in. apart on parchment paper-lined baking sheets. Whisk the egg white and water; brush over bagels. Bake 15-20 minutes or until golden brown. Remove from the pans to wire racks to cool.

Shaping Dough Into Bagels

Think creating bagels from scratch is too complicated or time-consuming? The Cranberry Whole Wheat Bagels recipe at left makes it easy. Follow the steps below to form each little ring in a snap.

1. Shape the dough into balls. Push your thumb through the center of the dough, forming a 1½-in. hole.

2. Stretch and shape the dough to form an even ring.

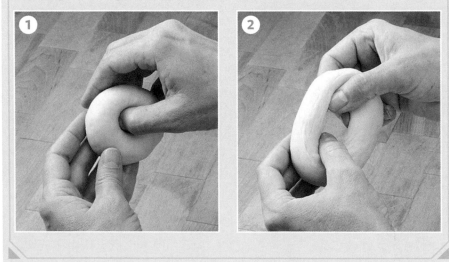

Ginger-Almond Pear Bread

When we moved to our property years ago, we inherited a bountiful pear tree. The fresh-picked fruit is especially good in this moist quick bread spiced with ginger and dotted with crunchy almonds.

—**RUTH EALY** PLAIN CITY, OH

PREP: 20 MIN. • **BAKE:** 50 MIN. + COOLING
MAKES: 1 LOAF (16 SLICES)

- 1½ cups all-purpose flour
- ¾ cup sugar
- 1 teaspoon baking powder
- ½ teaspoon baking soda
- ½ teaspoon salt
- ½ teaspoon ground ginger
- ½ teaspoon ground cinnamon
- 3 tablespoons finely chopped crystallized ginger
- 2 eggs
- ⅓ cup canola oil
- ½ teaspoon almond extract
- 2 cups finely chopped peeled ripe pears (about 2 large)
- ½ cup chopped almonds

1. Preheat oven to 350°. In a large bowl, whisk the first seven ingredients. Stir in crystallized ginger. In another bowl, whisk eggs, oil and extract. Add to flour mixture; stir just until moistened. Fold in the pears and almonds (batter will be stiff).

2. Transfer to a greased 9x5-in. loaf pan. Bake 50-60 minutes or until a toothpick inserted in center comes out clean. Cool in pan 10 minutes before removing to a wire rack to cool.

Holiday Helper

Crystallized ginger (also referred to as candied ginger) is the root of the ginger plant that has been cooked in a sugar syrup. Look in your grocery store's produce department or spice section for crystallized ginger. Store it in an airtight container in a cool, dark place for up to 3 months.

Sweet Italian Holiday Bread

This is authentic *ciambellotto*, a sweet loaf my great-grandmother used to bake in Italy. I still use her traditional recipe—the only update I made was for modern appliances.

—DENISE PERRIN VANCOUVER, WA

PREP: 15 MIN. • **BAKE:** 45 MIN.
MAKES: 1 LOAF (20 SLICES)

- 4 **cups all-purpose flour**
- 1 **cup sugar**
- 2 **tablespoons grated orange peel**
- 3 **teaspoons baking powder**
- 3 **eggs**
- ½ **cup 2% milk**
- ½ **cup olive oil**
- 1 **egg yolk**
- 1 **tablespoon coarse sugar**

1. Preheat oven to 350°. In a large bowl, whisk the flour, sugar, orange peel and baking powder. In another bowl, whisk the eggs, milk and oil until blended. Add to the flour mixture; stir just until moistened.

2. Shape into a 6-in. round loaf on a greased baking sheet. Brush the top with egg yolk; sprinkle with coarse sugar. Bake 45-50 minutes or until a toothpick inserted in center comes out clean. Cover top loosely with foil during the last 10 minutes if needed to prevent overbrowning. Remove from pan to a wire rack; serve warm.

seasonal
GET-TOGETHERS

Christmas In Paradise

Whatever the weather may be in your locale, celebrate the holiday season with friends in sunny style by throwing a festive tropical bash. Guests will feel like doing the hula when you serve mouthwatering grilled kabobs, pineapple-filled sliders, citrusy cocktails and coconut cream pie. Grab your sandals and sunglasses—life's a beach!

Pineapple Chicken Sliders

For fun appetizers that will tide over even the hungriest of partygoers, try these mini sandwiches. My youngest daughter is one of their biggest fans—she likes the small size and the sweet-tangy pineapple.

—**MARIA VASSEUR** VALENCIA, CA

PREP: 25 MIN. • **BROIL:** 10 MIN.
MAKES: 4 SERVINGS

- 1   **can (8 ounces) unsweetened crushed pineapple**
- ¼   **cup shredded carrot**
- 2   **tablespoons grated onion**
- 1   **tablespoon plus ½ teaspoon reduced-sodium soy sauce, divided**
- ¼   **teaspoon garlic powder**
- 1   **pound ground chicken**
- 8   **whole wheat dinner rolls, split**
- ¼   **cup reduced-fat sour cream**
- 2   **tablespoons mayonnaise**
- ¼   **teaspoon ground ginger**
- 1   **cup shredded lettuce**

1. Drain the pineapple, reserving 2 teaspoons juice. In a large bowl, combine carrot, onion, 1 tablespoon soy sauce, garlic powder and drained pineapple. Add the chicken; mix lightly but thoroughly. Shape mixture into eight ½-in.-thick patties.
2. Place rolls on a greased 15x10x1-in. baking pan, cut side up. Broil 4 in. from heat 30-60 seconds or until toasted. Remove from pan; keep warm.
3. Add burgers to same pan. Broil 4 in. from heat 4-6 minutes on each side or until a thermometer reads 165°.
4. Meanwhile, in a small bowl, mix the sour cream, mayonnaise, ginger, remaining soy sauce and reserved pineapple juice. Serve burgers on rolls with lettuce and sauce.

Holiday Helper

I love the flavor of fresh ginger. To always have that ingredient on hand, I store unpeeled gingerroot in my freezer. When I need some, I simply peel the root and slice, chop, mince or grate as needed.

—**SHEILA M.** MESA, AZ

Ginger-Orange Refresher

"A sunset in a glass" is how guests might describe this two-tone cocktail. With or without rum, it's a great thirst-quencher.

—**MARYBETH MANK** MESQUITE, TX

PREP: 15 MIN. • **COOK:** 15 MIN. + COOLING
MAKES: 10 SERVINGS

- 3   **medium oranges**
- 1½ **cups turbinado (washed raw) sugar**
- 1½ **cups water**
- 1   **cup fresh mint leaves**
- 8   **slices fresh gingerroot**
       Crushed ice
- 5   **ounces spiced rum, optional**
- 1   **bottle (1 liter) club soda, chilled**

1. Using a vegetable peeler, remove the colored layer of the peel from the oranges in strips, leaving the white pith. Cut oranges crosswise in half; squeeze juice from oranges.
2. In a small saucepan, combine the turbinado sugar, water and orange juice; bring to a boil. Stir in the mint leaves, sliced ginger and orange peel; return to a boil. Reduce the heat; simmer, uncovered, for 10 minutes. Cool completely.
3. Strain the syrup, discarding the solids. To serve, fill 10 highball glasses halfway with ice. Add 2 ounces syrup and, if desired, ½ ounce rum to each glass; top with club soda.

Teriyaki Glazed Pork & Vegetable Kabobs

Here's a colorful, fresh and fun-to-eat entree. Cook the unused Asian-style marinade into a zippy sauce and serve it alongside the kabobs for dipping.

—JANE MCMILLAN DANIA BEACH, FL

PREP: 40 MIN. + MARINATING
GRILL: 10 MIN. • **MAKES:** 16 KABOBS

- ⅔ **cup unsweetened pineapple juice**
- ⅔ **cup reduced-sodium teriyaki sauce**
- ⅓ **cup white wine or chicken broth**
- 3 **tablespoons sweet chili sauce**
- 4 **garlic cloves, minced**
- 5 **teaspoons rice vinegar**
- 5 **teaspoons sesame oil**
- 2 **pork tenderloin (1 pound each), cut into 1¼-inch cubes**

KABOBS

- 4 **cups cubed fresh pineapple**
- 2 **medium zucchini, cut into 1-inch pieces**
- 1 **large sweet red pepper, cut into 1-inch pieces**
- 1 **large red onion, cut into 1-inch pieces**
- ⅓ **cup sesame oil**

1. In a small bowl, whisk the first seven ingredients until blended. Pour 1 cup marinade into a large resealable plastic bag. Add pork; seal bag and turn to coat. Refrigerate pork and the remaining marinade, covered, for 2 hours.

2. In a small saucepan, bring reserved marinade to a boil; cook 8-10 minutes or until the liquid is reduced by half. Reserve for serving.

3. Drain the pork, discarding the marinade in the bag. On 16 metal or soaked wooden skewers, alternately thread pork, pineapple and vegetables. Brush kabobs with oil.

4. Grill the kabobs, covered, over medium heat or broil 4 in. from the heat 8-10 minutes or until the pork and zucchini are tender, turning occasionally. Remove from the grill. Brush kabobs with some of the glaze; serve with remaining glaze.

Tropical Snap Pea & Mango Salad

Want an extra-special salad? Toss romaine with mango, avocado, sugar snap peas, red onion and a homemade honey-lime dressing. Toasted coconut sprinkled on top adds crunch.
—TASTE OF HOME TEST KITCHEN

START TO FINISH: 25 MIN. • **MAKES:** 6 SERVINGS

- 3 **cups torn romaine**
- 1½ **cups fresh sugar snap peas, trimmed**
- 1 **medium mango, peeled and cubed**
- 1 **medium ripe avocado, peeled and cubed**
- ½ **cup thinly sliced red onion**

DRESSING

- 3 **tablespoons honey**
- 1 **teaspoon grated lime peel**
- 2 **tablespoons lime juice**
- 1 **tablespoon canola oil**
- ½ **cup flaked coconut, toasted**

In a large bowl, combine the first five ingredients. In a small bowl, whisk honey, lime peel, lime juice and oil until blended. Drizzle over salad and toss to coat. Sprinkle with coconut. Serve immediately.

NOTE *To toast coconut, spread it in a 15x10x1-in. baking pan. Bake at 350° for 5-10 minutes or until golden brown, stirring frequently.*

Lime & Coconut Cream Pie

My custard pie features two tropical flavors I love. Plus, it's a breeze to make. I throw most of the ingredients into the blender to whip up the filling, then pour it into a purchased crust.
—MANDY RIVERS LEXINGTON, SC

PREP: 30 MIN. • **BAKE:** 50 MIN. + CHILLING • **MAKES:** 8 SERVINGS

- **Pastry for single-crust pie (9 inches)**
- 3 **medium limes**
- 2 **cups flaked coconut, divided**
- 1 **can (13.66 ounces) coconut milk**
- 4 **eggs**
- 1 **cup sugar**
- ¼ **cup all-purpose flour**
- ¼ **teaspoon salt**
- ½ **teaspoon coconut extract, optional**
- 1 **cup heavy whipping cream**
- 1 **tablespoon confectioners' sugar**
  Toasted flaked coconut

1. Preheat oven to 350°. On a lightly floured surface, roll pastry dough to a ⅛-in.-thick circle; transfer to a 9-in. pie plate. Trim pastry to ½ in. beyond rim of plate; flute edge. Refrigerate while preparing filling.

2. Finely grate peel and squeeze juice from limes; place both in a blender. Add 1 cup coconut, coconut milk, eggs, sugar, flour, salt and, if desired, extract. Cover and process until blended. Add remaining 1 cup coconut; cover and pulse just until combined. Pour into pastry-lined plate (pie will be full).

3. Bake on a lower oven rack 50-55 minutes or until a knife inserted near the center comes out clean. Cool on a wire rack; refrigerate until cold.

4. In a small bowl, beat cream until it begins to thicken. Add confectioners' sugar; beat until soft peaks form. Spread over pie. Sprinkle with toasted coconut before serving.

NOTE *To toast coconut, spread it in a 15x10x1-in. baking pan. Bake at 350° for 5-10 minutes or until golden brown, stirring frequently.*

Holiday Helper

Before whipping heavy cream for recipes such as Lime & Coconut Cream Pie (below left), chill the bowl and beaters for about 30 minutes. Keep the cream in the refrigerator until you're ready to use it.

Vermicelli Rice Pilaf

I love preparing this recipe for holidays, just as my mom and generations of Armenian women did. It's a versatile side dish that pairs well with many different main courses.

—JEAN ECOS HARTLAND, WI

START TO FINISH: 30 MIN. • **MAKES:** 8 SERVINGS

- 3 **tablespoons butter**
- ½ **cup broken uncooked vermicelli (1-inch pieces)**
- 2 **cups uncooked basmati rice**
- 3 **cups reduced-sodium chicken broth**
- 1 **cup water**
- 1 **teaspoon salt**
- ½ **teaspoon pepper**
  Fresh chives, optional

1. In a large saucepan, heat butter over medium-high heat. Add the vermicelli; cook and stir 4-5 minutes or until golden brown. Add the rice, chicken broth, water, salt and pepper. Bring to a boil. Reduce heat; simmer, covered, 15-20 minutes or until the rice is tender. Remove from heat; let stand, covered, 5 minutes.

2. Fluff with a fork. If desired, top with fresh chives.

Beachy Candle Lantern

This fun party accent uses a medium-to-large mason jar. Add a wire hanger as described below, or just set the filled jar on a table. Here's how to make your own:

To fill the lantern, pour a small amount of loose sand or aquarium gravel into the bottom of the jar. Place a small pillar candle inside and press it firmly in place.

For a hanger, cut a piece of 12-gauge aluminum floral wire that is 1 in. larger than the circumference of the jar opening. Wrap the piece around the base of the opening. Twist the wire ends tightly together once, then push them against the jar to secure the wire.

For the handle, cut an 18-in. piece of wire and insert about 1 in. of an end under the wire on the jar. Push the short end of the wire upward and wrap it a few times around the long end to secure it. Repeat with the other wire end on the opposite side of the jar.

(Be sure to hang your candlelit lanterns away from flammable material and set them only on heat-proof surfaces—the glass will get hot.)

Shrimp & Sweet Potato Appetizer Kabobs

Roasted sweet potatoes and marinated shrimp combine for a fantastic party starter—especially when you thread them onto skewers and pop them on the grill!

—PAUL WARGASKI CHICAGO, IL

PREP: 40 MIN. + MARINATING
GRILL: 10 MIN. • **MAKES:** 1 DOZEN

- 2 **medium sweet potatoes (about 1¼ pounds)**
- 2 **tablespoons plus ¼ cup olive oil, divided**
- 1½ **teaspoons minced fresh rosemary**
- 1 **teaspoon chili powder, divided**
- 3 **tablespoons lemon juice**
- 12 **uncooked jumbo shrimp (about ¾ lb.), peeled and deveined**
- ¼ **teaspoon salt**
- ¼ **teaspoon pepper**

1. Preheat oven to 400°. Peel and cut the sweet potatoes into 1-inch cubes (about 24 cubes). Toss with 2 tablespoons oil, rosemary and ½ teaspoon chili powder. Transfer to a greased 15x10x1-in. baking pan. Roast 20-25 minutes or until almost tender, stirring occasionally. Cool slightly.

2. Meanwhile, in a small bowl, whisk the lemon juice and remaining oil and chili powder until blended. Reserve 2 tablespoons marinade for basting. Add shrimp to remaining marinade and toss to coat. Refrigerate, covered, 20 minutes.

3. On each of 12 soaked wooden appetizer skewers, thread the sweet potatoes and shrimp. Brush reserved marinade over kabobs; sprinkle with salt and pepper.

4. Grill, covered, over medium heat or broil 4 in. from heat 3-4 minutes on each side or until shrimp turn pink.

North Woods Breakfast

A fireplace crackling at a rustic log cabin in a snow-covered forest… bring the cozy feeling of the North Woods to your holiday table with a scrumptious breakfast of hearty fare. From bacon-filled pancakes and cheesy potatoes to a special egg scramble and sticky buns, these filling recipes will satisfy even the biggest appetites.

Apple-Cheddar Pancakes with Bacon

After sampling a scrumptious grilled apple-and-cheese sandwich, I decided to try the same flavors in pancakes. The idea of adding bacon came from my sister—a bacon fanatic!

—KIM KORVER ORANGE CITY, IA

PREP: 15 MIN. • **COOK:** 5 MIN./BATCH • **MAKES:** 16 PANCAKES

- 2 eggs
- 1 cup 2% milk
- 2 cups biscuit/baking mix
- 8 bacon strips, cooked and crumbled
- 2 large apples, peeled and shredded
- 1½ cups (6 ounces) shredded cheddar cheese
  Butter and maple syrup, optional

1. In a large bowl, whisk the eggs and milk until blended. Add biscuit mix and bacon; stir just until moistened. Fold in apples and cheese.

2. Lightly grease a griddle; heat over medium heat. Drop batter by ¼ cupfuls onto griddle, spreading with the back of a spoon as necessary. Cook until bubbles on top begin to pop and bottoms are golden brown. Turn; cook until second side is golden brown. If desired, serve with butter and syrup.

Birch Place Cards

Branch out for forest-inspired fun! Use a few natural materials to create rustic place cards. They're sure to charm guests at your North Woods-themed breakfast.

To start, cut a ¾-in.-thick slice from a 1½-in.-diameter birch branch. Drill a ⅛-in. hole in the center and insert a juniper sprig in the hole. With a 1¼-in. star paper punch, punch a star from a thin layer of birch bark or birch-print paper. Use a black marker to write a guest's name on the star, then glue it to the top of the sprig.

Three-Cheese Hash Brown Bake

Serve up comfort food for breakfast with this golden casserole featuring convenient frozen hash browns. The creamy side dish requires just 10 minutes of prep before you pop it in the oven.

—NANCY SIDHU FRANKLIN, WI

PREP: 10 MIN. • **BAKE:** 55 MIN. + STANDING • **MAKES:** 12 SERVINGS

- 2 cans (10¾ ounces each) condensed cream of potato soup, undiluted
- 1 cup (8 ounces) sour cream
- 1 teaspoon garlic powder
- ½ teaspoon pepper
- 1 package (32 ounces) frozen cubed hash brown potatoes, thawed
- 2 cups (8 ounces) shredded cheddar cheese
- 1 cup grated Parmesan cheese
- ½ cup shredded Swiss cheese

1. Preheat oven to 350°. In a large bowl, mix soup, sour cream, garlic powder and pepper until blended. Stir in remaining ingredients.

2. Transfer to a greased 13x9-in. baking dish. Bake, uncovered, 55-65 minutes or until golden brown and potatoes are tender. Let stand 10 minutes before serving.

Creamy Eggs &
Mushrooms Au Gratin

When I'm looking for a brunch dish that
has the crowd appeal of scrambled eggs
but is a little more special, I turn to this
skillet recipe. The rich Parmesan sauce
is simple but delicious, and lots of fresh
mushrooms add heartiness.

—DEBORAH WILLIAMS PEORIA, AZ

PREP: 15 MIN. • **COOK:** 25 MIN.
MAKES: 8 SERVINGS

- 9 **tablespoons butter, divided**
- 1 **pound sliced fresh mushrooms**
- 2 **green onions, finely chopped and divided**
- 3 **tablespoons all-purpose flour**
- ¾ **teaspoon salt, divided**
- ¼ **teaspoon pepper, divided**
- 1 **cup 2% milk**
- ½ **cup heavy whipping cream**
- 2 **tablespoons plus ½ cup grated Parmesan cheese, divided**
- 16 **eggs**

1. In a large broiler-safe skillet, heat
3 tablespoons butter over medium-
high heat. Add mushrooms; cook and
stir 4-6 minutes or until browned. Add
half of the green onions; cook 1 minute
longer. Remove from pan with a slotted
spoon. Wipe skillet clean.

2. In a small saucepan, melt
2 tablespoons butter over medium
heat. Stir in the flour, ½ teaspoon salt
and ⅛ teaspoon pepper until smooth;
gradually whisk in the milk and heavy
whipping cream. Bring to a boil,
stirring constantly; cook and stir 2-4
minutes or until thickened. Remove
from the heat; stir in 2 tablespoons
Parmesan cheese.

3. Preheat broiler. In a large bowl,
whisk eggs and the remaining salt
and pepper. In the same skillet, heat
remaining 4 tablespoons butter over
medium heat. Pour in egg mixture;
cook and stir until eggs are thickened
and no liquid egg remains. Remove
from heat.

4. Spoon half of the sauce over the
eggs; top with the mushrooms. Add
the remaining sauce; sprinkle with the
remaining cheese. Broil 4-5 in. from
the heat 4-6 minutes or until the top
is lightly browned. Sprinkle with the
remaining green onions.

Homemade Biscuits & Maple Sausage Gravy

I remember digging into a mouthwatering breakfast of flaky, gravy-smothered biscuits on Christmas and other holidays when I was a child. What a way to start the day!

—JENN TIDWELL FAIR OAKS, CA

PREP: 30 MIN. • **BAKE:** 15 MIN.
MAKES: 8 SERVINGS

- 2 **cups all-purpose flour**
- 3 **teaspoons baking powder**
- 1 **tablespoon sugar**
- 1 **teaspoon salt**
- ¼ **teaspoon pepper, optional**
- 3 **tablespoons cold butter, cubed**
- 1 **tablespoon shortening**
- ¾ **cup 2% milk**

SAUSAGE GRAVY

- 1 **pound bulk maple pork sausage**
- ¼ **cup all-purpose flour**
- 3 **cups 2% milk**
- 2 **tablespoons maple syrup**
- ½ **teaspoon salt**
- ¼ **teaspoon ground sage**
- ¼ **teaspoon coarsely ground pepper**

1. Preheat oven to 400°. In a large bowl, whisk the flour, baking powder, sugar, salt and, if desired, pepper. Cut in the cold butter and shortening until the mixture resembles coarse crumbs. Add the milk; stir just until moistened. Turn onto a lightly floured surface; knead gently 8-10 times.

2. Pat or roll biscuit dough to 1-in. thickness; cut with a floured 2-in. biscuit cutter. Place 1 in. apart on an ungreased baking sheet. Bake 15-17 minutes or until golden brown.

3. Meanwhile, in a large skillet, cook sausage over medium heat 6-8 minutes or until no longer pink, breaking into crumbles. Stir in flour until blended; gradually stir in the milk. Bring to a boil, stirring constantly; cook and stir 4-6 minutes or until sauce is thickened. Stir in the remaining ingredients. Serve with warm biscuits.

Maple-Walnut Sticky Buns

Mmm! These ooey-gooey goodies will have the whole family licking maple syrup from their fingers—and grabbing seconds.

—NANCY FOUST STONEBORO, PA

PREP: 45 MIN. + RISING • **BAKE:** 30 MIN.
MAKES: 2 DOZEN

- 1 package (¼ ounce) active dry yeast
- 1 cup warm water (110° to 115°)
- ½ cup mashed potatoes (without added milk and butter)
- 1 egg
- 2 tablespoons shortening
- 2 tablespoons sugar
- 1 teaspoon salt
- 3 to 3½ cups all-purpose flour

TOPPING
- 1 cup maple syrup
- ¾ cup coarsely chopped walnuts

FILLING
- ⅓ cup sugar
- 1½ teaspoons ground cinnamon
- 3 tablespoons butter, softened

1. In a small bowl, dissolve the yeast in warm water. In a large bowl, combine the mashed potatoes, egg, shortening, sugar, salt, yeast mixture and 1 cup flour; beat on medium speed until smooth. Stir in enough remaining flour to form a soft dough.

2. Turn the dough onto a floured surface; knead until smooth and elastic, about 6-8 minutes. Place in a greased bowl, turning once to grease the top. Cover with plastic wrap and refrigerate overnight.

3. Pour syrup into a greased 13x9-in. baking dish; sprinkle with walnuts. In a small bowl, mix sugar and cinnamon. Punch down dough. Turn onto a lightly floured surface. Roll into a 24x8-in. rectangle. Spread with butter to within ½ in. of the edges; sprinkle with the cinnamon-sugar. Roll up jelly-roll style, starting with a long side; pinch seam to seal. Cut into 24 slices.

4. Place in prepared pan, cut side down. Cover with a kitchen towel; let rise in a warm place until doubled, about 30 minutes. Preheat oven to 350°. Bake 30-35 minutes or until golden brown. Cool in dish 5 minutes before inverting onto a serving plate.

Ham Steaks with Gruyere, Bacon & Mushrooms

Here's a satisfying choice for meat lovers. It's one of my favorite dishes because the bacon, Gruyere and mushrooms in the topping are an exceptional combination.
—**LISA SPEER** PALM BEACH, FL

START TO FINISH: 25 MIN.
MAKES: 4 SERVINGS

- 2 tablespoons butter
- ½ pound sliced fresh mushrooms
- 1 shallot, finely chopped
- 2 garlic cloves, minced
- ¼ teaspoon salt
- ⅛ teaspoon coarsely ground pepper
- 1 fully cooked boneless ham steak (about 1¼ pounds), cut into four pieces
- 1 cup (4 ounces) shredded Gruyere cheese
- 4 bacon strips, cooked and crumbled
- 1 tablespoon minced fresh parsley

1. In a large nonstick skillet, heat butter over medium-high heat. Add mushrooms and shallot; cook and stir 4-6 minutes or until tender. Add garlic, salt and pepper; cook 1 minute longer. Remove from the pan; keep warm. Wipe skillet clean.

2. In the same pan, cook the pieces of ham over medium heat 3 minutes. Turn; sprinkle with the Gruyere cheese and bacon. Cook, covered, 2-4 minutes longer or until the cheese is melted and the ham is heated through. Serve with the mushroom mixture; sprinkle with minced parsley.

Orange Fritters

My daughter made a citrusy version of apple fritters for 4-H demonstrations at our county and state fairs. The crowd-sized recipe yields 11 dozen, but it can easily be cut in half to suit a smaller group.
—**DEBBIE JOHNSON** CENTERTOWN, MO

PREP: 15 MIN. • **COOK:** 5 MIN./BATCH
MAKES: ABOUT 11 DOZEN

- 6 cups all-purpose flour
- 6 cups biscuit/baking mix
- 2 cups sugar
- 2 tablespoons baking powder
- 6 eggs
- 2 to 3 tablespoons grated orange peel
- 4 cups orange juice
  Oil for deep-fat frying
  Confectioners' sugar

1. In a large bowl, whisk the flour, biscuit mix, sugar and baking powder. In another bowl, whisk eggs, orange peel and orange juice until blended. Add to dry ingredients, stirring just until moistened.

2. In an electric skillet or deep fryer, heat oil to 375°. Drop the batter by rounded tablespoonfuls, a few at a time, into hot oil. Fry about 1-2 minutes on each side or until golden brown. Drain on paper towels; cool slightly. Dust with confectioners' sugar.

seasonal get-togethers ❄ 77

Reindeer Games Party

On Dasher, on Dancer, on Prancer and Vixen! Treat the "deer" little ones in your life to a merry reindeer-themed Christmas party. Young children will love joining in fun-filled games and having a yummy lunch featuring noodle-filled Spiral Pepperoni Pizza Bake. Don't forget a team of red-nosed Rudolph Cupcakes for dessert!

Rudolph Cupcakes

Our son needed treats for his class at school but forgot to tell me about it until the day before. It's the sort of situation every mom finds herself in at one time or another! We improvised and created little Rudolph faces on cupcakes.
—**KAREN GARDINER** EUTAW, AL

PREP: 20 MIN. • **BAKE:** 25 MIN. + COOLING
MAKES: 2 DOZEN

- 1 **package white cake mix (regular size)**
- 1 **can (16 ounces) chocolate frosting**
- 24 **each brown and blue M&M's minis**
- 24 **miniature marshmallows, halved**
- 24 **red jelly beans**
- 24 **miniature vanilla wafers**
- 48 **miniature pretzels**

1. Prepare and bake the white cake mix according to package directions for cupcakes.
2. Reserve 2-3 teaspoons frosting; spread the remaining frosting over the cooled cupcakes. For the eyes, using reserved frosting, press an M&M mini into each marshmallow half. Place two eyes on each cupcake. For nose, attach a red jelly bean onto each vanilla wafer; place on cupcake. Insert pretzels into cupcakes for antlers.

Spiral Pepperoni Pizza Bake

My grandmother used to make this cheesy, pepperoni-topped casserole for my Girl Scout troop when I was growing up. Now, I fix the pizza bake for my stepdaughters' troop. The kids beg me to make it!
—**KIMBERLY HOWLAND** FREMONT, MI

PREP: 30 MIN. • **BAKE:** 40 MIN.
MAKES: 12 SERVINGS

- 1 **package (16 ounces) spiral pasta**
- 2 **pounds ground beef**
- 1 **large onion, chopped**
- 1 **teaspoon salt**
- ½ **teaspoon garlic salt**
- ½ **teaspoon Italian seasoning**
- ½ **teaspoon pepper**
- 2 **cans (15 ounces each) pizza sauce**
- 2 **eggs, lightly beaten**
- 2 **cups 2% milk**
- ½ **cup shredded Parmesan cheese**

- 4 **cups (16 ounces) shredded part-skim mozzarella cheese**
- 1 **package (3½ ounces) sliced pepperoni**

1. Preheat oven to 350°. Cook pasta according to package directions.
2. Meanwhile, in a Dutch oven, cook the beef and onion over medium heat 8-10 minutes or until beef is no longer pink, breaking up beef into crumbles; drain. Sprinkle with seasonings. Stir in pizza sauce; remove from heat.

3. In a large bowl, mix eggs, milk and Parmesan cheese. Drain pasta; add to the egg mixture and toss to combine. Transfer to a greased 3-qt. baking dish. Top with beef mixture, mozzarella cheese and pepperoni.
4. Bake, covered, 20 minutes. Bake, uncovered, 20-25 minutes longer or until golden brown and heated through.

1. In a small bowl, mix the first seven ingredients. Transfer to a 4-ounce jar. Store in a cool dry place up to 1 year. Shake well before using. Makes: about 6 tablespoons mix.

2. To prepare one batch salad dressing: In a small bowl, whisk mayonnaise, buttermilk and 1 tablespoon mix. Refrigerate, covered, at least 1 hour to allow flavors to blend.

3. To prepare one batch dip: In a small bowl, combine mayonnaise, sour cream and 2 tablespoons mix; stir until blended. Refrigerate, covered, at least 2 hours before serving.

Fruit & Cereal Snack Mix

I combine dried fruit with cinnamon cereal for a kid-friendly treat. At parties, present it in Rudolph Cones (see the tip box below).
—**JOHN LANCASTER** UNION GROVE, WI

START TO FINISH: 10 MIN.
MAKES: 2½ QUARTS

- 8 **cups Cinnamon Toast Crunch cereal**
- ¾ **cup dried cranberries**
- ¾ **cup raisins**
- ½ **cup dried cherries**
- 1 **package (2½ ounces) dried apple chips, broken into large pieces**

Place all ingredients in a large bowl; toss to combine. Store in airtight containers.

Ranch Dressing and Dip Mix

Keep this versatile blend handy to whip up a delicious vegetable dip or salad dressing at a moment's notice. Children will love it served with veggies as a snack or side dish.

—**JOAN HALLFORD**

NORTH RICHLAND HILLS, TX

START TO FINISH: 10 MIN.
MAKES: 1 CUP DRESSING OR 2 CUPS DIP PER BATCH

- 2 **tablespoons dried parsley flakes**
- 1 **tablespoon minced chives**
- 1 **tablespoon garlic powder**
- 2 **teaspoons lemon-pepper seasoning**
- 1½ **teaspoons dried oregano**
- 1½ **teaspoons dried tarragon**
- 1 **teaspoon salt**

ADDITIONAL INGREDIENTS FOR DRESSING (PER BATCH)
- ½ **cup mayonnaise**
- ½ **cup buttermilk**

ADDITIONAL INGREDIENTS FOR DIP (PER BATCH)
- 1 **cup mayonnaise**
- 1 **cup (8 ounces) sour cream**

Rudolph Cones

Thrill young guests with a fun party favor or take-home treat. Just fix Fruit & Cereal Snack Mix (recipe above right), package it in sandwich bags and place them in cute cones.

For each cone, cut a 6-in. square of card stock. (To easily cut four at a time, use 12-in.-square sheets of card stock.)

Roll a square into a wide cone (the back will be slightly open) and tape it closed. Poke two holes and twist a chenille stem in each for antlers. Then just glue on wiggle eyes and a pompom nose—red, of course!

Orange Cream Fruit Salad

A bowl of fruit becomes a special treat when you stir in a creamy citrus dressing. It's a bright, refreshing salad for breakfast, brunch, lunch—any meal at all.

—**GAYLE GRIGG** PHOENIX, AZ

PREP: 10 MIN. + CHILLING
MAKES: 10 SERVINGS

- 1½ cups cold 2% milk
- ⅓ cup thawed orange juice concentrate
- 1 package (3.4 ounces) instant vanilla pudding mix
- ¾ cup sour cream
- 1 can (20 ounces) pineapple tidbits, drained
- 1 can (15¼ ounces) sliced peaches, drained
- 1 can (11 ounces) mandarin oranges, drained
- 2 firm bananas, sliced
- 1 medium apple, chopped

1. In a large bowl, whisk milk, orange juice concentrate and vanilla pudding mix for 2 minutes. Stir in sour cream.
2. Add remaining ingredients; toss gently to coat. Refrigerate, covered, at least 2 hours before serving.

Cherry Cranberry Punch

This festive thirst-quencher is one of my favorite beverages to make for functions at our church, where my husband serves as pastor. Serve each cup with or without a scoop of lemon sherbet on top.

—**CHRISTINE FLETCHER** BRONX, NY

PREP: 10 MIN. + CHILLING
MAKES: 16 SERVINGS (3 QUARTS)

- 1 cup boiling water
- 1 package (3 ounces) cherry gelatin
- 4 cups cranberry juice
- 3 cups cold water
- ¾ cup thawed lemonade concentrate
- 3½ cups chilled club soda
  Lemon sherbet, optional

1. In a small bowl, add the boiling water to the cherry gelatin; stir 2 minutes to completely dissolve. Stir in the cranberry juice, cold water and concentrate. Refrigerate, covered, until cold.
2. To serve, transfer gelatin mixture to a punch bowl or large pitcher. Stir in club soda. If desired, top with scoops of lemon sherbet.

sides to
MIX & MATCH

Triple-Mushroom Au Gratin Potatoes

When I first started cooking, the only mushrooms I used were the button variety. Now I love experimenting with different types. This three-times-as-good recipe is so filling, it can make a meatless entree.

—NADINE MESCH MOUNT HEALTHY, OH

PREP: 30 MIN. • **BAKE:** 1 HOUR + STANDING
MAKES: 10 SERVINGS

- **6** tablespoons butter, divided
- **½** pound each sliced fresh shiitake, baby portobello and button mushrooms
- **1** tablespoon sherry, optional
- **5** tablespoons all-purpose flour
- **3** cups half-and-half cream
- **3** tablespoons minced fresh rosemary
- **1½** teaspoons salt
- **1** teaspoon pepper
- **2** cups (8 ounces) shredded Gruyere cheese
- **2** pounds red potatoes, thinly sliced
- **½** teaspoon paprika

1. Preheat oven to 350°. In a large skillet, heat 1 tablespoon butter over medium-high heat. Add the sliced mushrooms; cook and stir until tender. If desired, stir in the sherry and cook 1-2 minutes longer or until evaporated. Remove from the pan.

2. In the same pan, melt remaining butter over medium heat. Stir in the flour until smooth; gradually whisk in the cream. Bring to a boil, stirring constantly; cook and stir 2 minutes or until thickened. Reduce the heat to medium-low. Stir in rosemary, salt and pepper. Gradually add cheese, stirring until melted. Remove from heat.

3. Arrange potatoes in an even layer in a greased 13x9-in. baking dish. Top with mushrooms and sauce mixture; sprinkle with paprika.

4. Bake, covered, 40 minutes. Bake, uncovered, 20-25 minutes longer or until golden brown and bubbly. Let stand 15 minutes before serving.

Creamy Carrot Bake

PREP: 20 MIN. • **BAKE:** 25 MIN.
MAKES: 8 SERVINGS

- 2 **pounds fresh carrots, thinly sliced**
- ¼ **cup butter, cubed**
- ¼ **cup finely chopped onion**
- ¼ **cup all-purpose flour**
- ¼ **teaspoon ground mustard**
- 2 **cups 2% milk**
- 1 **cup (4 ounces) shredded Monterey Jack cheese**
- 1 **cup (4 ounces) shredded sharp cheddar cheese**
- 1 **tablespoon prepared horseradish**
- 1 **teaspoon salt**
- ½ **teaspoon pepper**
- ¼ **teaspoon celery salt**
- 1 **cup soft bread crumbs**
- 2 **tablespoons butter, melted**

1. Preheat oven to 350°. In a Dutch oven, bring 1 in. of water to a boil. Add the carrots; cook, covered, 5-7 minutes or until crisp-tender. Drain; set aside.

2. In the same pan, heat butter over medium heat. Add onion; cook and stir 1-2 minutes or until tender.

3. Stir in the flour and mustard until blended; gradually whisk in milk. Bring to a boil, stirring constantly; cook and stir 1-2 minutes or until thickened. Add cheeses, horseradish and seasonings; cook and stir until the cheese is melted. Stir in carrots.

4. Transfer to a greased 11x7-in. baking dish. In a small bowl, toss the bread crumbs with melted butter; sprinkle over the top. Bake, uncovered, 25-30 minutes or until heated through and bread crumbs are lightly browned.

NOTE *To make soft bread crumbs, tear bread into pieces and place in a food processor or blender. Cover and pulse until crumbs form. One slice of bread yields ½ to ¾ cup crumbs.*

"Wondering what vegetable to serve for your Christmas feast? Here's a special way of preparing sliced fresh carrots. The bonus is, it goes with just about any main course."

—SANDY O'NEAL BOALSBURG, PA

Holiday Creamed Spinach

My mother made a variety of spinach dishes when I was growing up, but her delicious creamed version is the one that has stayed with me through the years.

—EDIE DESPAIN LOGAN, UT

PREP: 20 MIN. • **COOK:** 15 MIN.
MAKES: 12 SERVINGS (½ CUP EACH)

- 4 packages (10 ounces each) fresh spinach, trimmed
- 2 tablespoons butter
- 2 medium onions, finely chopped
- 3 tablespoons all-purpose flour
- 1 teaspoon salt
- ½ teaspoon white pepper
- 2 cups whole milk
- ½ cup heavy whipping cream
- ½ cup grated Parmesan cheese

1. In a Dutch oven, place steamer basket over 1 in. of water. Place a fourth of the spinach in basket. Bring water to a boil. Reduce heat to maintain a low boil; steam, covered, 3-4 minutes or just until spinach is wilted. Transfer to a colander; drain. Repeat with the remaining spinach.

2. When the spinach is cool enough to handle, squeeze dry. Coarsely chop the spinach.

3. In a large skillet, heat the butter over medium-high heat. Add onions; cook and stir until tender. Stir in the flour, salt and pepper until blended; gradually whisk in the milk and cream. Bring to a boil, stirring constantly; cook and stir 1-2 minutes or until thickened. Stir in the Parmesan cheese and spinach; heat through.

Holiday Helper

Orzo is a rice-shaped pasta that cooks quickly and can make a fast side dish for the holidays or anytime. With its similar shape and mild flavor, orzo can often be substituted for rice. Ounce for ounce, the two contain similar amounts of sodium, fat, sugar and carbohydrates.

Orzo Timbales with Fontina Cheese

Take mac and cheese to a whole new level using tiny orzo pasta and fontina. These delightfully different timbales bake in ramekins for perfect single servings.

—GILDA LESTER MILLSBORO, DE

PREP: 20 MIN. • **BAKE:** 30 MIN.
MAKES: 6 SERVINGS

- 1 cup uncooked orzo pasta
- 1½ cups (6 ounces) shredded fontina cheese
- ½ cup finely chopped roasted sweet red peppers
- 1 can (2¼ ounces) sliced ripe olives, drained
- 2 eggs
- 1½ cups 2% milk
- ¼ teaspoon salt
- ⅛ teaspoon ground nutmeg
  Minced fresh parsley, optional

1. Preheat oven to 350°. Cook orzo according to package directions for al dente; drain. Transfer to a bowl. Stir in cheese, peppers and olives. Divide among six greased 10-oz. ramekins or custard cups. Place on a baking sheet.

2. In a small bowl, whisk eggs, milk, salt and nutmeg; pour over pasta mixture. Bake 30-35 minutes or until golden brown. Let stand 5 minutes before serving. If desired, run a knife around the sides of ramekins and invert onto serving plates; sprinkle with parsley.

Mixed Greens with Bacon & Cranberries

When my holiday menu calls for a tossed salad, I dress up a mix of leafy greens with peppered bacon, dried cranberries and blue cheese. A zesty homemade vinaigrette is the finishing touch.

—**TERESA RALSTON** NEW ALBANY, OH

START TO FINISH: 20 MIN. • **MAKES:** 8 SERVINGS (¾ CUP EACH)

- ½ cup orange juice
- ½ cup dried cranberries
- 4 cups fresh arugula or baby spinach
- 4 cups spring mix salad greens
- ½ cup crumbled blue cheese
- 6 thick-sliced peppered bacon strips, cooked and crumbled

VINAIGRETTE
- 2 tablespoons balsamic vinegar
- 2 tablespoons olive oil
- 1 tablespoon honey
- 1½ teaspoons orange juice
- 1½ teaspoons Dijon mustard
- 1 teaspoon grated orange peel
- ⅛ teaspoon salt
- ⅛ teaspoon pepper

1. In a small saucepan, bring orange juice to a boil; remove from heat. Stir in cranberries; let stand 5 minutes. Drain, discarding remaining juice or saving for another use.

2. In a large bowl, combine the arugula and salad greens; top with the blue cheese, bacon and cranberries. In a small bowl, whisk the vinaigrette ingredients. Drizzle over salad; toss to coat. Serve immediately.

Fresh Cranberry Relish

This no-cook fruit medley spiced with cinnamon and ginger is a wonderfully refreshing complement to a savory main course. The tartness mellows as the relish chills overnight.

—**DEBORAH WILLIAMS** PEORIA, AZ

PREP: 15 MIN. + CHILLING • **MAKES:** 4 CUPS

- 1 package (12 ounces) fresh or frozen cranberries, chopped
- 1 can (8 ounces) unsweetened crushed pineapple, drained
- 1 medium apple, chopped
- 1 medium orange, chopped
- 1 cup sugar
- ¾ cup chopped pecans, toasted
- 1 tablespoon lemon juice
- ½ teaspoon ground cinnamon
- ½ teaspoon minced fresh gingerroot

Place all ingredients in a large bowl; toss to combine. Refrigerate, covered, overnight to blend.

NOTE *To toast nuts, spread them in a 15x10x1-in. baking pan. Bake at 350° for 5-10 minutes or until lightly browned, stirring occasionally. Or, spread in a dry nonstick skillet; heat over low heat until lightly browned, stirring occasionally.*

sides to mix & match ✳ 87

Brussels Sprouts Au Gratin

In our house, Brussels sprouts have always been a popular vegetable. I tried roasting them and adding a cream sauce, shredded Swiss and bread crumbs. The result was a new holiday dinner tradition.
—**GWEN GREGORY** RIO OSO, CA

PREP: 30 MIN. • **BAKE:** 15 MIN.
MAKES: 6 SERVINGS

- 2 pounds fresh Brussels sprouts, quartered
- 1 tablespoon olive oil
- ½ teaspoon salt, divided
- ¼ teaspoon pepper, divided
- ¾ cup cubed sourdough or French bread
- 1 tablespoon butter
- 1 tablespoon minced fresh parsley
- 2 garlic cloves, coarsely chopped
- 1 cup heavy whipping cream
- ⅛ teaspoon crushed red pepper flakes
- ⅛ teaspoon ground nutmeg
- ½ cup shredded white sharp cheddar or Swiss cheese

1. Preheat oven to 450°. Place the Brussels sprouts in a large bowl. Add oil, ¼ teaspoon salt and ⅛ teaspoon pepper; toss to coat. Transfer to two ungreased 15x10x1-in. baking pans. Roast 8-10 minutes or until lightly browned and crisp-tender. Reduce oven setting to 400°.

2. Meanwhile, place the bread, butter, parsley and garlic in a food processor; pulse until fine crumbs form.

3. Place roasted Brussels sprouts in a greased 8-in.-square baking dish. In a small bowl, mix the heavy whipping cream, red pepper flakes, nutmeg and remaining salt and pepper. Pour over the sprouts; sprinkle with cheese. Top with crumb mixture. Bake, uncovered, 15-20 minutes or until bubbly and topping is lightly browned.

Cheese Fondue Mac & Cheese

When my husband was a missionary kid living with his family in Switzerland, his mother learned how to make fondue. I thought of combining that favorite of his with one of mine: macaroni and cheese!
—**KATHY LEE** ELK RAPIDS, MI

PREP: 20 MIN. • **COOK:** 25 MIN.
MAKES: 8 SERVINGS

- ¼ cup panko (Japanese) bread crumbs
- 1½ teaspoons plus 1 tablespoon olive oil, divided
- 4 ounces sliced pancetta, finely chopped
- 3 cups uncooked elbow macaroni (about 12 ounces)
- 3 tablespoons butter
- 1 shallot, finely chopped
- 1 garlic clove, minced
- 3 tablespoons all-purpose flour
- ½ teaspoon salt
- ¼ teaspoon pepper
  Dash ground nutmeg
- 1½ cups 2% milk
- ½ cup white wine or chicken broth
- 1 cup (4 ounces) shredded Emmenthaler or Swiss cheese
- 1 cup (4 ounces) shredded Gruyere or Swiss cheese

1. In a small skillet, toss panko bread crumbs with 1½ teaspoons oil; cook and stir over medium-high heat until golden brown. Remove from pan.

2. In same skillet, heat the remaining oil over medium heat. Add pancetta; cook until crisp, stirring occasionally. Remove with a slotted spoon; drain on paper towels.

3. Cook the macaroni according to the package directions. Meanwhile, in a large saucepan, heat the butter over medium heat. Add the shallot and garlic; cook and stir 1-2 minutes or until tender. Stir in the flour and seasonings until blended; gradually whisk in the milk and wine. Bring to a boil, stirring constantly; cook and stir 2-3 minutes or until thickened. Stir in the cheeses until melted.

4. Drain the macaroni; add to sauce. Add the pancetta; toss to combine. Sprinkle with toasted bread crumbs.

Apricot, Cranberry & Walnut Pilaf

With dried fruit, nuts and Italian seasoning, this rice medley is a delightfully different mix of tastes and textures. It's always on the menu for our big holiday feasts.

—EVA SORRENTINO CRAIG, CO

START TO FINISH: 25 MIN.
MAKES: 4 SERVINGS

- 1 tablespoon canola oil
- ¼ cup chopped onion
- ¼ cup chopped celery
- 1 garlic clove, minced
- 2 cups instant brown rice
- 2 cups reduced-sodium chicken broth
- 1 tablespoon Italian seasoning
- ¼ cup chopped walnuts
- ¼ cup finely chopped dried apricots
- ¼ cup dried cranberries

1. In a large skillet, heat the oil over medium-high heat. Add the onion and celery; cook and stir until tender. Add garlic; cook 1 minute longer.

2. Stir in the brown rice, chicken broth and Italian seasoning. Bring to a boil. Reduce the heat; simmer, covered, 5 minutes or until liquid is absorbed. Stir in remaining ingredients.

Grecian Potato Cups

Tired of having the same old spuds? If you like stuffed potato skins, you'll love these little cups filled with feta cheese, spinach, onion and more. They're easy for guests to take from a buffet table, too.

—NICOLE FILIZETTI JACKSONVILLE, FL

PREP: 25 MIN. • **BAKE:** 70 MIN.
MAKES: 8 SERVINGS

- 8 medium red potatoes (about 2¼ pounds)
- 4 tablespoons olive oil, divided
- 1 teaspoon salt
- ¾ teaspoon pepper
- 1 medium onion, finely chopped
- 1 teaspoon dried oregano
- 2 garlic cloves, minced
- 1 package (10 ounces) frozen chopped spinach, thawed and squeezed dry
- 1 tablespoon lemon juice
- 1½ cups (6 ounces) crumbled feta cheese

1. Preheat oven to 425°. Scrub the potatoes; pierce several times with a fork. Place in a foil-lined 15x10x1-in. baking pan; bake 40-45 minutes or until tender.

2. Increase oven setting to 450°. When cool enough to handle, cut each potato crosswise in half. Scoop out the pulp, leaving ¼-in.-thick shells. (Save the removed potato for another use.) If necessary, carefully trim the bottom of the cups so the potatoes will sit upright. Rub 3 tablespoons oil over inside and outside of potatoes.

3. Place potatoes on two 15x10x1-in. baking pans, cut side down; sprinkle with salt and pepper. Bake 8-10 minutes or until the potato skin is crisp. Turn the potatoes over; bake 10-12 minutes longer or until golden brown. Remove from oven. Reduce oven setting to 350°.

4. In a large skillet, heat the remaining oil over medium-high heat. Add the onion and oregano; cook and stir 2-3 minutes or until the onion is tender. Add the garlic; cook 1 minute longer. Stir in the spinach and lemon juice; heat through. Remove from the heat; stir in the feta cheese. Spoon into the potato cups. Bake 8-10 minutes or until heated through.

Lemon-Roasted Squash with Tarragon

Roasting really brings out the flavor of butternut squash and zucchini. I drizzle them with lemon juice, oil, garlic and seasonings, then pop them into the oven.
—**CARRIE FARIAS** OAK RIDGE, NJ

PREP: 15 MIN. • **BAKE:** 20 MIN.
MAKES: 8 SERVINGS

- 1 **medium butternut squash (about 3 pounds), peeled and cut into ¾-inch cubes**
- 2 **medium zucchini, halved lengthwise and cut into ¾-inch slices**
- 2 **tablespoons lemon juice**
- 2 **tablespoons olive oil**
- 2 **garlic cloves, minced**
- ¾ **teaspoon salt**
- ½ **teaspoon pepper**
- 2 **teaspoons minced fresh tarragon**

1. Preheat oven to 425°. Place squash and zucchini in a shallow roasting pan. In a small bowl, whisk lemon juice, oil, garlic, salt and pepper until blended; drizzle over vegetables and toss to coat.
2. Roast 20-25 minutes or until tender, stirring occasionally. Sprinkle with tarragon.

Warm Cannellini Bean & Bacon Salad

My husband and son enjoy all kinds of bean dishes. For a change of pace, I whipped up this hearty salad. Feel free to replace the peppered bacon with the regular kind.
—**LOU SURIANO** TWINSBURG, OH

START TO FINISH: 20 MIN.
MAKES: 4 SERVINGS

- 4 **thick-sliced peppered bacon strips, chopped**
- ¼ **cup chopped onion**
- 3 **garlic cloves, minced**
- 1 **tablespoon chopped fresh sage**
- 1 **teaspoon minced fresh thyme**
- ½ **teaspoon onion powder**
- 2 **cans (15 ounces each) cannellini beans, rinsed and drained**
- 1 **can (14½ ounces) Italian diced tomatoes, undrained**

1. In a large skillet, cook the bacon over medium heat until crisp, stirring occasionally. Remove with a slotted spoon; drain on paper towels. Discard bacon drippings, reserving 1 tablespoon in the pan.
2. Add the onion to bacon drippings; cook and stir over medium heat 2-3 minutes or until tender. Add the garlic and seasonings; cook 1 minute longer. Stir in the cannellini beans and diced tomatoes; heat through. Stir in the bacon. Serve warm.

Smoked Sausage & Potato Dressing

I first tried this recipe for Thanksgiving dinner. My husband can be a picky eater and I wasn't sure he'd like the stuffing, but he ended up eating more of that than the turkey! If you have leftovers, top them with an over-easy egg the next day for breakfast.

—ADRIANA TORRES EL PASO, TX

PREP: 30 MIN. • **BAKE:** 20 MIN.
MAKES: 12 CUPS

- 1 tablespoon canola oil
- 1 medium sweet red pepper, chopped
- 1 medium green pepper, chopped
- 1 small onion, chopped
- 4 garlic cloves, minced
- 3 medium red potatoes (about ¾ pound), cubed
- 3 cups reduced-sodium chicken broth
- 1 tablespoon chicken bouillon granules
- ½ teaspoon pepper
- 1 package (12 ounces) seasoned stuffing cubes
- 8 ounces smoked kielbasa or Polish sausage, chopped

1. Preheat oven to 350°. In a Dutch oven, heat oil over medium-high heat. Add peppers and onion; cook and stir until peppers are crisp-tender. Stir in garlic; cook 1 minute longer.

2. Add the potatoes, chicken broth, chicken bouillon and pepper. Bring to a boil. Reduce heat; cook, uncovered, 8-10 minutes or just until the potatoes are tender. Remove from heat; stir in stuffing cubes and kielbasa.

3. Transfer to a greased 13x9-in. baking dish. Bake 18-22 minutes or until golden brown.

Parsnip & Celery Root Bisque

Here's an earthy yet elegant soup for fall and winter. Pomegranate seeds and minced chives make a festive red-and-green garnish.

—MERRY GRAHAM NEWHALL, CA

PREP: 25 MIN. • **COOK:** 45 MIN.
MAKES: 8 SERVINGS (2 QUARTS)

- 2 tablespoons olive oil
- 2 medium leeks (white portion only), chopped (about 2 cups)
- 1¼ to 1½ pounds medium parsnips, chopped (about 4 cups)
- 1 medium celery root, peeled and cubed (about 1½ cups)
- 4 garlic cloves, minced
- 6 cups chicken stock
- 1½ teaspoons salt
- ¾ teaspoon coarsely ground pepper
- 1 cup heavy whipping cream
- 2 tablespoons minced fresh parsley
- 2 teaspoons lemon juice
- 2 tablespoons minced fresh chives
  Pomegranate seeds, optional

1. In a large saucepan, heat oil over medium-high heat. Add leeks; cook and stir 3 minutes. Add parsnips and celery root; cook and stir 3-4 minutes. Add garlic; cook 1-2 minutes longer. Stir in stock, salt and pepper. Bring to a boil. Reduce heat; simmer, covered, 25-30 minutes or until the vegetables are tender.

2. Remove the soup from heat; cool slightly. Process in batches in a blender until smooth. Return all to the pan. Stir in the heavy whipping cream, parsley and lemon juice; heat through. Top servings with chives and, if desired, pomegranate seeds

Maple-Bourbon Roasted Sweet Potatoes

Let sweet potatoes shine underneath a simple but delectable drizzle of butter, maple syrup, bourbon and seasonings. No added sugar or marshmallows are needed!

—LAUREEN PITTMAN RIVERSIDE, CA

PREP: 10 MIN. • **BAKE:** 40 MIN.
MAKES: 6 SERVINGS

- 5 medium sweet potatoes (about 2½ pounds), peeled and cut into 1-inch pieces
- 2 tablespoons butter
- ⅓ cup maple syrup
- 2 tablespoons bourbon
- ½ teaspoon salt
- ¼ teaspoon pepper

1. Preheat oven to 400°. Place sweet potatoes in a large bowl. In microwave, melt the butter; stir in the remaining ingredients. Drizzle over the potatoes and toss to coat.

2. Transfer to a foil-lined 15x10x1-in. baking pan. Roast 40-45 minutes or until tender, stirring occasionally.

Peach Gelatin Salad

My mom always asked us what we wanted to have on the menu for our holiday feasts. Without exception, our list of requests included her golden peach gelatin. It's a refreshing counterpoint to a savory meal.

—DENNIS KING NAVARRE, FL

PREP: 15 MIN. + CHILLING
MAKES: 8 SERVINGS

- **1 can (29 ounces) sliced peaches, drained**
- **1½ cups boiling water**
- **2 packages (3 ounces each) lemon gelatin**
- **1 can (12 ounces) ginger ale, chilled**
- **⅓ cup chopped walnuts, toasted**

1. Arrange half of peaches in a 6-cup ring mold coated with cooking spray. In a small bowl, add boiling water to the gelatin; stir 2 minutes to dissolve.

2. Stir in the ginger ale. Pour half of the mixture over the peaches in the mold; sprinkle with the walnuts. Refrigerate 30 minutes or until set but not firm.

Let remaining gelatin mixture stand at room temperature.

3. Carefully arrange the remaining peach slices over the gelatin in mold. Spoon remaining gelatin mixture over the top. Refrigerate until firm. Unmold onto a serving plate.

NOTE *To toast nuts, spread them in a 15x10x1-in. baking pan. Bake at 350° for 5-10 minutes or until lightly browned, stirring occasionally. Or, spread in a dry nonstick skillet; heat over low heat until lightly browned, stirring occasionally.*

Parmesan Kale Casserole

I wanted to create a new way to use kale and did some experimenting. The result was a hearty casserole with sausage, garlic and cheese. My husband loved it!

—DIANA JOHNSON AUBURN, WA

PREP: 10 MIN. • **BAKE:** 25 MIN.
MAKES: 6 SERVINGS

- 1½ cups heavy whipping cream
- ½ cup finely chopped summer sausage
- 3 garlic cloves, minced
- 2 packages (16 ounces each) frozen cut kale, thawed and squeezed dry (about 3 cups total)
- ¾ cup panko (Japanese) bread crumbs
- ¾ cup grated Parmesan cheese

1. Preheat oven to 350°. In a large skillet, combine the cream, sausage and garlic; bring to a boil. Reduce heat; simmer, uncovered, 3-5 minutes or until slightly thickened. Stir in the kale. Add the bread crumbs and cheese; toss to combine.

2. Transfer to a greased 8-in.-square baking dish. Bake 25-30 minutes or until edges are golden brown.

Lemony Couscous with Toasted Nuts

Dressed up with lemon and two kinds of nuts, my couscous is ready to eat in less than half an hour. Sometimes I stir in a little chopped parsley after cooking.

—MARIE MCCONNELL SHELBYVILLE, IL

START TO FINISH: 25 MIN.
MAKES: 6 SERVINGS

- ¼ cup pine nuts
- ¼ cup sliced almonds
- 1¾ cups chicken stock
- 3 tablespoons lemon juice
- 2 tablespoons butter
- ¼ teaspoon salt
- ⅛ teaspoon pepper
- 1 package (10 ounces) couscous

1. In a dry large saucepan, toast pine nuts and almonds over medium heat 4-5 minutes or until lightly browned, stirring frequently. Remove from pan.

2. In same pan, combine stock, lemon juice, butter, salt and pepper; bring to a boil. Stir in couscous. Remove from heat; let stand, covered, 5-10 minutes or until liquid is absorbed. Stir in nuts.

New Orleans-Style Scalloped Corn

This colorful corn bake is popular in many New Orleans homes. I started making it years ago, and now our sons do, too.

—PRISCILLA GILBERT
INDIAN HARBOUR BEACH, FL

PREP: 20 MIN. • **BAKE:** 35 MIN.
MAKES: 8 SERVINGS

- 4 teaspoons butter
- 1 large onion, finely chopped
- 1 large sweet red pepper, finely chopped
- 4 cups frozen corn
- 2 eggs
- 1 cup fat-free milk
- 1 tablespoon sugar
- 1 to 2 teaspoons hot pepper sauce
- ½ teaspoon dried thyme
- ¼ teaspoon salt
- ¼ teaspoon pepper
- 1¼ cups crushed reduced-fat butter-flavored crackers (about 30 crackers)
- 5 green onions, sliced

1. Preheat oven to 350°. In a large skillet, heat butter over medium-high heat. Add the onion and pepper; cook and stir until tender. Add the corn; heat through, stirring occasionally. Remove from heat.

2. In a small bowl, whisk eggs, milk, sugar, hot pepper sauce, thyme, salt and pepper; add to the corn mixture. Stir in crackers and onions.

3. Transfer to a 2-qt. baking dish coated with cooking spray. Bake, uncovered, 35-40 minutes or until a knife inserted near the center comes out clean.

Opening a Pomegranate

Pomegranate seeds bring added flavor and bright color to Festive Three-Grain Salad (recipe below right). Follow these directions to easily remove the seeds:

1. Cut off the crown of the fruit and score the fruit in quarters, taking care not to cut into the red juice sacs (arils).

2. Place the sections in a bowl of water and soak for 5 minutes. Use your fingers to break open the sections and gently push out the seed clusters. Discard the skin and white membrane. Drain the water, reserving the arils. Dry them on paper towels. The arils may be used whole, seeds and all.

Festive Three-Grain Salad

Wholesome ingredients and festive color make this unique side one of my Christmas staples. I can assemble it the night before and store it in the refrigerator.

—TERI KREYCHE TUSTIN, CA

PREP: 15 MIN. • **COOK:** 1 HOUR + COOLING
MAKES: 8 SERVINGS

- ¾ cup uncooked wheat berries
- 5 cups water
- ½ cup uncooked medium pearl barley
- ⅓ cup uncooked long grain brown rice
- 1 medium apple, chopped
- ½ cup pomegranate seeds, dried cherries or dried cranberries
- 4 green onions, chopped
- ¼ cup finely chopped carrot
- ¼ cup finely chopped celery
- ¼ cup minced fresh parsley

DRESSING
- ⅓ cup cider vinegar
- 3 tablespoons finely chopped red onion
- 3 tablespoons canola oil
- 2 to 3 tablespoons sugar
- 1 tablespoon Worcestershire sauce
- 2 garlic cloves, minced
- ½ teaspoon salt
- ¼ teaspoon pepper

1. In a large saucepan, combine the wheat berries and water; bring to a boil. Reduce the heat; simmer, covered, 10 minutes.
2. Stir in the pearl barley; simmer, covered, 5 minutes. Stir in the brown rice; simmer, covered, 40-45 minutes or until the grains are tender. Drain; transfer to a large bowl. Cool mixture to room temperature.
3. Add the apple, pomegranate seeds, green onions, carrot, celery and parsley to the wheat berry mixture; toss to combine. In a small bowl, whisk the dressing ingredients until blended. Pour the dressing over the salad; toss to coat. Serve immediately or refrigerate and serve cold.

Garlic-Sesame Green Beans

Sauteed bits of garlic and shallot, plus a sprinkling of toasted sesame seeds, turn ordinary green beans into something special. Keep this recipe handy when you pick a fresh crop from your vegetable garden during summer, too.
—**DEIRDRE COX** KANSAS CITY, MO

PREP: 25 MIN. • **COOK:** 10 MIN.
MAKES: 12 SERVINGS

- 3 pounds fresh green beans, trimmed
- 1 tablespoon sesame oil
- 1 tablespoon canola oil
- 1 shallot, finely chopped
- 6 garlic cloves, minced
- 1½ teaspoons salt
- ½ teaspoon pepper
- 2 tablespoons sesame seeds, toasted

1. In a Dutch oven, bring 10 cups of water to a boil. Add the green beans; cook, uncovered, 6-8 minutes or until tender.

2. Meanwhile, in a small skillet, heat the oils over medium heat. Add the shallot, garlic, salt and pepper; cook and stir 2-3 minutes or until tender.

3. Drain the green beans and return to the Dutch oven. Add the shallot mixture; toss to coat. Sprinkle with sesame seeds.

Holiday Helper

Sometimes the garlic in stores is last year's crop. If the cloves start to sprout, they develop a very strong, bitter taste. I cut my cloves in half before using them and remove the green sprout in the middle. Then the garlic tastes just like it was fresh-picked.

—**SHIRLEY S.** GILBERT, AZ

Brie Mushroom Soup

Simmer up the richness of Brie cheese and the earthy flavor of fresh mushrooms in one delicious soup. I serve big bowlfuls to warm us up on chilly days. If you like, add extra minced parsley as a garnish.

—MARIA EMMERICH RIVER FALLS, WI

PREP: 15 MIN. • **COOK:** 20 MIN.
MAKES: 4 SERVINGS

- ¼ **cup butter, cubed**
- 1 **pound sliced fresh mushrooms**
- 2 **large onions, chopped**
- 1 **can (14½ ounces) chicken broth**
- 1 **tablespoon paprika**
- 1 **tablespoon reduced-sodium soy sauce**
- 2 **teaspoons dill weed**
- 3 **tablespoons all-purpose flour**
- 1 **cup milk**
- 4 **ounces Brie cheese, rind removed, cubed**
- ¼ **cup minced fresh parsley**
- 2 **teaspoons lemon juice**
- ½ **teaspoon salt**
- ¼ **teaspoon pepper**

1. In a Dutch oven, heat butter over medium-high heat. Add mushrooms and onions; cook and stir until tender. Stir in the chicken broth, paprika, soy sauce and dill. Bring to a boil. Reduce heat; simmer, covered, 5 minutes.
2. In a small bowl, whisk the flour and milk until smooth. Stir into the mushroom mixture. Bring to a boil; cook and stir 1-2 minutes or until thickened. Reduce the heat; add the remaining ingredients. Cook and stir until cheese is melted (do not boil).

slow cooker
CHRISTMAS

Buffalo Shrimp Mac & Cheese

Here's a yummy twist on ever-popular macaroni and cheese. Hot sauce, salad shrimp and blue cheese make it deliciously different—and filling enough to serve as the main course of your meal.

—ROBIN HAAS CRANSTON, RI

PREP: 15 MIN. • **COOK:** 3½ HOURS
MAKES: 6 SERVINGS

- 2 cups 2% milk
- 1 cup half-and-half cream
- 2 tablespoons Louisiana-style hot sauce
- 1 tablespoon butter
- 1 teaspoon ground mustard
- ½ teaspoon onion powder
- ¼ teaspoon white pepper
- ¼ teaspoon ground nutmeg
- 2 cups (8 ounces) finely shredded cheddar cheese
- 1 cup (4 ounces) shredded Gouda or Swiss cheese
- 1½ cups uncooked elbow macaroni
- ¾ pound frozen cooked salad shrimp, thawed
- 1 cup (4 ounces) crumbled blue cheese
- 2 tablespoons minced fresh chives
- 2 tablespoons minced fresh parsley
  Additional Louisiana-style hot sauce, optional

1. In a 3-qt. slow cooker, combine the first eight ingredients; stir in shredded cheeses and macaroni. Cook, covered, on low 3 to 3½ hours or until macaroni is almost tender.

2. Stir in shrimp and blue cheese; cook, covered, 30-35 minutes longer or until heated through. Just before serving, stir in chives, parsley and, if desired, additional hot sauce.

Sweet Kahlua Coffee

Want to perk up java for the holidays? A splash of Kahlua and creme de cacao will do just that! Garnished with a dollop of whipped cream and grated chocolate, this indulgent coffee is the perfect after-dinner treat on chilly winter evenings.

—RUTH GRUCHOW YORBA LINDA, CA

PREP: 10 MIN. • **COOK:** 3 HOURS
MAKES: 8 SERVINGS (2¼ QUARTS)

- 2 quarts hot water
- ½ cup Kahlua (coffee liqueur)
- ¼ cup creme de cacao
- 3 tablespoons instant coffee granules
- 2 cups heavy whipping cream
- ¼ cup sugar
- 1 teaspoon vanilla extract
- 2 tablespoons grated semisweet chocolate

1. In a 4-qt. slow cooker, mix the hot water, Kahlua, creme de cacao and coffee granules. Cook, covered, on low 3-4 hours or until heated through.

2. In a large bowl, beat the whipping cream until it begins to thicken. Add the sugar and vanilla; beat until soft peaks form. Serve warm coffee with whipped cream and grated chocolate.

Turkey with Mushroom Sauce

When my husband and I were newlyweds, we didn't have an oven, so I prepared a turkey breast in our slow cooker. With a stovetop mushroom sauce, this fuss-free recipe is still a family favorite.

—MYRA INNES AUBURN, KS

PREP: 20 MIN. • **COOK:** 3 HOURS + STANDING
MAKES: 8 SERVINGS

- 1 boneless skinless turkey breast half (2½ pounds)
- 2 tablespoons butter, melted
- 2 tablespoons dried parsley flakes
- ½ teaspoon salt
- ½ teaspoon dried tarragon
- ⅛ teaspoon pepper
- 1 jar (4½ ounces) sliced mushrooms, drained or 1 cup sliced fresh mushrooms
- ½ cup white wine or chicken broth
- 2 tablespoons cornstarch
- ¼ cup cold water

1. Place turkey in a 5-qt. slow cooker. Brush with melted butter. Sprinkle with seasonings. Top with mushrooms. Pour wine over all. Cook, covered, on low 3-4 hours (a thermometer inserted in turkey should read at least 165°).

2. Remove turkey to a serving platter; tent with foil. Let stand 10 minutes before slicing.

3. Transfer the cooking juices to a small saucepan; bring to a boil. In a small bowl, mix the cornstarch and water until smooth; gradually stir into the cooking juices. Bring to a boil; cook and stir 2 minutes or until thickened. Serve turkey with sauce.

Slow-Cooked Fish Stew

I love fish and chowder, so this stew is one of my favorites. If you like, garnish each serving with a little grated cheddar.

—**JANE MCMILLAN** DANIA BEACH, FL

PREP: 25 MIN. • **COOK:** 6½ HOURS
MAKES: 8 SERVINGS (3 QUARTS)

- 1 pound potatoes (about 2 medium), peeled and finely chopped
- 1 package (10 ounces) frozen corn, thawed
- 1½ cups frozen lima beans, thawed
- 1 large onion, finely chopped
- 1 celery rib, finely chopped
- 1 medium carrot, finely chopped
- 4 garlic cloves, minced
- 1 bay leaf
- 1 teaspoon lemon-pepper seasoning
- 1 teaspoon dried parsley flakes
- 1 teaspoon dried rosemary, crushed
- ½ teaspoon salt
- 1½ cups vegetable or chicken broth
- 1 can (10¾ ounces) condensed cream of celery soup, undiluted
- ½ cup white wine or additional vegetable broth
- 1 pound cod fillets, cut into 1-inch pieces
- 1 can (14½ ounces) diced tomatoes, undrained
- 1 can (12 ounces) fat-free evaporated milk

1. In a 5-qt. slow cooker, combine the first 15 ingredients. Cook, covered, on low 6-8 hours or until the potatoes are tender.

2. Remove the bay leaf. Stir in the cod, tomatoes and milk; cook, covered, 30-35 minutes longer or until fish just begins to flake easily with a fork.

Christmas Punch

A co-worker brought her wonderfully refreshing punch to our office holiday party, and she shared the recipe with me. Red Hots spice up every glassful with cinnamon flavor and rosy color.

—**PATRICIA DICK** ANDERSON, IN

PREP: 15 MIN. • **COOK:** 3 HOURS
MAKES: 20 SERVINGS (¾ CUP EACH)

- 1 quart brewed tea
- 1 quart apple juice
- 1 quart orange juice
- 1 quart pineapple juice
- 1 package (9 ounces) Red Hots

Place all ingredients in a 6-qt. slow cooker. Cook, covered, on low 3-4 hours or until heated through and candies are melted, stirring occasionally.

Chicken Wild Rice Soup with Spinach

Whenever we're craving something warm and comforting, I fix my chicken-and-rice soup. Reduced-fat and reduced-sodium ingredients make it a healthier option.

—**DEBORAH WILLIAMS** PEORIA, AZ

PREP: 10 MIN. • **COOK:** 5¼ HOURS
MAKES: 6 SERVINGS (ABOUT 2 QUARTS)

- 3 cups water
- 1 can (14½ ounces) reduced-sodium chicken broth
- 1 can (10¾ ounces) reduced-fat reduced-sodium condensed cream of chicken soup, undiluted
- ⅔ cup uncooked wild rice
- 1 garlic clove, minced
- ½ teaspoon dried thyme
- ½ teaspoon pepper
- ¼ teaspoon salt
- 3 cups cubed cooked chicken breast
- 2 cups fresh baby spinach

1. In a 3-qt. slow cooker, mix the first eight ingredients until blended. Cook, covered, on low 5-7 hours or until rice is tender.

2. Stir in chicken and spinach. Cook, covered, on low 15 minutes longer or until heated through.

Cranberry Pork & Sweet Potatoes

PREP: 10 MIN. • **COOK:** 6 HOURS
MAKES: 6 SERVINGS

- 1⅔ cups sweetened applesauce (about 15 ounces)
- 3 pounds sweet potatoes (about 3 large), peeled and cut into 1-inch slices
- ¾ teaspoon salt, divided
- ¼ teaspoon pepper, divided
- ¼ cup packed brown sugar
- 6 bone-in pork loin chops (6 ounces each)
- 1 can (14 ounces) whole-berry cranberry sauce

1. Place applesauce in a 6-qt. slow cooker. Top with sweet potatoes; sprinkle with ¼ teaspoon salt, ⅛ teaspoon pepper and brown sugar.

2. Place the pork chops over sweet potatoes; sprinkle with the remaining salt and pepper. Spoon the cranberry sauce over pork chops. Cook, covered, on low 6-8 hours or until pork chops and sweet potatoes are tender.

Holiday Helper

Select sweet potatoes that are heavy for their size. They should have a thin, smooth skin. Avoid any with shriveled skin, cracks, soft spots or bruises. Handle the potatoes gently to avoid bruising.

When stored in a cool, dark, well-ventilated place, sweet potatoes will stay fresh for about 2 weeks. If the temperature is above 60°, they'll sprout sooner or become woody. Cooked sweet potatoes can be stored for up to 1 week in the refrigerator.

To prepare sweet potatoes for use, scrub them with a vegetable brush under cold water.

"Sit down to a delicious dinner *from the slow cooker—tender pork chops and sweet potatoes with applesauce, cranberries and brown sugar. It's a wonderful meal for the holiday season."*

—DORIS BRANHAM KINGSTON, TN

Taste of Home ❄ CHRISTMAS

Pecan-Coconut Sweet Potatoes

This easy-to-prepare side dish cooks for 5 hours. Then just sprinkle some miniature marshmallows on top, and you're done!

—**REBECCA CLARK** WARRIOR, AL

PREP: 20 MIN. • **COOK:** 5 HOURS
MAKES: 6 SERVINGS

- ¼ **cup packed brown sugar**
- 2 **tablespoons flaked coconut**
- 2 **tablespoons chopped pecans, toasted**
- 1 **teaspoon vanilla extract**
- ½ **teaspoon salt**
- ¼ **teaspoon ground cinnamon**
- 2 **pounds sweet potatoes, peeled and cut into ¾-inch cubes**
- 1 **tablespoon butter, melted**
- ½ **cup miniature marshmallows**

1. In a small bowl, mix the first six ingredients. Place sweet potatoes in a 3-qt. slow cooker coated with cooking spray; sprinkle with brown sugar mixture. Drizzle with butter.

2. Cook, covered, on low 5-6 hours or until the sweet potatoes are tender. Turn off the slow cooker. Sprinkle miniature marshmallows over the potatoes; let stand, covered, 5 minutes before serving.

Amaretto Cherries with Dumplings

Treat your family and friends to a dessert of comfort food—warm tart cherries drizzled with amaretto and covered with fluffy from-scratch dumplings. A scoop of vanilla ice cream melting on top of each bowlful is the perfect finishing touch.
—TASTE OF HOME TEST KITCHEN

PREP: 15 MIN. • **COOK:** 7¾ HOURS
MAKES: 6 SERVINGS

- 2 cans (14½ ounces each) pitted tart cherries
- ¾ cup sugar
- ¼ cup cornstarch
- ⅛ teaspoon salt
- ¼ cup amaretto or ½ teaspoon almond extract

DUMPLINGS
- 1 cup all-purpose flour
- ¼ cup sugar
- 1 teaspoon baking powder
- ½ teaspoon grated lemon peel
- ⅛ teaspoon salt
- ⅓ cup 2% milk
- 3 tablespoons butter, melted
  Vanilla ice cream, optional

1. Drain the tart cherries, reserving ¼ cup juice. Place cherries in a 3-qt. slow cooker.

2. In a small bowl, mix the sugar, cornstarch and salt; stir in reserved juice until smooth. Stir into cherries. Cook, covered, on high 7 hours. Drizzle amaretto over cherry mixture.

3. For the dumplings, in a small bowl, whisk the flour, sugar, baking powder, lemon peel and salt. In another bowl, whisk milk and melted butter. Add to flour mixture; stir just until moistened.

4. Drop by tablespoonfuls on top of the hot cherry mixture. Cook, covered, 45 minutes or until a toothpick inserted in the center of dumplings comes out clean. If desired, serve warm with vanilla ice cream.

Slow-Cooked Reuben Spread

I'm a big fan of Reuben sandwiches and anything with that flavor combination. For an appetizer, I like to blend chopped corned beef with cheese, sauerkraut and Thousand Island salad dressing to make a spread for rye bread or crackers.
—JUNE HERKE WATERTOWN, SD

PREP: 10 MIN. • **COOK:** 4 HOURS
MAKES: 30 SERVINGS (2 TABLESPOONS EACH)

- 2 packages (8 ounces each) cream cheese, cubed
- 4 cups (16 ounces) shredded Swiss cheese
- 1 can (14 ounces) sauerkraut, rinsed and well drained
- 4 packages (2 ounces each) thinly sliced deli corned beef, chopped
- ½ cup Thousand Island salad dressing
  Snack rye bread or rye crackers

1. Place the first five ingredients in a 1½-qt. slow cooker; stir to combine. Cook, covered, on low 4 to 4½ hours or until heated through.

2. Stir to blend. Serve with rye bread.

Spinach Artichoke Dip

Here's a recipe you'll want to keep close at hand for every special occasion. The rich, creamy dip always goes over well and is ready to cook in just 10 minutes.

—**JAN HABERSTICH** WATERLOO, IA

PREP: 10 MIN. • **COOK:** 2 HOURS
MAKES: 12 SERVINGS (¼ CUP EACH)

- 1 can (14 ounces) water-packed artichoke hearts, drained and chopped
- 1 cup fresh baby spinach, chopped
- ½ cup sour cream
- ½ cup mayonnaise
- ½ cup shredded part-skim mozzarella cheese
- ½ cup shredded Parmesan cheese
- ⅓ cup chopped red onion
- ¼ teaspoon garlic powder
  Assorted crackers or sliced breads

1. Place the first eight ingredients in a 1½-qt. slow cooker; stir to combine. Cook, covered, on low 2 to 2½ hours or until heated through.

2. Stir to blend. Serve with crackers.

Holiday Helper

Slow cooking is even easier when you keep these tips in mind:

● Unless your slow cooker recipe instructs otherwise, do not lift the lid while the slow cooker is cooking. Every time you lift the lid, steam is lost and you add 15 to 30 minutes of cooking time.

● Make sure that the lid is sealed properly and not tilted or askew. The steam creates a seal.

● When food is finished cooking, remove it from the slow cooker within 1 hour and refrigerate the leftovers promptly.

Barbecued Party Starters

You'll need only six simple ingredients and 30 minutes to get these sweet-tangy morsels into the slow cooker. The saucy homemade meatballs, miniature hot dogs and pineapple chunks are just filling enough to tide over everyone until dinner. Place some festive holiday picks nearby that guests can grab for easy nibbling.

—**ANASTASIA WEISS** PUNXSUTAWNEY, PA

PREP: 30 MIN. • **COOK:** 2¼ HOURS
MAKES: 16 SERVINGS (⅓ CUP EACH)

- 1 **pound ground beef**
- ¼ **cup finely chopped onion**
- 1 **package (16 ounces) miniature hot dogs, drained**
- 1 **jar (12 ounces) apricot preserves**
- 1 **cup barbecue sauce**
- 1 **can (20 ounces) pineapple chunks, drained**

1. In a large bowl, combine the ground beef and onion, mixing lightly but thoroughly. Shape the mixture into 1-in. balls. In a large skillet over medium heat, cook the meatballs in two batches until cooked through, turning occasionally.

2. Using a slotted spoon, transfer the meatballs to a 3-qt. slow cooker. Add the miniature hot dogs; stir in apricot preserves and barbecue sauce. Cook, covered, on high 2-3 hours or until heated through.

3. Stir in the pineapple chunks; cook, covered, 15-20 minutes longer or until heated through.

Vegetarian Stuffed Peppers

These flavorful meatless peppers are an updated version of my mom's. Whenever I make them, I'm reminded of home.

—MELISSA MCCABE LONG BEACH, CA

PREP: 30 MIN. **COOK:** 3½ HOURS
MAKES: 6 SERVINGS

- 2 **cups cooked brown rice**
- 3 **small tomatoes, chopped**
- 1 **cup frozen corn, thawed**
- 1 **small sweet onion, chopped**
- ¾ **cup cubed Monterey Jack cheese**
- 1 **can (4¼ ounces) chopped ripe olives**
- ⅓ **cup canned black beans, rinsed and drained**
- ⅓ **cup canned red beans, rinsed and drained**

- 4 **fresh basil leaves, thinly sliced**
- 3 **garlic cloves, minced**
- 1 **teaspoon salt**
- ½ **teaspoon pepper**
- 6 **large sweet peppers**
- ¾ **cup meatless spaghetti sauce**
- ½ **cup water**
- 4 **tablespoons grated Parmesan cheese, divided**

1. Place the first 12 ingredients in a large bowl; mix lightly to combine. Cut and discard the tops from the sweet peppers; remove seeds. Fill peppers with rice mixture.

2. In a small bowl, mix sauce and water; pour half of mixture into an oval 5-qt. slow cooker. Add filled peppers. Top with remaining sauce. Sprinkle with 2 tablespoons Parmesan cheese.

3. Cook, covered, on low 3½ to 4 hours or until heated through and peppers are tender. Sprinkle with remaining Parmesan cheese.

Holiday Helper

For Vegetarian Stuffed Peppers (at left) that are baked instead, preheat the oven to 350° and fill the peppers as directed. Spoon half of the sauce mixture into an ungreased 3-qt. baking dish. Add the filled peppers; top with the remaining sauce. Add cheese as directed. Bake, covered, 30-35 minutes or until heated through and the peppers are tender.

Gooey Peanut Butter-Chocolate Cake

Here in Wisconsin, winter weather is always frigid and a hot dessert is just the ticket to chase away the chill of ice-cold temperatures. My chocolaty cake sprinkled with salted peanuts is a favorite.

—**LISA ERICKSON** RIPON, WI

PREP: 20 MIN. • **COOK:** 2 HOURS
MAKES: 8 SERVINGS

- 1¾ **cups sugar, divided**
- 1 **cup 2% milk**
- ¾ **cup creamy peanut butter**
- 3 **tablespoons canola oil**
- 2 **cups all-purpose flour**
- ¾ **cup baking cocoa, divided**
- 3 **teaspoons baking powder**
- 2 **cups boiling water**
  Chopped salted peanuts, optional

1. In a large bowl, beat 1 cup sugar, milk, peanut butter and oil until well blended. In another bowl, whisk the flour, ½ cup cocoa and baking powder; gradually beat into the peanut butter mixture (batter will be thick). Transfer to a greased 5-qt. slow cooker.

2. In a small bowl, mix the remaining sugar and cocoa. Stir in the boiling water. Pour over batter (do not stir).

3. Cook, covered, on high 2 to 2½ hours or until a toothpick inserted in the cake portion comes out with moist crumbs. If desired, sprinkle with peanuts. Serve warm.

Butterscotch-Pecan Bread Pudding

Bread pudding fans are sure to love this rich and delectable version from the slow cooker. Add a dollop of whipped cream and a drizzle of butterscotch topping.

—**LISA VARNER** EL PASO, TX

PREP: 15 MIN. • **COOK:** 3 HOURS
MAKES: 8 SERVINGS

- 9 **cups cubed day-old white bread (about 8 slices)**
- ½ **cup chopped pecans**
- ½ **cup butterscotch chips**
- 4 **eggs**
- 2 **cups half-and-half cream**
- ½ **cup packed brown sugar**
- ½ **cup butter, melted**
- 1 **teaspoon vanilla extract**
  Whipped cream and butterscotch ice cream topping

1. Place the cubed bread, pecans and butterscotch chips in a greased 4-qt. slow cooker. In a large bowl, whisk the eggs, half-and-half cream, brown sugar, melted butter and vanilla until blended. Pour over the bread mixture; stir gently to combine.

2. Cook, covered, on low 3-4 hours or until a knife inserted in center comes out clean. Serve warm with whipped cream and butterscotch topping.

Spiced Acorn Squash

PREP: 15 MIN. • **COOK:** 3½ HOURS
MAKES: 4 SERVINGS

- ¾ **cup packed brown sugar**
- 1 **teaspoon ground cinnamon**
- 1 **teaspoon ground nutmeg**
- 2 **small acorn squash, halved and seeded**
- ¾ **cup raisins**
- 4 **tablespoons butter**
- ½ **cup water**

1. In a small bowl, mix the brown sugar, cinnamon and nutmeg; spoon into the squash halves. Sprinkle with raisins. Top each with 1 tablespoon butter. Wrap each half individually in heavy-duty foil, sealing tightly.

2. Pour the water into a 5-qt. slow cooker. Place squash in slow cooker, cut side up (packets may be stacked). Cook, covered, on high 3½ to 4 hours or until squash is tender. Open foil carefully to allow steam to escape.

Preparing Acorn Squash

The ridged shell of an acorn squash can be dark green, golden/orange or cream colored, and the orange flesh is mild. For the Spiced Acorn Squash recipe (above), wash each squash and pat it dry with paper towels. Use a sharp knife to cut it in half, then scrape out the seeds and fibrous strings with a spoon.

"With a full-time job, my days were hectic and I wasn't always able to fix my family's favorite dishes. So I adapted many of them, including this yummy squash, for the slow cooker."

—**CAROL GRECO** CENTEREACH, NY

cheesecake
CHEER

Italian Chocolate-Hazelnut Cheesecake Pie

I first made an Italian-style cheese pie years ago. When I added a chocolate-hazelnut topping, I got requests for the recipe!
—**STEVE MEREDITH** STREAMWOOD, IL

PREP: 25 MIN. • **BAKE:** 30 MIN. + CHILLING
MAKES: 8 SERVINGS

- 2 **packages (8 ounces each) cream cheese, softened**
- ½ **cup sugar**
- ½ **cup mascarpone cheese**
- ¼ **cup sour cream**
- 1 **teaspoon lime juice**
- 1 **teaspoon vanilla extract**
- 2 **eggs, lightly beaten**
- 1 **chocolate crumb crust (9 inches)**

TOPPING
- ½ **cup semisweet chocolate chips**
- ⅓ **cup heavy whipping cream**
- ½ **teaspoon vanilla extract**
  Whole or chopped hazelnuts, toasted

1. Preheat oven to 350°. In a large bowl, beat the cream cheese and sugar until smooth. Beat in the mascarpone cheese, sour cream, lime juice and vanilla. Add the eggs; beat on low speed just until blended. Pour into the chocolate crumb crust. Place on a baking sheet.

2. Bake 30-35 minutes or until the center of pie is almost set. Cool 1 hour on a wire rack.

3. Meanwhile, for topping, place chocolate chips in a small bowl. In a small saucepan, bring cream just to a boil. Pour over chips; stir with a whisk until smooth. Stir in vanilla. Cool to room temperature or until mixture thickens to a spreading consistency, stirring occasionally.

4. Spread the chocolate mixture over pie; refrigerate overnight. Just before serving, top with hazelnuts.

NOTE *To toast nuts, spread them in a 15x10x1-in. baking pan. Bake at 350° for 5-10 minutes or until lightly browned, stirring occasionally. Or, spread in a dry nonstick skillet and heat over low heat until lightly browned, stirring occasionally.*

Peanut Butter Cheesecake Ice Cream

After a big holiday feast, an ice cream dessert is always cool and refreshing. I freeze mine in a springform pan and cut it into wedges.
—**TERRYANN MOORE** VINELAND, NJ

PREP: 35 MIN. + FREEZING • **MAKES:** 16 SERVINGS

- 2 cups whole milk
- 1½ cups packed brown sugar
- 2 packages (8 ounces each) cream cheese, softened
- 1 cup creamy peanut butter
- 1½ cups heavy whipping cream
- 3 teaspoons vanilla extract
- 24 Oreo cookies, coarsely chopped
- 1 cup coarsely chopped salted peanuts
  Chocolate and caramel ice cream topping
  Whipped cream, optional

1. In a small saucepan, combine the milk and brown sugar; cook and stir over medium heat until the sugar is dissolved. Cool to room temperature.

2. In a large bowl, beat cream cheese and peanut butter until blended. Gradually add the milk mixture, cream and vanilla; beat until smooth. Press waxed paper onto surface of mixture. Refrigerate several hours or overnight.

3. Pour half of the cream cheese mixture into the cylinder of ice cream freezer; freeze according to the manufacturer's directions, adding half of the chopped cookies and half of the peanuts during the last 2 minutes of processing. (Refrigerate remaining mixture until ready to freeze.) Transfer ice cream to a 9-in. springform pan. Repeat with remaining cream cheese mixture, cookies and peanuts. Transfer to pan. Freeze until firm, about 4 hours.

4. To serve, remove the rim from the pan. Drizzle ice cream with chocolate and caramel ice cream toppings. If desired, serve with whipped cream.

No-Bake Oreo Cheesecake

Crunchy Oreos and a decadent cheesecake filling—how can you go wrong? I prepared 20 of these crowd pleasers in different sizes for my wedding, and they got rave reviews.
—**LEANNE STINSON** CARNDUFF, SK

PREP: 40 MIN. + CHILLING • **MAKES:** 8 SERVINGS

- 24 Oreo cookies, crushed
- 6 tablespoons butter, melted

FILLING

- 1 envelope unflavored gelatin
- ¼ cup cold water
- 1 package (8 ounces) cream cheese, softened
- ½ cup sugar
- ¾ cup 2% milk
- 1 cup whipped topping
- 10 Oreo cookies, coarsely chopped

1. In a small bowl, mix crushed cookies and butter. Press onto bottom of a greased 9-in. springform pan. Refrigerate until ready to use.

2. In a small saucepan, sprinkle the gelatin over cold water; let stand 1 minute. Heat and stir over low heat until gelatin is dissolved. Let stand 5 minutes.

3. In a large bowl, beat the cream cheese and sugar until smooth; gradually add milk. Beat in gelatin mixture. Fold in whipped topping and chopped cookies. Spoon over crust.

4. Refrigerate, covered, overnight. Loosen the sides of the cheesecake with a knife; remove rim from pan.

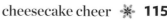

Feta-Olive Tartlets

When the occasion calls for elegant party starters, rely on ready-made phyllo tart shells. They are easy to fill and always look fancy on a serving platter.

—DARIA BURCAR ROCHESTER, MI

PREP: 30 MIN. • **BAKE:** 15 MIN.
MAKES: 2½ DOZEN

- 2 packages (1.9 ounces each) frozen miniature phyllo tart shells
- 1 egg
- 1 cup (4 ounces) crumbled feta cheese
- 3 ounces cream cheese, softened
- 2 teaspoons lemon juice
- 1 teaspoon all-purpose flour
- ⅓ cup chopped ripe olives
- 1 garlic clove, minced
- ½ teaspoon dried oregano
- ½ teaspoon olive oil
- ¼ teaspoon balsamic vinegar
  Dash cayenne pepper

1. Preheat oven to 325°. Place the phyllo tart shells on an ungreased 15x10x1-in. baking pan. In a small bowl, beat the egg, feta cheese, cream cheese, lemon juice and flour until blended. Spoon 1½ teaspoons filling into each tart shell. Bake 12-15 minutes or until golden brown.

2. In a small bowl, mix the remaining ingredients. Spoon about ½ teaspoon mixture over each tartlet. Serve warm.

Muffuletta Cheesecake

Fans of the traditional Italian muffuletta sandwich will love this appetizer. We spread it on crackers or baguette slices.

—HELEN FLAMM DAYTON, OH

PREP: 25 MIN. + CHILLING
BAKE: 35 MIN. + CHILLING
MAKES: 24 SERVINGS

- 1½ cups crushed butter-flavored crackers (40–45 crackers)
- ⅓ cup butter, melted
- 2 packages (8 ounces each) cream cheese, softened
- 1½ cups (12 ounces) sour cream
- ½ teaspoon Italian seasoning
- 1 egg, lightly beaten
- 1 egg yolk
- 2 cups (8 ounces) shredded provolone cheese
- 1 cup chopped salami

OLIVE SALAD
- ½ cup pimiento-stuffed olives
- ¼ cup pitted Greek olives
- 4 pickled onions
- 2 tablespoons capers, drained
- 2 tablespoons olive oil
- 1 pepperoncini, stem removed
- 2 teaspoons lemon juice
- 1 teaspoon Italian seasoning
- 1 garlic clove

SERVING
  Assorted crackers or baguette slices

1. Preheat oven to 375°. In a small bowl, mix cracker crumbs and butter. Press onto bottom and 1 in. up sides of a greased 9-in. springform pan. Place pan on a baking sheet.

2. In a large bowl, beat cream cheese until smooth. Gradually beat in sour cream and Italian seasoning. Add egg and egg yolk; beat on low speed just until blended. Fold in provolone and salami. Pour into crust. Bake 35-45 minutes or until center is almost set.

3. Place the olive salad ingredients in a food processor; process until coarsely chopped. Refrigerate, covered, overnight.

4. Cool the cheesecake on a wire rack 10 minutes. Loosen the sides from the pan with a knife. Cool 1 hour longer. Refrigerate overnight, covering when completely cooled.

5. Remove rim of pan. Top cheesecake with olive salad. Serve with crackers.

Butterscotch-Cappuccino Cream Cheese Pie

PREP: 15 MIN. + CHILLING
BAKE: 5 MIN. + COOLING
MAKES: 8 SERVINGS

- 1 chocolate crumb crust (9 inches)
- 2 tablespoons instant espresso powder
- 2 tablespoons hot water
- 2 packages (8 ounces each) cream cheese, softened
- ⅓ cup confectioners' sugar
- ½ cup sour cream
- ½ cup whipped topping
- 1 teaspoon vanilla extract
- ¾ cup butterscotch chips, chopped
- 2 tablespoons butterscotch ice cream topping
  Additional whipped topping and butterscotch ice cream topping, optional

1. Bake crust according to package directions. Cool completely.

2. In a small bowl, dissolve espresso powder in hot water. In a large bowl, beat cream cheese and confectioners' sugar until smooth. Beat in sour cream, whipped topping, vanilla and espresso mixture. Fold in butterscotch chips.

3. Drizzle the butterscotch topping over the crust; top with cream cheese mixture. Refrigerate, loosely covered, 2 hours or until filling is set. If desired, serve with toppings.

"Here's my favorite way to satisfy sweet-tooth cravings. The rich, creamy no-bake pie blends butterscotch flavor and espresso in a chocolate crumb crust."

—AYSHA SCHURMAN AMMON, ID

Holiday Helper

To achieve the best results when baking a cheesecake, use regular cream cheese unless your recipe specifically calls for the reduced-fat or fat-free kind. For a no-bake pie recipe such as Butterscotch-Cappuccino Cream Cheese Pie (above), feel free to experiment.

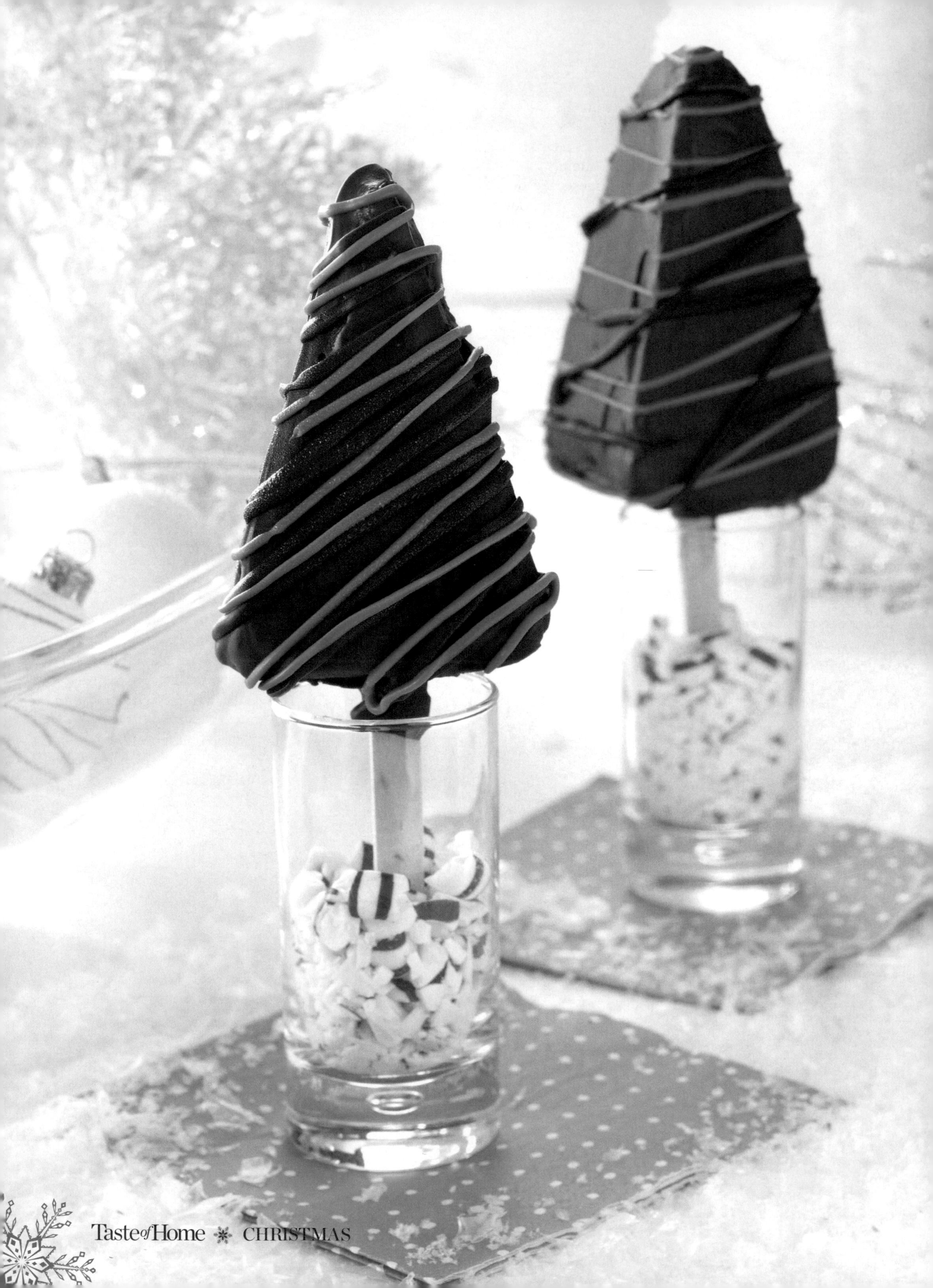

Peppermint Cheesecake on a Stick

Surprise Christmastime guests with a fun holiday treat: dipped cheesecake wedges you can nibble without a fork. Whenever I serve them to my son, he jokes that he wants to quit his job and sell them!

—MARIA MORELLI KELOWNA, BC

PREP: 1¼ HOURS + FREEZING
BAKE: 1 HOUR + CHILLING • **MAKES:** 1 DOZEN

- 1¼ cups graham cracker crumbs
- ¼ cup sugar
- ¼ cup butter, melted

CHEESECAKE

- 4 packages (8 ounces each) cream cheese, softened
- ¾ cup sugar
- ⅓ cup sour cream
- ¼ cup eggnog or half-and-half cream
- 2 tablespoons cornstarch
- 1 teaspoon vanilla extract
- 3 eggs, lightly beaten
- 1 cup crushed peppermint candies (about 35 candies)

ASSEMBLY

- 12 wooden pop sticks
- 28 ounces semisweet chocolate, chopped
- 3 tablespoons shortening
- ½ cup green candy coating disks, melted
- ¼ cup red candy coating disks, melted

1. Preheat oven to 325°. Place a greased 9-in. springform pan on a double thickness of heavy-duty foil (about 18 in. square). Wrap foil securely around pan. Place on a baking sheet.

2. In a small bowl, mix the graham cracker crumbs and sugar; stir in the butter. Press onto bottom of prepared pan. Bake 10-12 minutes or until lightly browned. Cool on a wire rack.

3. In a large bowl, beat cream cheese and sugar until smooth. Beat in sour cream, eggnog, cornstarch and vanilla. Add eggs; beat on low speed just until blended. Fold in peppermint candies. Pour over crust. Place springform pan in a larger baking pan; add 1 in. of hot water to larger pan.

4. Bake 60-65 minutes or until the center is just set and the top appears dull. Remove the springform pan from the water bath. Cool cheesecake on a wire rack 10 minutes. Loosen the sides from pan with a knife; remove foil. Cool 1 hour longer. Refrigerate overnight, covering when completely cooled.

5. Remove the rim from the pan. Cut cheesecake into 12 slices; gently insert a stick into wide end of each. Place on a waxed paper-lined 15x10x1-in. baking pan; freeze until firm.

6. In a microwave, melt chocolate and shortening; stir until smooth. Spoon chocolate mixture over each slice until all sides are coated; allow excess to drip off. (Keep remaining slices in freezer until ready to coat.) Place on a waxed paper-lined baking pan. Seal any gaps by drizzling with chocolate mixture, reheating the mixture if necessary. Refrigerate 10 minutes or until set.

7. Decorate with melted candy coating as desired. Refrigerate until serving.

NOTE *This recipe was tested with commercially prepared eggnog.*

Decorating Cheesecake Slices

Turning each piece of cheesecake (recipe at left) into a treat on a stick is easier than you might think. Just refer to the photos here!

1. After cutting the cheesecake into 12 slices, gently insert a wooden stick into the wide end of each slice.

2. Hold each frozen cheesecake slice over the bowl of melted chocolate, then spoon the chocolate over the slice, coating all sides completely.

3. Cut the tip from a pastry bag or cut a hole in a corner of a freezer bag. Spoon the melted green candy coating inside and drizzle it onto the slices. Use another bag to drizzle red candy coating in the same way.

Pineapple Cheesecake-Topped Cake

My brother-in-law asked if I could make a cheesecake version of an old-fashioned favorite: pineapple upside-down cake. After a lot of experimentation, I came up with one we all like. It's a rich, creamy twist on a traditional dessert.

—REBECCA EVERETT KANSAS CITY, MO

PREP: 30 MIN. • **BAKE:** 1 HOUR + CHILLING
MAKES: 16 SERVINGS

- ¼ **cup butter, melted**
- ⅓ **cup packed brown sugar**
- 8 **canned unsweetened pineapple slices**
- 4 **maraschino cherries, halved**

CHEESECAKE

- 3 **packages (8 ounces each) cream cheese, softened**
- 1 **cup sugar**
- 2 **tablespoons all-purpose flour**
- 1 **teaspoon vanilla extract**
- 3 **eggs, lightly beaten**

CAKE

- ½ **cup butter, softened**
- 1 **cup sugar**
- 2 **eggs**
- 1 **teaspoon vanilla extract**
- 1½ **cups all-purpose flour**
- 1½ **teaspoons baking powder**
- ¼ **teaspoon salt**
- ½ **cup 2% milk**

1. Preheat oven to 325°. Place a greased 10-in. springform pan on a double thickness of heavy-duty foil (about 18 in. square). Wrap the foil securely around the pan. Place on a baking sheet.

2. Pour the melted butter into the prepared pan; sprinkle with the brown sugar. Arrange the pineapple slices in a single layer over the sugar; place a maraschino cherry half in the center of each pineapple slice.

3. For the cheesecake, in a large bowl, beat the cream cheese and sugar until smooth. Beat in the flour and vanilla. Add eggs; beat on low speed just until blended. Spoon over fruit.

4. For the cake, in another bowl, cream the butter and sugar until light and fluffy. Add the eggs, one at a time, beating well after each addition. Beat in the vanilla. In a small bowl, whisk the flour, baking powder and salt; add to the creamed mixture alternately with the milk, beating well after each addition. Spoon over the cheesecake. Bake 60-70 minutes or until golden brown and a toothpick inserted into the cake portion comes out clean.

5. Cool on a wire rack 20 minutes. Remove foil. Loosen the sides of the cake with a knife; remove rim from pan. Invert cake onto a serving plate; remove bottom of pan. Cool 1 hour longer. Refrigerate overnight, covering when completely cooled.

Glazed Strawberry Cheesecake

This berry-topped showstopper has been a "must" at family functions for more than 30 years. We devour every bite!

—JAN DECARLANTONIO CENTREVILLE, MD

PREP: 30 MIN. • **BAKE:** 70 MIN. + CHILLING
MAKES: 16 SERVINGS

- ¾ **cup ground pecans**
- ¾ **cup crushed vanilla wafers (about 25 wafers)**
- 3 **tablespoons unsalted butter, melted**

FILLING
- 4 **packages (8 ounces each) cream cheese, softened**
- 1⅔ **cups sugar, divided**
- 3 **teaspoons vanilla extract, divided**
- 4 **eggs, lightly beaten**
- 1 **cup (8 ounces) sour cream**

GLAZE
- 4 **teaspoons cornstarch**
- ⅓ **cup orange liqueur**
- 1 **jar (10 ounces) seedless raspberry spreadable fruit**
- 1 **pound fresh strawberries, hulled and sliced**

1. Preheat oven to 325°. Place a greased 9-in. springform pan on a double thickness of heavy-duty foil (about 18 in. square). Wrap the foil securely around the pan.

2. In a small bowl, mix the pecans and wafer crumbs; stir in the butter. Press onto the bottom and ½ in. up the sides of the prepared pan.

3. In a large bowl, beat cream cheese and 1⅓ cups sugar until smooth. Beat in 2 teaspoons vanilla. Add the eggs; beat on low speed just until blended. Pour into the crust. Place springform pan in a larger baking pan; add 1 in. of hot water to larger pan.

4. Bake 65-75 minutes or until center is almost set. Let stand 5 minutes on a wire rack. In a small bowl, mix the sour cream and remaining sugar and vanilla; spread over the top of cheesecake. Bake 5 minutes longer.

5. Remove the springform pan from the water bath. Cool the cheesecake on a wire rack 10 minutes. Loosen the sides from the springform pan with a knife; remove foil. Cool 1 hour longer. Refrigerate overnight, covering when completely cooled.

6. In a small saucepan, whisk the cornstarch and orange liqueur until smooth. Stir in the spreadable fruit; bring to a boil over medium heat. Cook and stir 2 minutes or until thickened. Cool to room temperature, stirring occasionally.

7. Remove the rim from springform pan. Arrange the strawberries over the cheesecake; top with some of the glaze, allowing glaze to drip down the sides. Refrigerate until glaze is set, about 1 hour. To serve, gently warm remaining glaze; serve with cheesecake.

Sweet & Savory Mini Apple Cheesecakes

Serve my miniature cheesecakes as a dinnertime hors d'oeuvre, brunch treat or dessert. The savory flavor of blue cheese complements the sweetness of the apples.
—**JAMIE JONES** MADISON, GA

PREP: 35 MIN. + COOLING
BAKE: 25 MIN. + CHILLING
MAKES: 8 SERVINGS

- ¾ cup quick-cooking oats
- ¼ cup finely chopped walnuts
- ¼ cup packed brown sugar
- 3 tablespoons butter, melted

FILLING
- 1 package (8 ounces) cream cheese, softened
- ¼ cup sour cream
- 1 egg, lightly beaten
- ½ cup crumbled blue cheese

TOPPING
- ½ cup packed brown sugar
- ½ cup heavy whipping cream
- 2 tablespoons butter
- ⅛ teaspoon salt
- 4 medium apples, peeled and sliced
- ¼ teaspoon vanilla extract
- ½ cup finely chopped walnuts, toasted

1. Preheat oven to 375°. In a small bowl, mix oats, nuts and brown sugar; stir in butter. Divide mixture among eight paper-lined muffin cups; press onto the bottoms to form a crust. Bake 7-9 minutes or until light brown. Cool on a wire rack. Reduce oven to 325°.

2. In a large bowl, beat cream cheese and sour cream until smooth. Add egg; beat on low speed just until blended. Fold in blue cheese. Pour over crusts.

3. Bake 15-20 minutes or until centers are almost set. Cool in the pan on a wire rack 30 minutes. Refrigerate overnight, covering after the cheesecakes are completely cooled.

4. In a large skillet, combine brown sugar, cream, butter and salt; bring to a boil. Add apples; return to a boil. Cook 8-10 minutes or until apples are tender, stirring occasionally. Remove from heat; stir in vanilla. Cool completely.

5. To serve, remove the liners from the cheesecakes. Top cheesecakes with the apple mixture; sprinkle with nuts.

NOTE *To toast nuts, spread them in a 15x10x1-in. baking pan. Bake at 350° for 5-10 minutes or until lightly browned, stirring occasionally. Or, spread in a dry nonstick skillet and heat over low heat until lightly browned, stirring occasionally.*

Creole Shrimp & Crab Cheesecake

We live on the beach and love to eat seafood. I created this chunky spread and accompanying sauce as a special appetizer.
—**CHRISTY HUGHES** SUNSET BEACH, NC

PREP: 30 MIN. • **BAKE:** 1 HOUR + CHILLING
MAKES: 24 SERVINGS

¾ cup dry bread crumbs
¼ cup grated Parmesan cheese

½ teaspoon dill weed
2 tablespoons butter, melted

CHEESECAKE

2 tablespoons butter
1 medium sweet red pepper, finely chopped
1 small onion, finely chopped
1 medium carrot, finely chopped
½ teaspoon dill weed
½ teaspoon Creole seasoning
¼ teaspoon salt

¼ teaspoon pepper
3 packages (8 ounces each) cream cheese, softened
½ cup heavy whipping cream
1 tablespoon sherry or additional cream
4 eggs, lightly beaten
1 pound peeled and deveined cooked small shrimp, chopped
2 cans (6 ounces each) lump crabmeat, drained
1 cup (4 ounces) shredded Gouda cheese

SAUCE

1 cup mayonnaise
2 tablespoons Dijon mustard
½ teaspoon Creole seasoning
Assorted crackers

1. Preheat oven to 350°. In a small bowl, mix crumbs, Parmesan cheese and dill; stir in butter. Press onto the bottom of a greased 9-in. springform pan. Place pan on a baking sheet.
2. For cheesecake, in a large skillet, heat butter over medium-high heat. Add red pepper, onion and carrot; cook and stir until tender. Stir in seasonings. Cool slightly.
3. In a large bowl, beat cream cheese, cream and sherry until smooth. Add eggs; beat on low just until combined. Fold in vegetable mixture, shrimp, crab and Gouda cheese. Pour over crust.
4. Bake 60-65 minutes or until the center is almost set. Cool on a wire rack 10 minutes. Loosen the sides from the pan with a knife. Cool 1 hour longer. Refrigerate overnight, covering when completely cooled.
5. In a small bowl, mix mayonnaise, Dijon mustard and Creole seasoning. Remove the rim from the springform pan. Serve the cheesecake with sauce and crackers.

NOTE *The following spices may be substituted for 1 teaspoon Creole seasoning: ¼ teaspoon each salt, garlic powder and paprika, and a pinch each of dried thyme, ground cumin and cayenne pepper.*

Cheesecake Sandwich Wafers

I put together these super-easy, no-bake cookies one day while trying out some new ideas in the kitchen. I was so pleased with the results, I gave a batch of these treats to my boss for Christmas.
—**GINGER YOUNG** HUNTSVILLE, AL

PREP: 20 MIN. + CHILLING
MAKES: ABOUT 3 DOZEN

- 1 package (8 ounces) cream cheese, softened
- ½ cup butter, softened
- ½ teaspoon vanilla extract
- 1 cup confectioners' sugar
- 1 package (12 ounces) vanilla wafers

1. In a small bowl, beat cream cheese, butter and vanilla until blended. Beat in confectioners' sugar until smooth.
2. Spread on the bottoms of half of the wafers; cover with the remaining wafers. Refrigerate at least 1 hour or until the filling is firm.

White Chocolate Cheesecake with Cherry Topping

Cheesecake is even more decadent with rich white chocolate. If you like, substitute cookies for the graham crackers or use a different pie filling in place of cherry.
—**SUSAN CLEMENTS** CONWAY, AR

PREP: 35 MIN. • **BAKE:** 65 MIN. + CHILLING
MAKES: 16 SERVINGS

- 2½ cups cinnamon graham cracker crumbs (about 13 whole crackers)
- ¼ cup packed brown sugar
- ½ cup butter, melted

FILLING
- 4 packages (8 ounces each) cream cheese, softened
- 1⅓ cups sugar
- 1 teaspoon vanilla extract
- 4 eggs, lightly beaten
- 3 ounces white baking chocolate, finely chopped

TOPPING
- 1½ cups (12 ounces) sour cream
- ¼ cup sugar
- 1 ounce white baking chocolate, melted and cooled slightly
- 1 can (21 ounces) cherry pie filling
  Whipped cream

1. Preheat oven to 325°. In a small bowl, mix graham cracker crumbs and brown sugar; stir in butter. Press onto bottom and 1½ in. up sides of a greased 10-in. springform pan. Place pan on a baking sheet.
2. In a large bowl, beat the cream cheese and sugar until smooth. Beat in the vanilla. Add the eggs; beat on low speed just until blended. Fold in the white chocolate. Pour into crust.
3. Bake 55-60 minutes or until center is almost set. Let stand 5 minutes on a wire rack. In a small bowl, mix sour cream, sugar and melted chocolate; spread over top of cheesecake. Bake 10 minutes longer.
4. Cool on wire rack 10 minutes. Loosen the sides from the springform pan with a knife. Cool 1 hour longer. Refrigerate overnight, covering when completely cooled.
5. Remove the rim from springform pan. Serve cheesecake with cherry pie filling and whipped cream.

Cream Cheese Mocha Cupcakes

To perk up cupcakes made from a boxed mix, I add coffee, a cream cheese filling and a silky ganache on top. My family members and friends can't get enough of them!
—**ANDREA FRANKS** CARROLLTON, TX

PREP: 20 MIN. + COOLING
BAKE: 20 MIN. + COOLING • **MAKES:** 2 DOZEN

- 1 package chocolate cake mix (regular size)
- 2 tablespoons instant coffee granules
- 1 package (8 ounces) cream cheese, softened
- ⅓ cup sugar
- 1 egg
- 1 cup semisweet chocolate chunks

GANACHE
- 4 ounces bittersweet chocolate, chopped
- ½ cup heavy whipping cream
- 2 teaspoons corn syrup

1. Preheat oven to 350°. Line 24 muffin cups with paper liners. Prepare cake mix according to package directions, adding coffee granules before mixing batter. Fill paper-lined muffin cups two-thirds full.
2. In a small bowl, beat cream cheese and sugar until smooth. Beat in egg. Stir in chocolate chunks. Drop filling by rounded teaspoonfuls into center of each cupcake.
3. Bake 20-25 minutes or until the cake springs back when lightly touched. Cool in the pans 10 minutes before removing to wire racks to cool completely.
4. For the ganache, place bittersweet chocolate in a small bowl. In a small saucepan, bring the cream just to a boil. Pour over the chocolate; stir with a whisk until smooth. Stir in the corn syrup. Cool 10 minutes or until slightly thickened, stirring occasionally.
5. Dip the tops of the cupcakes into the ganache. Refrigerate leftovers.

Apple Cobbler Cheesecake

I call this combination of two classic desserts my "lucky" recipe. It won top honors in the baking contest held during my hometown's apple festival.

—JAY HOOVER THE VILLAGES, FL

PREP: 50 MIN. • **BAKE:** 1¼ HOURS + COOLING
MAKES: 16 SERVINGS

- 2 **cups graham cracker crumbs**
- ¼ **cup sugar**
- ½ **cup butter, melted**

COBBLER LAYER

- 1 **cup butter, softened**
- 1 **cup sugar**
- 2 **eggs**
- 2 **cups all-purpose flour**
- 2 **tablespoons baking powder**
- 2 **medium tart apples, peeled and thinly sliced**

- 1 **jar (12 ounces) hot caramel ice cream topping, divided**

CHEESECAKE LAYER

- 3 **packages (8 ounces each) cream cheese, softened**
- 1 **cup sugar**
- ¼ **cup all-purpose flour**
- ¼ **cup water**
- 3 **eggs, lightly beaten**
  Whipped cream

1. Preheat oven to 325°. In a small bowl, mix the crumbs and sugar; stir in butter. Press onto bottom and 1 in. up sides of a greased 10-in. springform pan. Place pan on a 15x10x1-in. baking pan.

2. For cobbler layer, in a large bowl, cream butter and sugar until light and fluffy. Add eggs, one at a time, beating well after each addition. In a small bowl, whisk flour and baking powder; add to creamed mixture. Drop half of the dough by tablespoonfuls into crust. Top with half of the apple slices; drizzle with ⅓ cup caramel topping.

3. For the cheesecake layer, in a large bowl, beat the cream cheese and sugar until smooth. Beat in the flour and water. Add the eggs; beat on low speed just until combined. Pour over the caramel. Repeat the cobbler layer with the remaining dough, apple and an additional ⅓ cup caramel.

4. Bake 1¼ to 1½ hours or until the cheesecake layer no longer jiggles when moved. Cool on a wire rack 30 minutes.

5. Serve warm or refrigerate overnight, covering when completely cooled, and serve cold. Loosen sides of cheesecake with a knife. Remove rim from pan. Warm remaining caramel. Serve with cheesecake; top with whipped cream.

quick & easy
COOKIES

Hazelnut Chocolate Cookies

With ground hazelnuts in the dough, these sugar-dusted sweets also have a whole nut in the center. They're popular with everyone, from our family to the members of our Bible study group.
—**ELISA LOCHRIDGE** BEAVERTON, OR

PREP: 20 MIN.
BAKE: 15 MIN./BATCH + COOLING
MAKES: 2 DOZEN

- ½ cup butter, softened
- 6 tablespoons sugar
- 1 teaspoon vanilla extract
- ¾ cup cake flour
- ¼ cup baking cocoa
- ¾ cup ground hazelnuts (about 3 ounces)
- 24 whole hazelnuts, toasted and skins removed
  Confectioners' sugar

1. Preheat oven to 325°. In a bowl, cream butter and sugar until light and fluffy. Beat in vanilla. In another bowl, whisk the cake flour and cocoa; gradually beat into the creamed mixture. Stir in ground hazelnuts.

2. Shape dough into twenty-four 1-in. balls; place 2 in. apart on ungreased baking sheets. Press a whole hazelnut onto the center of each ball.

3. Bake cookies 15-19 minutes or until firm to the touch. Cool on pans 2 minutes. Remove from pans to wire racks to cool completely. Dust cookies with confectioners' sugar.

NOTE *To toast whole hazelnuts, spread hazelnuts in a 15x10x1-in. baking pan. Bake in a 350° oven 7-10 minutes or until fragrant and lightly browned, stirring occasionally. To remove skins, wrap hazelnuts in a tea towel; rub with towel to loosen skins.*

Toffee-Almond Cookie Slices

Crispy cookie slices are the perfect shape and texture for dunking into hot coffee. Invite friends over and enjoy!
—**JULIE PLUMMER** SYKESVILLE, MD

PREP: 15 MIN. • **BAKE:** 45 MIN. + COOLING
MAKES: 2½ DOZEN

- 1 package (17½ ounces) sugar cookie mix
- ½ cup all-purpose flour
- ½ cup butter, softened
- 1 egg
- ⅓ cup slivered almonds, toasted
- ⅓ cup miniature semisweet chocolate chips
- ⅓ cup English toffee bits or almond brickle chips

1. Preheat oven to 350°. In a large bowl, mix the sugar cookie mix, flour, butter and egg to form a stiff dough. Stir in the slivered almonds, chocolate chips and toffee bits.

2. Divide cookie dough in half. On an ungreased baking sheet, shape each portion into a 10x2½-in. rectangle. Bake 25-30 minutes or until light brown. Cool on pans on wire racks 10 minutes.

3. Transfer the baked rectangles to a cutting board. Using a serrated knife, cut diagonally into 15 slices. Place on baking sheets, cut sides down.

4. Bake 8-10 minutes on each side or until golden brown. Remove from pans to wire racks to cool completely. Store in an airtight container.

Fudgy Mint Cookies

Chocolate fanatics, get ready for love at first bite! These doubly delectable treats start with a convenient devil's food cake mix and feature thin mints on top.

—RENEE SCHWEBACH DUMONT, MN

PREP: 15 MIN. • **BAKE:** 10 MIN./BATCH
MAKES: ABOUT 3 DOZEN

- 1 package devil's food cake mix (regular size)
- ½ cup butter, softened
- 2 eggs
- 1 tablespoon water
- 2 tablespoons confectioners' sugar
- 2 packages (5 ounces each) chocolate-covered thin mints

1. Preheat oven to 375°. In a large bowl, mix cake mix, butter, eggs and water to form a soft dough. Shape the dough into 1-in. balls; roll in confectioners' sugar. Place 2 in. apart on ungreased baking sheets.

2. Bake 8-10 minutes or until set. Immediately press a mint into the center of each cookie. Cool on pans 2 minutes. Remove from pans to wire racks to cool.

Holiday Helper

No time to bake? Here are tricks for turning store-bought cookies into your own festive works of art for Christmas:

- Melt white baking chips, then dip gingersnaps halfway into the chips...or drizzle the melted chips over the cookies.

- Tint vanilla frosting with food coloring and use it to pipe holiday designs on sugar cookies.

- Add a drizzle of melted white chocolate to chocolate-covered mint cookies.

- Frost chocolate chip cookies with chocolate frosting; decorate with colored sugar or sprinkles.

Almond Macaroons

I dress up my golden brown macaroons with a drizzle of melted milk chocolate. The little coconut bites are crisp on the outside and chewy on the inside.

—DEENA DILLION OSSIAN, IN

PREP: 20 MIN.
BAKE: 20 MIN./BATCH + COOLING
MAKES: 3 DOZEN

- 1 **package (14 ounces) flaked coconut**
- 1 **can (14 ounces) sweetened condensed milk**
- ¼ **cup sliced almonds, chopped**
- 1 **teaspoon almond extract**
- 1 **teaspoon vanilla extract**
- 1 **cup milk chocolate chips, melted**

1. Preheat oven to 325°. In a large bowl, mix the first five ingredients until blended. Drop the mixture by tablespoonfuls 2 in. apart onto parchment paper-lined baking sheets.

2. Bake 16-20 minutes or until light brown. Remove from the pans to wire racks to cool completely.

3. Drizzle cookies with melted milk chocolate chips; let stand until set. Store in an airtight container.

Raspberry Almond Strips

Thanks to refrigerated dough, it's easy to bake a batch of sweet almond cookie strips. A cup of tea is the perfect complement.

—TASTE OF HOME TEST KITCHEN

START TO FINISH: 30 MIN. • **MAKES:** 16 COOKIES

- ½ tube refrigerated sugar cookie dough, softened
- ⅓ cup all-purpose flour
- ¼ cup finely chopped almonds
- 3 tablespoons raspberry cake and pastry filling

OPTIONAL ICING

- ¼ cup confectioners' sugar
- 1½ teaspoons 2% milk
- ⅛ teaspoon almond extract

1. Preheat oven to 350°. In a small bowl, beat the sugar cookie dough, flour and almonds until blended. Roll into a 13½x2-in. rectangle on an ungreased baking sheet.

2. Using a wooden spoon handle, make a ¼-in.-deep indentation lengthwise down the center of the rectangle. Bake 5 minutes.

3. Spoon the raspberry filling into the indentation. Bake 8-10 minutes longer or until cookie is golden brown. Cool on the pan 2 minutes.

4. Remove from the pan to a cutting board; cut crosswise into 16 slices. Transfer to a wire rack to cool. If desired, in a small bowl, mix the remaining ingredients until smooth; drizzle icing over warm cookies.

Thumbprint Butter Cookies

Fill the thumbprint in the center of these jewel-toned goodies with any fruit preserves you like. The buttery little rounds bring a lovely burst of color to a platter of Christmas treats.

—TASTE OF HOME TEST KITCHEN

PREP: 20 MIN. • **BAKE:** 10 MIN./BATCH + COOLING • **MAKES:** 2½ DOZEN

- 6 tablespoons butter, softened
- ½ cup sugar
- 1 egg
- 2 tablespoons canola oil
- 1 teaspoon vanilla extract
- ¼ teaspoon butter flavoring
- 1½ cups all-purpose flour
- ¼ cup cornstarch
- 1 teaspoon baking powder
- ¼ teaspoon salt
- 3 tablespoons apricot preserves or fruit preserves of your choice

1. Preheat oven to 350°. In a large bowl, cream the butter and sugar until light and fluffy. Beat in the egg, oil, vanilla and butter flavoring. In another bowl, whisk the flour, cornstarch, baking powder and salt; gradually beat into creamed mixture.

2. Shape dough into 1-in. balls; place 2 in. apart on greased baking sheets. Press a deep indentation in the center of each with the end of a wooden spoon handle.

3. Bake 8-10 minutes or until edges are light brown. Remove from pans to wire racks to cool. Fill each cookie with about ¼ teaspoon preserves.

Peppermint Puff Pastry Sticks

I wanted to impress my husband's family with something you might expect to find in a European bakery. The chocolaty sticks I came up with are surprisingly easy to make using frozen puff pastry.
—**DARLENE BRENDEN** SALEM, OR

PREP: 15 MIN.
BAKE: 15 MIN./BATCH + COOLING
MAKES: ABOUT 3 DOZEN

- 1 sheet frozen puff pastry, thawed
- 1½ cups crushed peppermint candies
- 10 ounces milk chocolate candy coating, coarsely chopped

1. Preheat oven to 400°. Unfold the sheet of puff pastry. Cut in half to form two rectangles. Cut each rectangle crosswise into 18 strips, about ½ in. wide. Place on ungreased baking sheets. Bake 12-15 minutes or until golden brown. Remove from pans to wire racks to cool completely.
2. Place crushed candies in a shallow bowl. In a microwave, melt the candy coating; stir until smooth. Dip each cookie halfway in coating; allow excess to drip off. Sprinkle with peppermint candies. Place on waxed paper; let stand until set. Store in an airtight container.

Chocolate-Dipped Orange Spritz

Tired of your usual spritz cookies? Add a burst of tangy citrus with this two-tone dipped variation. It's scrumptious and looks extra special for Christmas.
—**ALISSA STEHR** GAU-ODERNHEIM, GERMANY

PREP: 20 MIN.
BAKE: 10 MIN./BATCH + COOLING
MAKES: 4 DOZEN

- ¾ cup butter, softened
- 1 cup sugar
- 1 egg
- 2 tablespoons orange juice
- 4 teaspoons grated orange peel
- 2¾ cups all-purpose flour
- 1 teaspoon baking powder
- ¼ teaspoon salt
- ½ cup ground walnuts
- 1 cup (6 ounces) semisweet chocolate chips
- 1 tablespoon shortening

1. Preheat oven to 350°. In a bowl, cream butter and sugar until light and fluffy. Gradually beat in egg, orange juice and peel. In another bowl, whisk flour, baking powder and salt; gradually add to creamed mixture, mixing well.
2. Using a cookie press fitted with a bar disk, press long strips of dough onto ungreased baking sheets; cut the ends to release from the disk. Cut each strip into 3-in. lengths (there is no need to separate them).
3. Bake 8-10 minutes or until set (do not brown). Re-cut the cookies if necessary. Remove from pans to wire racks to cool completely.
4. Place the walnuts in a shallow bowl. In a microwave, melt the chocolate chips and shortening; stir until smooth. Dip each cookie halfway in the melted chocolate; allow excess to drip off. Sprinkle with walnuts. Place on waxed paper; let stand until set.

Quick Decorating

Want fancy cutouts fast? Whisk 2 cups confectioners' sugar with ⅓ cup evaporated milk to create a quick icing you can use for the decorating ideas here:

1. Cut a small hole in a corner of a freezer bag. Fill it with plain icing (or icing tinted with food coloring) and drizzle away.

2. Simply dip the tops of cookies into the bowl of icing. Decorate the dipped cookies with colored sugar or sprinkles.

3. Create a marbled look. Dip the cookie tops in plain icing, pipe on lines of tinted icing and drag a toothpick through the lines.

Shortbread Cutouts

These are the cutout cookies I've been baking for more than 30 years. With only four ingredients, they're easy to fit into a hectic holiday-season schedule.

—JEAN HENDERSON MONTGOMERY, TX

PREP: 20 MIN. • **BAKE:** 20 MIN./BATCH
MAKES: ABOUT 2 DOZEN

- 1 **cup butter, softened**
- ½ **cup sugar**
- 2½ **cups all-purpose flour**
  Colored sugar, optional

1. Preheat oven to 300°. In a large bowl, cream the butter and sugar until light and fluffy. Gradually beat in the flour. Transfer dough to a clean work surface; knead gently to form a smooth dough, about 2 minutes. (The mixture will be very crumbly at first, but will come together and form a dough as it's kneaded.)

2. Divide the dough in half. Roll each portion between two sheets of waxed paper to ¼-in. thickness. Cut with floured 2- to 3-in. cookie cutters. Place 1 in. apart on ungreased baking sheets. If desired, sprinkle with colored sugar.

3. Bake 20-25 minutes until golden brown. Remove from the pans to wire racks to cool.

Lemon-on-Lemon Iced Cookies

I collect recipes from all over the world, and when I come across a new favorite, it goes in a binder so I can enjoy it again and again. My iced lemon triangles are one of the best discoveries I've made.

—SHARON DELANEY-CHRONIS

SOUTH MILWAUKEE, WI

PREP: 20 MIN.
BAKE: 15 MIN./BATCH + COOLING
MAKES: 4 DOZEN

- 2½ **cups all-purpose flour**
- ⅓ **cup sugar**
- 1 **tablespoon grated lemon peel**
- 1 **cup cold butter, cubed**

ICING

- 1 **cup confectioners' sugar**
- ½ **teaspoon grated lemon peel**
- 4 **to 6 teaspoons lemon juice**

1. Preheat oven to 325°. In a large bowl, mix the flour, sugar and lemon peel; cut in the butter until crumbly. Transfer the mixture to a clean work surface; knead gently to form a smooth dough, about 2 minutes. (The mixture will be very crumbly at first, but will come together and form a dough as it's kneaded.) Divide dough in half.

2. On a lightly floured surface, roll or pat each portion of dough into an 8x6-in. rectangle. Cut the rectangle into twelve 2-in. squares; cut squares diagonally in half to form twenty-four triangles. Place 1 in. apart on ungreased baking sheets.

3. Bake 15-18 minutes or until golden brown. Remove from the pans to wire racks to cool completely.

4. In a small bowl, mix confectioners' sugar, lemon peel and enough lemon juice to reach desired consistency. Drizzle over cookies; let stand until set.

Mocha Macaroon Cookies

Here's a coffeehouse version of the classic macaroon. With chocolate, java, vanilla and a dash of cinnamon, it tastes like a specialty brew from a barista.

—**JEANNE HOLT** MENDOTA HEIGHTS, MN

PREP: 20 MIN.
BAKE: 10 MIN./BATCH + COOLING
MAKES: 4 DOZEN

- 2 **teaspoons instant coffee granules**
- 2 **teaspoons hot water**
- 1 **can (14 ounces) sweetened condensed milk**
- 2 **ounces unsweetened chocolate, melted**
- 1 **teaspoon vanilla extract**
- ¼ **teaspoon ground cinnamon**
- ⅛ **teaspoon salt**
- 1 **package (14 ounces) flaked coconut**
- ⅔ **cup white baking chips, melted**
   Plain or chocolate-covered coffee beans

1. Preheat oven to 350°. In a large bowl, dissolve the instant coffee granules in hot water. Stir in the sweetened condensed milk, melted chocolate, vanilla, cinnamon and salt until blended. Stir in the coconut. Drop mixture by rounded teaspoonfuls 2 in. apart onto parchment paper-lined baking sheets.
2. Bake 10-12 minutes or until set. Cool on pans 1 minute. Remove from pans to wire racks to cool completely.
3. Drizzle cookies with melted baking chips. Top with coffee beans, attaching with melted chips if necessary.

Holiday Helper

Need a festive yuletide present for the coffee lover on your list? Pack a Christmasy basket with a tin of Mocha Macaroon Cookies (recipe above) and include the recipe, a favorite bag of java and a mug. For even more fun, add a personalized Recycled Sweater Coffee Sleeve (see page 207).

Chocolate-Peanut Butter Cookies

Five ingredients are all you'll need to whip up a batch of these rich, dense goodies topped with fudgy frosting. They go over big with kids and make a great pick-me-up for adults during afternoon break time.

—**ELAINE STEPHENS** CARMEL, IN

PREP: 20 MIN.
BAKE: 10 MIN./BATCH + COOLING
MAKES: 3½ DOZEN

- 2 **cans (16 ounces each) chocolate fudge frosting, divided**
- 1 **egg**
- 1 **cup chunky peanut butter**
- 1½ **cups all-purpose flour**
   Granulated sugar

1. Preheat oven to 375°. Reserve one can plus ⅓ cup chocolate fudge frosting for topping cookies. In a large bowl, mix the egg, peanut butter and remaining frosting until blended. Stir in the flour just until moistened.
2. Drop cookie dough by rounded tablespoonfuls 2 in. apart onto greased baking sheets. Flatten with a fork dipped in sugar.
3. Bake 8-11 minutes or until set. Remove from the pans to wire racks to cool completely. Spread with the reserved frosting.

Orange Cocoa Sandies

As a child, I helped my mom look through the food sections of newspapers and magazines for new dessert ideas. We created a big book with our collection, which included this sweet discovery.
—**NELLA PARKER** HERSEY, MI

PREP: 15 MIN. • **BAKE:** 15 MIN./BATCH
MAKES: ABOUT 2 DOZEN

- ½ **cup butter, softened**
- ½ **cup confectioners' sugar**
- ½ **teaspoon orange extract**
- 1 **cup all-purpose flour**
- 2 **tablespoons baking cocoa**
- ½ **cup finely chopped pecans**
  Additional confectioners' sugar

1. Preheat oven to 350°. In a large bowl, beat butter, ½ cup confectioners' sugar and extract until blended. In another bowl, whisk flour and cocoa; gradually beat into the butter mixture. Stir in pecans.
2. Shape dough into 1-in. balls; place 1 in. apart on ungreased baking sheets. Bake 12-14 minutes or until set. Cool on pans 1-2 minutes. Roll warm cookies in confectioners' sugar. Cool on wire racks. If desired, reroll cookies in confectioners' sugar after cooling.

Mocha Nut Balls

These tender, sugar-coated bites are so popular. I have to double the recipe—for a total of 9 dozen—every time I make them. My family demands it!
—**JANET SULLIVAN** BUFFALO, NY

PREP: 20 MIN. • **BAKE:** 15 MIN./BATCH
MAKES: 4½ DOZEN

- 1 **cup butter, softened**
- ½ **cup sugar**
- 2 **teaspoons vanilla extract**
- 1¾ **cups all-purpose flour**
- ⅓ **cup baking cocoa**
- 1 **tablespoon instant coffee granules**
- 1 **cup finely chopped pecans or walnuts**
  Confectioners' sugar

1. Preheat oven to 325°. In a large bowl, cream butter and sugar until light and fluffy. Beat in the vanilla. In another bowl, whisk flour, cocoa and coffee granules; gradually beat into

creamed mixture. Stir in pecans. Shape dough into 1-in. balls; place 2 in. apart on ungreased baking sheets.
2. Bake 14-16 minutes or until set. Cool on pans 1-2 minutes. Roll the warm cookies in confectioners' sugar. Cool on wire racks.

Gingerbread Fruitcake Cookies

I take two Christmas classics—fruitcake and gingerbread—and combine them into one yummy cookie. It's extra special spread with a simple homemade glaze.
—**JAMIE JONES** MADISON, GA

PREP: 20 MIN.
BAKE: 10 MIN./BATCH + COOLING
MAKES: 3 DOZEN

- 1 **package (14½ ounces) gingerbread cake/cookie mix**
- ¼ **cup butter, melted**
- ¼ **cup water**
- 1 **container (8 ounces) chopped mixed candied fruit**
- ½ **cup chopped pecans**
- ½ **cup raisins**
- 1¼ **cups confectioners' sugar**
- 1 **to 2 tablespoons orange juice**

1. Preheat oven to 350°. In a large bowl, mix the gingerbread cake/cookie mix, melted butter and water to form a soft dough. Stir in the candied fruit, pecans and raisins. Drop the dough by tablespoonfuls 2 in. apart onto ungreased baking sheets.
2. Bake 8-10 minutes or until set. Cool on pans 1 minute. Remove from pans to wire racks to cool completely.
3. In a small bowl, mix confectioners' sugar and enough orange juice to reach desired consistency. Spread or drizzle over cookies. Let stand until set.

Creme de Menthe Cheesecake Cookies

Stir cream cheese and creme de menthe baking chips into purchased dough for richness and a hint of mint. Candy-coating trees piped on top add a festive finish.
—**SHEILA SPORN** HOUSTON, TX

PREP: 15 MIN.
BAKE: 15 MIN./BATCH + COOLING
MAKES: 4 DOZEN

- 1 **tube (16½ ounces) refrigerated sugar cookie dough**
- 6 **tablespoons all-purpose flour**
- 1 **large egg**
- 1 **package (8 ounces) cream cheese, softened**
- 1⅓ **cups Andes creme de menthe baking chips**
  Green candy coating disks and sprinkles, optional

1. Preheat oven to 350°. In a large bowl, beat the cookie dough and flour until blended and dough is softened. Beat in the egg. Add the cream cheese; beat until smooth. Stir in the baking chips. (Dough will be soft.)

2. Drop dough by tablespoonfuls 2 in. apart onto ungreased baking sheets. Bake 11-13 minutes or until bottoms are golden brown. Cool 2 minutes before removing from pans to wire racks to cool completely.

3. If decorating the cookies, melt the green candy coating disks in a microwave. Cut a small hole in the tip of a pastry bag or in a corner of a food-safe plastic bag; insert a small round pastry tip. Fill the bag with the melted coating. Pipe designs onto the cookies; decorate with sprinkles.

Cinnamon-Sugar Crackle Cookies

These crackle treats are a tradition during the holiday season. Christmas wouldn't be the same without them! Everyone likes the generous coating of cinnamon and sugar.

—**SARAH MILLER** WAUCONDA, WA

PREP: 20 MIN. • **BAKE:** 10 MIN./BATCH
MAKES: 4 DOZEN

- 1 cup shortening
- 1¾ cups sugar, divided
- 2 eggs
- 2¾ cups all-purpose flour
- 2 teaspoons cream of tartar
- 1 teaspoon baking soda
- ½ teaspoon salt
- 4 teaspoons ground cinnamon

1. Preheat oven to 400°. In a large bowl, cream shortening and 1½ cups sugar until light and fluffy. Beat in eggs. In another bowl, whisk flour, cream of tartar, baking soda and salt; gradually beat into creamed mixture.
2. In a small bowl, mix cinnamon and remaining sugar. Shape dough into 1-in. balls; roll in cinnamon-sugar. Place 2 in. apart on ungreased baking sheets.
3. Bake 8-10 minutes or until golden brown. Cool 2 minutes before removing to wire racks to cool.

Holiday Helper

Want to send cookies in the mail? Those that are soft and even a little chewy are less likely to break or crumble during shipping. Bar cookies are also good choices.

Wrap cookies or bars individually or in pairs before packing to help them stay fresh. Pack them tightly in a sturdy box or cookie tin so they don't shift during shipping. Sometimes it's better to pack several smaller boxes or tins than one large box. Place small boxes or tins in a larger box filled with bubble wrap or shipping peanuts.

White Chocolate Cran-Pecan Cookies

Put a seasonal twist on classic chocolate chip cookies by stirring in pecans, white chips and cranberries. They're so good, your family will request them year-round.

—**BARB GARRETT** JACKSONVILLE, NC

PREP: 15 MIN. • **BAKE:** 10 MIN./BATCH
MAKES: ABOUT 2½ DOZEN

- ½ cup butter, softened
- ½ cup sugar
- ½ cup packed brown sugar
- 1 egg
- 1½ teaspoons vanilla extract
- 1½ cups all-purpose flour
- ½ teaspoon baking soda
- 1 cup dried cranberries
- ¾ cup white baking chips
- ½ cup chopped pecans

1. Preheat oven to 375°. In a large bowl, cream butter and sugars until light and fluffy. Beat in the egg and vanilla. In another bowl, whisk the flour and baking soda; gradually beat into the creamed mixture. Stir in the dried cranberries, white baking chips and pecans.
2. Drop the dough by tablespoonfuls 2 in. apart onto ungreased baking sheets. Bake 8-10 minutes or until light brown. Remove from the pans to wire racks to cool.

sweet
SENSATIONS

Marzipan Yule Logs

For an extra-special treat at Christmastime, I shape these sweet confections using homemade almond paste. Then I coat the logs with melted chocolate for the "bark" and decorate them with candied cherries and pecans. Everyone wants a slice!

—MARGERY RICHMOND FORT COLLINS, CO

PREP: 1 HOUR + CHILLING
MAKES: 2 YULE LOGS (10 SERVINGS EACH)

- **3** tablespoons golden raisins
- **3** tablespoons golden or light rum
- **1** teaspoon meringue powder
- **1** tablespoon water
- **1** cup blanched almonds
- **1** cup confectioners' sugar
- **1** teaspoon almond extract
- **1** teaspoon corn syrup
- **3** tablespoons chopped candied orange peel
- **4** ounces semisweet chocolate, melted
  Pecan halves and halved candied cherries

1. In a small bowl, combine raisins and rum. Cover and let stand overnight. Drain, reserving liquid.

2. In another small bowl, dissolve the meringue powder in the water. Place the almonds and ½ cup confectioners' sugar in a food processor; pulse until almonds are finely ground. Add the remaining confectioners' sugar; pulse until blended. Add the almond extract, corn syrup and meringue mixture; process until mixture forms a ball.

Remove and wrap in plastic wrap. Refrigerate 1 hour or until firm.

3. Crumble almond paste into a large bowl. Knead in the drained raisins and candied peel. If mixture is too stiff, add enough reserved rum as necessary to soften. Divide mixture in half; shape each into a 6-in. log. Wrap in plastic wrap. Refrigerate 4 hours or overnight until firm.

4. Unwrap the yule logs; brush all sides with the melted semisweet chocolate. Place on waxed paper. Decorate with the pecan halves and halved candied cherries. To serve, cut logs crosswise into slices.

NOTE *Meringue powder is available from Wilton Industries. Call 800-794-5866 or visit wilton.com.*

Pear Upside-Down Gingerbead

I usually prefer to bake from scratch, but this gingerbread made with a cake mix is a family favorite. For a change of pace, replace the pears and pecans with apples and walnuts.

—TRISHA KRUSE EAGLE, ID

PREP: 20 MIN. • **BAKE:** 55 MIN. + COOLING • **MAKES:** 9 SERVINGS

- ¾ **cup chopped pecans, toasted**
- ⅓ **cup packed brown sugar**
- ¼ **cup dark corn syrup**
- 3 **tablespoons butter, melted**
- 2 **medium pears, peeled and thinly sliced**
- 1 **package (14½ ounces) gingerbread cake mix**
- 2 **tablespoons crystallized ginger, finely chopped**

1. Preheat oven to 350°. In a small bowl, mix the pecans, brown sugar, corn syrup and butter. Pour into a greased 8-in.-square baking pan. Arrange the pear slices over the pecan mixture, overlapping slightly.

2. Prepare the gingerbread cake mix according to the package directions, folding the crystallized ginger into the batter. Pour over the pears. Bake 55-60 minutes or until a toothpick inserted in the center comes out with moist crumbs. Cool 10 minutes before inverting onto a serving plate. Serve warm.

NOTE *To toast nuts, spread them in a 15x10x1-in. baking pan. Bake at 350° for 5-10 minutes or until lightly browned, stirring occasionally. Or, spread in a dry nonstick skillet; heat over low heat until lightly browned, stirring occasionally.*

Eggnog Creams

When I discovered a creamy, dreamy truffle recipe in a cookbook, I came up with a yuletide variation to give as a holiday gift. Rum and nutmeg add a bit of classic eggnog flavor.

—CARLA MANNING GRANTSBURG, WI

PREP: 45 MIN. + CHILLING • **MAKES:** 2½ DOZEN

- 3½ **cups white baking chips, divided**
- ½ **cup butter, softened**
- 1 **package (3 ounces) cream cheese, softened**
- 2 **tablespoons dark rum**
- ¼ **teaspoon vanilla extract**
- 2 **tablespoons shortening**
  Ground nutmeg, optional

1. In a microwave, melt 1½ cups baking chips; stir until smooth. In a small bowl, cream butter and cream cheese until smooth. Add rum and vanilla. Beat in melted chips. Refrigerate, covered, 1 hour or until set.

2. Shape the mixture into 1-in. balls; place on a waxed paper-lined baking sheet. Refrigerate 2 hours or until firm and slightly dry to the touch.

3. In a microwave, melt shortening and remaining baking chips; stir until smooth. Dip the balls in the mixture; allow excess to drip off. Return to the baking sheet; if desired, sprinkle with nutmeg.

4. Refrigerate 2 hours or until set. Store between layers of waxed paper in an airtight container in the refrigerator.

NOTE *This recipe was tested with Ghirardelli white baking chips.*

White Chip Peanut-Pretzel Clusters

With lots of crunch and sweet-salty appeal, these colorful goodies always get snatched up quickly. The no-bake clusters require only six basic ingredients.

—**SANDY KLOCINSKI** SUMMERVILLE, SC

PREP: 20 MIN. + STANDING
MAKES: 5 DOZEN

- 2⅔ cups white baking chips
- ½ cup creamy peanut butter
- 3 cups Rice Krispies
- 1 cup lightly salted dry roasted peanuts
- ½ cup crushed pretzels
- ½ cup red and green milk chocolate M&M's

1. In a large heavy saucepan, melt the baking chips and peanut butter over medium-low heat; stir until smooth. Remove from heat. Stir in remaining ingredients.
2. Drop by tablespoonfuls onto waxed paper; let stand until set. Store in an airtight container.

Red Velvet Marble Cake

I watched my grandmother prepare her red velvet showstopper countless times for family get-togethers. The fluffy butter frosting perfectly complements the flavor of the gorgeous, chocolaty cake.

—**JODI ANDERSON** OVERBROOK, KS

PREP: 20 MIN. • **BAKE:** 30 MIN. + COOLING
MAKES: 12 SERVINGS

- ¾ cup butter, softened
- 2¼ cups sugar
- 3 eggs
- 4½ teaspoons white vinegar
- 1½ teaspoons vanilla extract
- 3¾ cups cake flour
- 1½ teaspoons baking soda
- 1½ cups buttermilk
- 3 tablespoons baking cocoa
- 4½ teaspoons red food coloring

FROSTING

- 1 cup butter, softened
- 9 cups confectioners' sugar
- 3 teaspoons vanilla extract
- ⅔ to ¾ cup 2% milk

1. Preheat oven to 350°. Line bottoms of two greased 9-in. round baking pans with parchment paper; grease paper.
2. In a large bowl, cream butter and sugar until light and fluffy. Add eggs, one at a time, beating well after each addition. Beat in vinegar and vanilla. In another bowl, whisk the flour and baking soda; add to creamed mixture alternately with buttermilk, beating well after each addition.
3. Transfer half of the batter to another bowl; stir in cocoa and food coloring until blended. Alternately drop the plain and chocolate batters by ¼ cupfuls into prepared pans, dividing batter evenly between pans. To make the batter level in the pans, bang pans several times on counter.
4. Bake 30-35 minutes or until a toothpick inserted in center comes out clean. Cool 10 minutes before removing from the pans to wire racks to cool completely.
5. In a large bowl, beat the butter, confectioners' sugar, vanilla and enough milk to reach a spreading consistency. Spread frosting between layers and over top and sides of cake.

Almond Macaroon Tart

My husband is a fan of his aunt's almond cake, but she's very secretive about her recipe. I tried adapting the same idea and came up with something new—a nutty, golden brown tart we love.

—ELISA THORESEN ENGLISHTOWN, NJ

PREP: 25 MIN. • **BAKE:** 30 MIN. + COOLING
MAKES: 16 SERVINGS

- 1 cup slivered almonds
- 1 cup flaked coconut
- 2¼ cups all-purpose flour
- 1 cup sugar
- 1 cup butter, softened

FILLING
- 1¼ cups confectioners' sugar
- ¾ cup flaked coconut, divided
- 1 package (7 ounces) almond paste, crumbled
- 1 teaspoon almond extract
- 2 egg whites

1. Preheat the oven to 350°. Place the almonds and coconut in a food processor; process until finely ground. Add flour and sugar; pulse to combine. Add the butter; pulse until crumbly. Reserve 1½ cups crumb mixture for the topping. Press the remaining mixture onto the bottom and up the sides of a greased 11-in. fluted tart pan with removable bottom.

2. For the filling, place confectioners' sugar, ½ cup coconut, almond paste and extract in food processor; pulse until fine crumbs form. Add the egg whites; process until blended. Spread into the prepared crust; sprinkle with the reserved topping.

3. Bake 25-30 minutes or until golden brown. Sprinkle with the remaining coconut; bake 5-8 minutes longer or until coconut is lightly browned. Cool completely on a wire rack.

Pear & Maple Cream Pavlova

Delicate and creamy, this pear-covered pavlova makes an extra-special dessert for company. I prepare the filling using the maple syrup I buy from a local farm.
—**DIANE NEMITZ** LUDINGTON, MI

PREP: 35 MIN. • **BAKE:** 45 MIN. + STANDING
MAKES: 8 SERVINGS

- 4 egg whites
- ⅛ teaspoon cream of tartar
- ¾ cup sugar
- ¼ cup ground pecans
- 1⅓ cups half-and-half cream
- ½ cup plus 3 tablespoons maple syrup, divided
- 1 egg
- 1 egg yolk
- 2 tablespoons brown sugar
- 2 tablespoons cornstarch
- 8 canned pear halves in juice, well-drained

1. Place the egg whites in a large bowl; let stand at room temperature 30 minutes. Line a baking sheet with parchment paper. Trace a 9-in. circle on the parchment paper; invert paper.

2. Preheat oven to 275°. Add cream of tartar to egg whites; beat on medium speed until foamy. Gradually add sugar, 1 tablespoon at a time, beating on high after each addition until the sugar is dissolved. Continue beating until stiff glossy peaks form. Fold in pecans.

3. Spread the meringue over circle, shaping a shallow well in the center using the back of a spoon. Bake 45-50 minutes or until set and dry. Turn off oven (do not open oven door); leave meringue in oven 1 hour.

4. Meanwhile, in a small saucepan, heat the cream until bubbles form around the sides of pan. In a small bowl, whisk ½ cup maple syrup, egg, egg yolk, brown sugar and cornstarch until blended but not foamy. Slowly whisk in the hot cream. Return all to pan; cook and stir over medium heat until thickened and a thermometer reads 170°. Immediately transfer to a clean bowl. Cool 30 minutes, stirring occasionally. Press plastic wrap onto surface of filling; refrigerate until cold.

5. Remove meringue from oven; cool completely on baking sheet. Preheat broiler. Thinly slice wide end of each pear, leaving stem end attached. Blot dry. Place on a foil-lined baking sheet; spread slices to fan. Brush pears with remaining maple syrup. Broil 3-4 in. from heat 7-8 minutes or until lightly browned. Cool completely.

6. To serve, remove meringue from paper; place on a serving plate. Fill with maple cream. Arrange cooled pears over top. Refrigerate leftovers.

Cranberry Cashew Fudge

What berries say "Christmas" more than cranberries? I add those little red gems to a simple cashew fudge recipe, giving it a colorful and festive upgrade.
—**BETSY KING** DULUTH, MN

PREP: 25 MIN. + CHILLING
MAKES: ABOUT 1¾ POUNDS (64 PIECES)

- 2 teaspoons butter, softened
- ⅔ cup evaporated milk
- 1⅔ cups sugar
- ⅛ teaspoon salt
- 4 ounces semisweet chocolate, chopped
- 1½ cups miniature marshmallows
- ½ cup unsalted cashews, chopped
- ½ cup dried cranberries
- 1 teaspoon vanilla extract

1. Line an 8-in.-square baking dish with foil; grease foil with butter.

2. In a large heavy saucepan, combine the evaporated milk, sugar and salt. Bring to a rapid boil over medium heat, stirring constantly. Cook 5 minutes longer, stirring constantly. Remove from heat.

3. Stir in chocolate and marshmallows until melted. Stir in the cashews, dried cranberries and vanilla. Immediately spread into prepared pan. Refrigerate at least 2 hours or until firm.

4. Using the foil, lift the fudge out of the pan. Remove foil; cut fudge into 1-in. squares. Store between layers of waxed paper in an airtight container.

Making Meringue for Pavlova

Pear & Maple Cream Pavlova (recipe above) features a light-as-air layer of meringue that forms the base for the cream filling and pears. When making the meringue, refer to the helpful how-to photos here.

1. Beat until stiff glossy peaks form. To make sure the sugar is dissolved, rub a little meringue between your fingers—it should feel silky smooth.

2. After folding the ground pecans into the meringue, spread it over the parchment-paper circle, creating a shallow well in the center.

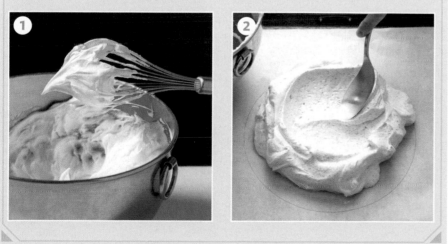

Dates-Under-a-Cloud Bars

When I was in elementary school, we had a community cookbook that included these yummy bars. Use a wet knife when cutting them to easily slice through the meringue.

—LORRAINE CALAND SHUNIAH, ON

PREP: 30 MIN. • **BAKE:** 25 MIN. + COOLING
MAKES: 2 DOZEN

- 2 eggs, separated
- 1¼ cups chopped dates
- ½ cup water
- 4 teaspoons grated orange peel
- ½ cup butter, softened
- ½ cup sugar
- 1 teaspoon vanilla extract
- 1½ cups all-purpose flour
- 1 teaspoon baking powder
- ⅔ cup packed brown sugar
- ¼ cup sliced almonds

1. Place the egg whites in a small bowl; let stand at room temperature 30 minutes. Preheat oven to 350°.

2. Meanwhile, in a small saucepan, combine dates, water and orange peel; bring to a boil. Reduce heat; simmer, uncovered, until thickened, stirring occasionally. Cool slightly.

3. For crust, in a large bowl, cream butter and sugar until light and fluffy. Beat in the egg yolks and vanilla. In another bowl, whisk flour and baking powder; gradually beat into creamed mixture. Press onto the bottom of a greased 13x9-in. baking pan. Spread date mixture over top.

4. With clean beaters, beat the egg whites on medium speed until foamy. Gradually add the brown sugar, 1 tablespoon at a time, beating on high after each addition until sugar is dissolved. Continue beating until stiff peaks form. Spread over date mixture; sprinkle with almonds.

5. Bake 25-30 minutes or until the top is golden brown. Cool completely on a wire rack.

Creamy Coconut Rice Pudding Parfait

My daughter likes to invite friends over for lunch and often treats them to her tropical parfaits. Made with coconut milk and brown rice, the desserts are creamy, fresh and comforting any time of year.

—SUZANNE CLARK PHOENIX, AZ

PREP: 15 MIN. **COOK:** 45 MIN.
MAKES: 6 SERVINGS

- 2 cups 2% milk
- 1½ cups coconut milk
- 1½ cups cooked cold brown rice
- ¼ cup maple syrup
- ¼ teaspoon salt
- 2 teaspoons vanilla extract
- ¼ teaspoon almond extract
- 2 medium oranges, peeled and sectioned
- 2 medium kiwifruit, peeled and sliced
- ¼ cup sliced almonds, toasted
  Toasted flaked coconut

1. In a large heavy saucepan, combine the first five ingredients; bring to a boil over medium heat. Reduce the heat to maintain a low simmer. Cook, uncovered, 35-45 minutes or until rice is soft and milk is almost absorbed, stirring occasionally.

2. Remove from heat; stir in extracts. Cool slightly. Serve warm or refrigerate, covered, and serve cold. To serve, spoon pudding into dishes. Top with fruit; sprinkle with almonds and coconut.

NOTE *To toast nuts and coconut, spread individually in a dry nonstick skillet and heat over low heat until lightly browned, stirring occasionally.*

Lemon Creme Brulee

Here's a tangy twist on a classic favorite. Don't have the kitchen torch traditionally used for creme brulee? Simply pop the ramekins under the broiler.

—**SARA SCHELER** HELENVILLE, WI

PREP: 15 MIN. • **BAKE:** 45 MIN. + CHILLING
MAKES: 5 SERVINGS

- 3 **cups heavy whipping cream**
- 6 **egg yolks**
- ½ **cup plus 5 teaspoons sugar, divided**
- ½ **teaspoon salt**
- 2 **tablespoons grated lemon peel**
- ½ **teaspoon lemon extract**

1. Preheat oven to 325°. In a large saucepan, heat cream until bubbles form around sides of pan; remove from heat. In a large bowl, whisk egg yolks, ½ cup sugar and salt until blended but not foamy. Slowly stir in hot cream. Stir in lemon peel and extract.

2. Place five 6-oz. broiler-safe ramekins in a baking pan large enough to hold them without touching. Pour egg mixture into ramekins. Place pan on oven rack; add very hot water to pan to within ½ in. of top of ramekins. Bake 45-50 minutes or until a knife inserted near the center comes out clean (the centers will still be soft).

3. Immediately remove the ramekins from the water bath to a wire rack; cool 10 minutes. Refrigerate until cold.

4. To caramelize the topping with a kitchen torch, sprinkle custards evenly with remaining sugar. Hold the torch flame about 2 in. above custard surface and rotate it slowly until the sugar is evenly caramelized. Refrigerate 30-60 minutes before serving.

5. To caramelize topping in a broiler, preheat broiler and place ramekins on a baking sheet; let stand at room temperature 15 minutes. Sprinkle custards evenly with remaining sugar. Broil 3-4 in. from heat 2-3 minutes or until sugar is caramelized. Refrigerate 30-60 minutes before serving.

Layered Chocolate-Raspberry Triangles

These chocolaty triangles layered with jam are a must in our house during the holiday season. The cakelike bars look fancy, and one batch goes a long way.

—MARY ANN LEE CLIFTON PARK, NY

PREP: 45 MIN. • **BAKE:** 15 MIN. + STANDING
MAKES: 4 DOZEN

- 6 **eggs, separated**
- 1½ **cups butter, softened**
- 1½ **cups sugar**
- 2 **teaspoons vanilla extract**
- 2½ **cups all-purpose flour**
- 3 **ounces unsweetened chocolate, melted and cooled slightly**
- 3 **ounces white baking chocolate, melted and cooled slightly**
- ¼ **cup seedless raspberry jam**
- 1 **cup (6 ounces) semisweet chocolate chips, melted**
  White baking chocolate shavings

1. Place the egg whites in a large bowl; let stand at room temperature 30 minutes. Preheat oven to 350°. Line the bottoms of two greased matching 13x9-in. baking pans (or reuse one pan) with parchment paper; grease papers.

2. In a large bowl, cream the butter and sugar until light and fluffy. Add egg yolks, one at a time, beating well after each addition. Add vanilla. Stir in flour.

3. With clean beaters, beat egg whites on medium speed until stiff peaks form. Fold into batter. Transfer half of the batter to another bowl. Fold melted unsweetened chocolate into one bowl; spread into a prepared pan. Fold melted white chocolate into remaining batter; spread into second prepared pan.

4. Bake 12-16 minutes or until a toothpick inserted in center comes out clean. Cool 5 minutes. Invert onto wire racks. Remove parchment paper; cool completely.

5. Transfer the chocolate layer to a baking sheet lined with a large piece of plastic wrap. Spread jam over the top; place the white chocolate layer over jam. Wrap securely with plastic wrap. Set a cutting board or heavy baking pan over the top to flatten the layers. Let stand at room temperature 3-4 hours. (Or, refrigerate overnight and return to room temperature before continuing).

6. Unwrap the cake; place on a cutting board. Spread the top with the melted chocolate chips. Top with the white chocolate shavings. Let stand until set. Trim the edges with a knife. Cut into 24 squares; cut the squares diagonally in half.

Sticky Bread Pudding Cups

Love bread pudding? Bake that comforting treat in a muffin pan for fun single servings.

—**MARY FREELAND** DAYTON, TX

PREP: 35 MIN. • **BAKE:** 35 MIN.
MAKES: 12 SERVINGS

2¼ cups pecan halves
¼ cup packed brown sugar
½ cup butter, cubed

BREAD PUDDING

2 eggs
1¼ cups 2% milk
⅓ cup packed brown sugar
2 tablespoons sugar
1 teaspoon vanilla extract
½ teaspoon ground cinnamon
¼ teaspoon salt
8 slices white bread, crusts removed and cut into ½-inch cubes (about 3 cups)

TOPPING

3 tablespoons butter
3 tablespoons brown sugar
Whipped cream

1. In a small bowl, toss the pecans with the brown sugar. In a small heavy saucepan, melt butter over medium heat. Heat 5-7 minutes or until golden brown, stirring constantly. Stir into pecan mixture.

2. Remove 12 of the pecans; place on foil to cool. Transfer half of the remaining pecan mixture to a food processor; process until smooth. Add the remaining pecan mixture; pulse until chopped.

3. Preheat oven to 350°. In a large bowl, whisk eggs, milk, sugars, vanilla, cinnamon and salt until blended. Stir in bread; let stand about 15 minutes or until bread is softened. Add pecan mixture, stirring gently to swirl (do not combine completely).

4. For the topping, divide the butter among 12 ungreased muffin cups; sprinkle with brown sugar. Spoon the bread mixture into cups. Bake 35-40 minutes or until a knife near the center comes out clean.

5. Remove from the oven; let stand 5 minutes. Run a knife around the edges of the cups; invert onto dessert plates. Serve warm; top with whipped cream and the reserved pecans.

Holiday Helper

When my loaf of white bread is down to the last few slices, I cube the bread, put it in a freezer bag and place it in the freezer. I keep adding to the bag when I can, so when I want to prepare bread pudding or stuffing, I have plenty of cubes ready to go.

—**HELEN R.** ROCKTON, IL

Zesty Citrus Cake

PREP: 30 MIN. • **BAKE:** 15 MIN. + COOLING
MAKES: 12 SERVINGS

- **1** package yellow cake mix (regular size)
- **½** cup sour cream
- **½** cup butter, melted
- **5** tablespoons lemon juice
- **¼** cup orange juice
- **3** eggs
- **1** tablespoon grated orange peel
- **2** teaspoons grated lemon peel

FROSTING

- **1** cup butter, softened
- **½** cup butter-flavored shortening
- **1** tablespoon grated orange peel
- **2** teaspoons grated lemon peel
- **5** cups confectioners' sugar
- **3** tablespoons lemon juice
- **1** tablespoon orange juice
- **1** cup toasted sliced almonds, optional
     Candied orange and lemon slices, optional

1. Preheat oven to 350°. Line bottoms of two greased 9-in. round baking pans with parchment paper; grease paper.

2. In a large bowl, combine the first eight ingredients; beat on low speed 30 seconds. Beat on medium 2 minutes. Transfer to prepared pans.

3. Bake 15-20 minutes or until a toothpick inserted in center comes out clean. Cool in pans 10 minutes before removing to wire racks; remove paper. Cool completely.

4. For the frosting, in a large bowl, beat the butter, shortening and citrus peels until blended. Gradually beat in the confectioners' sugar and juices until smooth. Beat until fluffy.

5. Spread frosting between layers and over top and sides of cake. If desired, gently press almonds into frosting on sides of cake and top with candied orange and lemon slices.

NOTE *To toast nuts, spread them in a 15x10x1-in. baking pan. Bake at 350° for 5-10 minutes or until lightly browned, stirring occasionally. Or, spread in a dry nonstick skillet and heat over low heat until lightly browned, stirring occasionally.*

"We grow our own citrus trees, so I'm always trying to come up with new recipes to showcase the fruit. My layer cake gets a nice tang from lemons and oranges."

—GENEVA GARRISON-BENNETT JACKSONVILLE, FL

Buttermilk Pie with Pecans

Want to branch out from the usual pecan pie? Consider this creamy-crunchy version that blends in buttermilk. Big slices are even better topped with whipped cream.

—**KATHY HARDING** RICHMOND, MO

PREP: 40 MIN. • **BAKE:** 50 MIN. + COOLING
MAKES: 8 SERVINGS

Pastry for single-crust pie (9 inches)
½ cup butter, softened
1¾ cups sugar
3 eggs
3 tablespoons all-purpose flour
¼ teaspoon salt
1 cup buttermilk
2 teaspoons vanilla extract
1 cup chopped pecans
Sweetened whipped cream, optional

1. Preheat oven to 425°. On a lightly floured surface, roll pastry dough to a ⅛-in.-thick circle; transfer to a 9-in. pie plate. Trim pastry to ½ in. beyond rim of plate; flute edge. Line unpricked pastry with a double thickness of foil. Fill with pie weights, dried beans or uncooked rice.

2. Place on a baking sheet; bake 20 minutes or until bottom is lightly browned. Remove foil and weights; bake 1-2 minutes longer or until golden brown. Cool the crust on a wire rack. Reduce oven setting to 325°.

3. In a large bowl, beat the butter and sugar until blended. Add eggs, one at a time, beating well after each addition. Beat in flour and salt. Gradually stir in buttermilk and vanilla.

4. Sprinkle the pecans into crust; add filling. Bake 50-60 minutes or until the center is set. Cover top loosely with foil during the last 15 minutes to prevent overbrowning if necessary.

5. Cool completely on a wire rack. If desired, serve with whipped cream. Serve or refrigerate within 2 hours.

Holiday Helper

To make pastry for a single-crust pie (9 inches) such as Buttermilk Pie with Pecans at left, combine 1¼ cups all-purpose flour and ¼ teaspoon salt; cut in ½ cup cold butter until crumbly. Gradually add 3-5 tablespoons ice water, tossing the dough with a fork until it holds together when pressed. Wrap the dough in plastic wrap and refrigerate 1 hour.

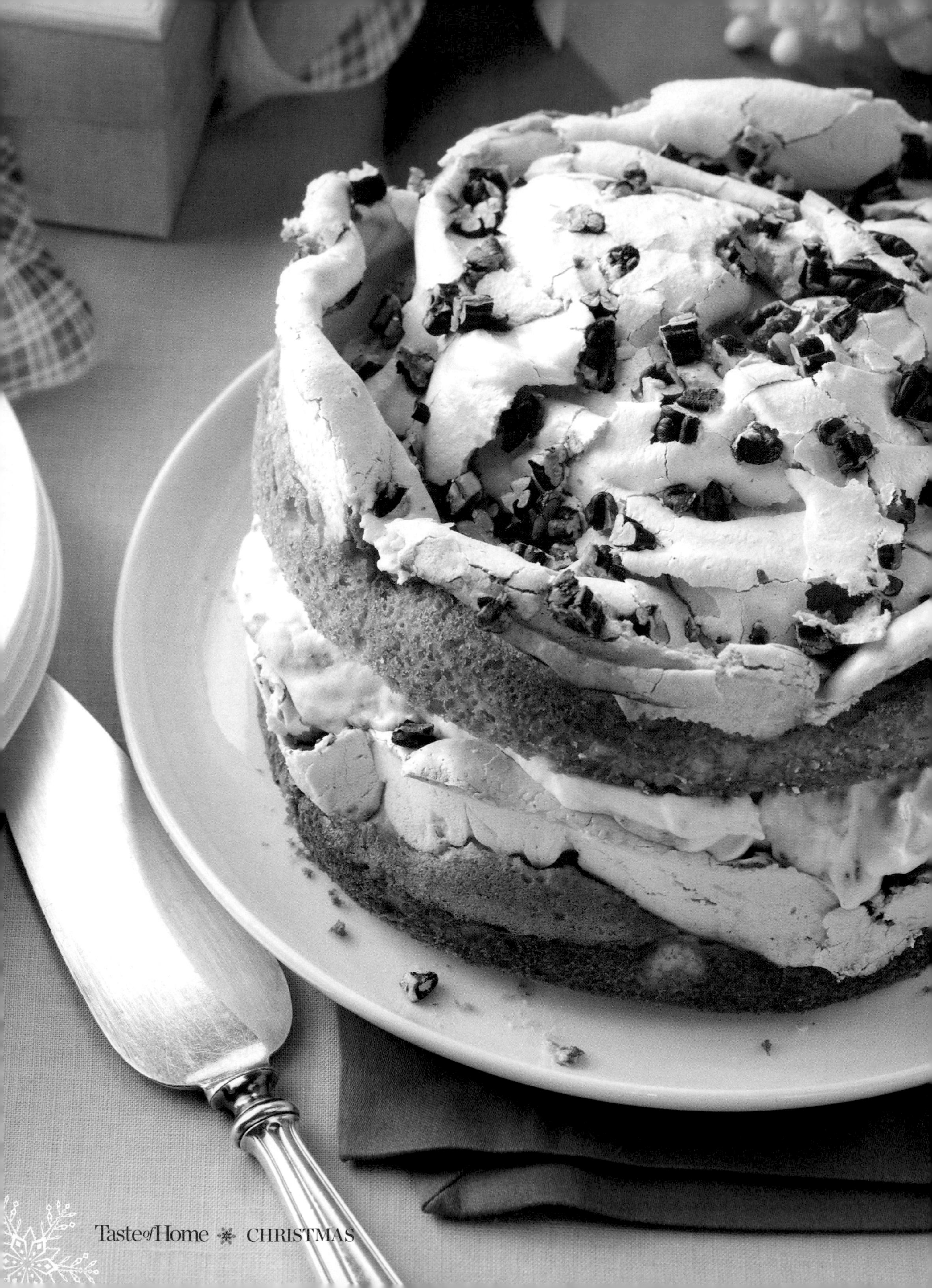

Cranberry Meringue Cake

A fan of Southern cooking, I love exchanging recipes while working at my beauty salon. I found my meringue cake in an old cookbook.
—**SANDY THOMAS** GUNTERSVILLE, AL

PREP: 40 MIN. • **BAKE:** 25 MIN. + COOLING • **MAKES:** 12 SERVINGS

- 4 eggs, separated
- ½ cup butter, softened
- 1½ cups sugar, divided
- 3 teaspoons vanilla extract, divided
- 1 cup cake flour
- 2 teaspoons baking powder
- ⅛ teaspoon salt
- 5 tablespoons 2% milk
- ¾ cup finely chopped pecans

FILLING
- ½ cup frozen cranberries
- ½ cup sugar
- 2 tablespoons grated orange peel
- 1 tablespoon orange juice
- 1 cup heavy whipping cream
- 2 tablespoons confectioners' sugar
- 1 teaspoon almond extract

1. Place the egg whites in a large bowl; let stand at room temperature 30 minutes. Preheat oven to 350°. Line the bottoms of two greased 8-in. round baking pans with parchment paper; grease paper.
2. In a large bowl, cream butter and ½ cup sugar until light and fluffy. Add egg yolks, one at a time, beating well after each addition. Beat in 2 teaspoons vanilla.
3. In another bowl, whisk flour, baking powder and salt; add to creamed mixture alternately with milk, beating well after each addition. Transfer to prepared pans.
4. With clean beaters, beat the egg whites on medium speed until foamy. Gradually add the remaining sugar, 1 tablespoon at a time, beating on high after each addition until the sugar is dissolved. Add the remaining vanilla; continue beating until stiff glossy peaks form. Spread over the batter in pans; sprinkle with pecans. Bake 25-30 minutes or until meringue is lightly browned.
5. Meanwhile, for the filling, combine cranberries, sugar, orange peel and orange juice in a small saucepan. Cook, uncovered, over medium heat 7-10 minutes or until berries pop, stirring occasionally. Remove from heat; cool slightly. Transfer to a food processor; pulse until berries are coarsely chopped. Cool completely.
6. In a bowl, beat cream until it begins to thicken. Add the confectioners' sugar and extract; beat until stiff peaks form. Fold in cranberry mixture.
7. Loosen sides of cakes from pans with a knife. Carefully invert each cake onto a plate (meringue will crack); remove paper. Invert again onto a wire rack; cool completely.
8. Place one cake layer on a serving plate. Gently spread with filling. Top with the remaining cake layer, meringue side up. Refrigerate leftovers.

Fluted Lemon Cake with Fresh Fruit

This citrusy, golden brown beauty looks especially impressive baked in a decorative tube pan. Serve each sugar-dusted slice with a dollop of whipped cream and your favorite fruit.
—**DONNA STELMACH** MORRISTOWN, NJ

PREP: 20 MIN. • **BAKE:** 1 HOUR + COOLING • **MAKES:** 12 SERVINGS

- 1 cup butter, softened
- 2 cups sugar
- 4 eggs
- 2 tablespoons grated lemon peel
- 1 teaspoon lemon extract
- 2½ cups all-purpose flour
- 2 teaspoons baking powder
- ½ teaspoon salt
- 1 cup (8 ounces) fat-free strawberry Greek yogurt
  Confectioners' sugar, optional
  Assorted fresh fruit
  Whipped cream

1. Preheat oven to 325°. Grease and flour a 10-in. fluted tube pan. In a large bowl, cream the butter and sugar until light and fluffy. Add eggs, one at a time, beating well after each addition. Beat in lemon peel and extract.
2. In another bowl, whisk the flour, baking powder and salt; add to creamed mixture alternately with yogurt, beating well after each addition.
3. Transfer to prepared pan. Bake 60-70 minutes or until a toothpick inserted in center comes out clean. Cool in pan 10 minutes before removing to a wire rack to cool completely. If desired, dust with confectioners' sugar. Serve with fresh fruit and whipped cream.
NOTE *For easier removal of cakes, use solid shortening to grease plain and fluted tube pans.*

Pumpkin Pie Spiced Blondies

My family loves pumpkin pie at holiday time and craves brownies all year long. So I always hear raves when I bring out a platter of my spiced blondies. The homemade frosting is a bonus!

—**AMY ANDREWS** MAPLE VALLEY, WA

PREP: 25 MIN. • **BAKE:** 25 MIN. + COOLING • **MAKES:** 16 SERVINGS

- ¾ cup butter, softened
- ¾ cup packed brown sugar
- 2 eggs
- 4 teaspoons light corn syrup
- 1½ teaspoons rum extract
- 1⅓ cups all-purpose flour
- 2 teaspoons pumpkin pie spice
- ½ teaspoon baking powder
- ¼ teaspoon salt
- 1 cup white baking chips
- ¾ cup chopped pecans, optional

FROSTING

- 1¼ cups confectioners' sugar
- 3 tablespoons cream cheese, softened
- ⅛ teaspoon vanilla extract
- 1½ to 2 teaspoons orange juice

1. Preheat oven to 350°. In a large bowl, cream butter and brown sugar until light and fluffy. Beat in eggs, corn syrup and extract. In another bowl, whisk flour, pie spice, baking powder and salt; gradually beat into creamed mixture. Stir in baking chips and, if desired, pecans.

2. Spread into a greased 8-in.-square baking pan. Bake 25-30 minutes or until a toothpick inserted in the center comes out clean (do not overbake). Cool completely in pan on a wire rack.

3. In a small bowl, beat the confectioners' sugar, cream cheese, vanilla and enough orange juice to reach a spreading consistency. Spread the frosting over the top; cut into bars. Refrigerate leftovers.

Apple-Cherry Cream Cheese Pie

A layer of sweetened cream cheese topped with a tart fruit filling makes this home-style dessert popular with relatives, friends, co-workers, neighbors—just about everyone! It also won a blue ribbon at a local fair. The ruby red tint from the cherries creates a festive look that suits the Christmas season.

—**DONNA RETTEW** JONESTOWN, PA

PREP: 45 MIN. + CHILLING • **BAKE:** 45 MIN. + COOLING
MAKES: 8 SERVINGS

- 2¼ cups all-purpose flour
- 2 teaspoons sugar
- ¾ teaspoon salt
- 1 cup cold unsalted butter, cubed
- 6 to 8 tablespoons ice water

FILLING

- 1 package (8 ounces) cream cheese, softened
- 1¼ cups sugar, divided
- 1 teaspoon vanilla extract
- 9 cups thinly sliced peeled McIntosh apples (about 11 medium)
- ½ cup all-purpose flour
- 1 teaspoon apple pie spice
- ¼ teaspoon salt
- 1 can (14½ ounces) pitted tart cherries, drained
- 2 tablespoons butter

1. In a large bowl, mix the flour, sugar and salt; cut in the butter until crumbly. Gradually add the ice water, tossing with a fork until dough holds together when pressed. Divide dough in half. Shape each into a disk; wrap in plastic wrap. Refrigerate 1 hour or overnight.

2. Preheat oven to 425°. For filling, in a small bowl, beat cream cheese, ¼ cup sugar and vanilla until blended. In a large bowl, toss the apples with the flour, pie spice, salt and remaining sugar. Stir in cherries.

3. On a lightly floured surface, roll one half of dough to a ⅛-in.-thick circle; transfer to a 9-in. pie plate. Trim pastry even with rim.

4. Spread the cream cheese mixture onto the bottom of the pastry. Add apple mixture; dot with butter. Roll remaining dough to a ⅛-in.-thick circle. Place over filling. Trim, seal and flute edge. Cut slits in top.

5. Bake 45-50 minutes or until the crust is golden brown and the filling is bubbly. Cover top loosely with foil during the last 10-15 minutes if needed to prevent overbrowning. Cool on a wire rack. Refrigerate leftovers.

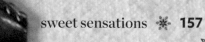

Flourless Chocolate Torte

Here's the ideal treat for chocoholics—like me! I bake the melt-in-your-mouth torte all the time for special occasions. It's so rich and decadent, the only topping I add is a dusting of confectioners' sugar.

—KAYLA ALBRECHT FREEPORT, IL

PREP: 20 MIN. • **BAKE:** 40 MIN. + COOLING
MAKES: 12 SERVINGS

- 5 eggs, separated
- 12 ounces semisweet chocolate, chopped
- ¾ cup butter, cubed
- ¼ teaspoon cream of tartar
- ½ cup sugar
  Confectioners' sugar, optional

1. Place the egg whites in a large bowl; let stand at room temperature 30 minutes. Preheat oven to 350°. In top of a double boiler or a metal bowl over barely simmering water, melt the chocolate and butter; stir until smooth. Remove from heat; cool slightly.

2. In another large bowl, beat egg yolks until thick and lemon-colored. Beat in chocolate mixture. With clean beaters, beat egg whites and cream of tartar on medium speed until foamy.

3. Gradually add sugar, 1 tablespoon at a time, beating on high after each addition until the sugar is dissolved. Continue beating until stiff glossy peaks form. Fold a fourth of the egg whites into chocolate mixture, then fold in remaining whites.

4. Transfer batter to a greased 9-in. springform pan. Bake 40-45 minutes or until toothpick inserted in center comes out with moist crumbs (do not overbake). Cool completely on wire rack.

5. Loosen sides from pan with a knife. Remove rim from pan. If desired, dust with confectioners' sugar.

Chocolate Pecan Pie Bars

These chunky pecan bars start with a homemade pastry crust and pile on a chocolate-chip filling. They're perfect for bake sales or casual get-togethers.

—HEATHER BIEDLER MARTINSBURG, WV

PREP: 30 MIN. + CHILLING
BAKE: 50 MIN. + COOLING
MAKES: 3 DOZEN

- 1¾ cups all-purpose flour
- ¼ teaspoon salt
- ¾ cup cold butter
- ¼ to ½ cup ice water

FILLING
- 4 eggs
- 2 cups sugar
- ½ teaspoon salt
- 1 cup all-purpose flour
- 1 cup butter, melted and cooled
- 4 teaspoons vanilla extract
- 2⅔ cups (16 ounces) semisweet chocolate chips
- 1⅓ cups chopped pecans

1. In a small bowl, mix flour and salt; cut in butter until crumbly. Gradually add ice water, tossing with a fork until dough holds together when pressed. Shape into a disk; wrap in plastic wrap. Refrigerate 1 hour or overnight.
2. Preheat oven to 350°. On a lightly floured surface, roll dough to fit bottom of a 13x9-in. baking pan; press into pan. Refrigerate while preparing filling.
3. In a large bowl, beat eggs, sugar and salt on high speed 2 minutes. Stir in the flour, melted butter and vanilla. Fold in chocolate chips. Pour over pastry; sprinkle with pecans.
4. Cover loosely with foil. Place on a lower oven rack; bake 20 minutes. Bake, uncovered, 30 minutes longer or until the top is golden brown and a knife inserted near the center comes out clean.
5. Cool in pan on a wire rack. Cut into bars. Refrigerate leftovers.

Orange-Pistachio Divinity

Old-fashioned divinity candy is even better when you add a hint of refreshing orange zest and bits of crunchy pistachios. Store-bought versions just can't compare!

—LORRI REINHARDT BIG BEND, WI

PREP: 15 MIN. + STANDING
COOK: 40 MIN. + STANDING
MAKES: 4 DOZEN (1⅓ POUNDS)

- 2 egg whites
- 2⅔ cups sugar
- ⅔ cup light corn syrup
- ½ cup water
- 1 teaspoon grated orange peel
- 1 teaspoon vanilla extract
- ⅔ cup pistachios, coarsely chopped

1. Place egg whites in bowl of a stand mixer; let stand at room temperature 30 minutes. Meanwhile, line two 15x10x1-in. pans with waxed paper.
2. In a large heavy saucepan, combine sugar, corn syrup and water; cook and stir until sugar is dissolved and mixture comes to a boil. Cook, without stirring, over medium heat until a candy thermometer reads 252° (hard-ball stage). Just before the temperature is reached, beat egg whites on medium speed until stiff peaks form.
3. Slowly add the hot sugar mixture in a thin stream over the egg whites, beating constantly and scraping the sides of bowl occasionally. Add orange peel and vanilla. Beat until the candy holds its shape, about 5-6 minutes. (Do not overmix or the candy will get stiff and crumbly.) Immediately fold in the pistachios.
4. Quickly drop the mixture by tablespoonfuls onto prepared pans. Let stand at room temperature until dry to the touch. Store between layers of waxed paper in an airtight container at room temperature.

Chocolate Drizzled Maple-Nut Tart

Here's a true indulgence! The rich, buttery crust holds a triple-nut filling flavored with maple and drizzled with chocolate.

—REBEKAH RADEWAHN WAUWATOSA, WI

PREP: 20 MIN. + CHILLING
BAKE: 40 MIN. + CHILLING
MAKES: 12 SERVINGS

- 2 **cups all-purpose flour**
- 3 **tablespoons sugar**
- ¾ **cup cold butter**
- ¼ **cup cold 2% milk**
- 2 **egg yolks**

FILLING

- 1 **can (14 ounces) sweetened condensed milk**
- ¾ **teaspoon maple flavoring**
- ½ **teaspoon ground cinnamon**
- ¼ **teaspoon salt**
- ⅔ **cup coarsely chopped pecans**
- ⅔ **cup coarsely chopped walnuts**
- ⅔ **cup sliced almonds**
- ⅓ **cup semisweet chocolate chips, melted**

1. Preheat oven to 375°. In a large bowl, mix flour and sugar; cut in butter until crumbly. In a small bowl, whisk milk and egg yolks; gradually add to flour mixture, tossing with a fork until dough holds together when pressed. Shape into a disk; wrap in plastic wrap. Refrigerate 30 minutes or overnight.

2. On a lightly floured surface, roll dough to a ¼-in.-thick circle; transfer to an ungreased 11-in. fluted tart pan with removable bottom. Trim pastry even with rim; refrigerate 15 minutes.

3. Line unpricked pastry with a double thickness of foil. Fill with pie weights, dried beans or uncooked rice. Bake 20-25 minutes or until the bottom is lightly browned. Remove the foil and weights; bake 5-7 minutes longer or until light brown.

4. Meanwhile, in a large bowl, mix the milk, maple flavoring, cinnamon and salt until blended. Stir in the pecans, walnuts and almonds; add to crust. Bake 15-20 minutes or until crust is golden brown and filling is set. Cool completely on a wire rack.

5. Drizzle with chocolate. Refrigerate 1 hour or until filling is firm.

kitchen treats
TO SHARE

Coconut Caramels

When I had an overabundance of coconut milk, I came up with the idea of using it to flavor my homemade caramels. The chewy wrapped candies loaded with almonds are always among the first treats to disappear from my Christmas platter.

—WENDY RUSCH TREGO, WI

PREP: 15 MIN. • **COOK:** 45 MIN. + STANDING
MAKES: 4 POUNDS

- 1 tablespoon butter
- 3 cups flaked coconut, divided
- 1½ cups coarsely chopped salted roasted almonds, divided
- 3 cups sugar
- 1 can (13.66 ounces) coconut milk
- 1½ cups light corn syrup
- ¾ cup butter, cubed
- ⅓ cup heavy whipping cream
- 3 teaspoons vanilla extract
- 1 teaspoon ground ginger
- ½ teaspoon salt

1. Line a 13x9-in. pan with foil; grease the foil with 1 tablespoon butter. Layer with 1 cup coconut and ¾ cup almonds; set aside.

2. In a Dutch oven, combine sugar, milk, corn syrup, cubed butter and cream. Cook and stir over medium heat until a candy thermometer reads 238° (soft-ball stage), about 40 minutes.

3. Using a pastry brush dipped in water, wash down the sides of pan to eliminate sugar crystals. Cook and stir until thermometer reads 244° (firm-ball stage), about 5 minutes longer.

4. Remove from heat; stir in 1 cup coconut, vanilla, ginger, salt and remaining almonds. Immediately pour into prepared pan (do not scrape saucepan). Sprinkle with remaining coconut. Let stand until firm, about 5 hours or overnight.

5. Using the foil, lift the caramel out of the pan; remove the foil. Using a buttered knife, cut the caramel into 1-in. squares. Wrap individually in waxed paper; twist the ends.

Seasoned Salt Mix

A co-worker gave me her terrific recipe for seasoned salt. I add ½ teaspoon of it to ¾ cup of flour, then coat fish before frying.

—FLORENCE BEER HOULTON, WI

START TO FINISH: 5 MIN.
MAKES: ABOUT ½ CUP

- ⅓ cup salt
- 1½ teaspoons garlic powder
- 1½ teaspoons celery seed
- 1½ teaspoons paprika
- ½ teaspoon onion powder
- ½ teaspoon ground mustard

In a small bowl, mix all ingredients. Store in an airtight container in a cool dry place for up to 1 year. Use to season fish, chicken and pork chops.

Mint Chocolate Bark

After sampling peppermint bark candy from an upscale store, I thought, *I can make that!* Using four basic ingredients, I hit on a simple but yummy version that won over family and friends.

—PATTI MAURER WISE, VA

PREP: 15 MIN. + CHILLING
MAKES: 1½ POUNDS

- 1 teaspoon plus 3 tablespoons shortening, divided
- 1 package (10 ounces) Andes creme de menthe baking chips
- 2 cups white baking chips
- ½ cup crushed peppermint candies

1. Line a 13x9-in. pan with foil; grease foil with 1 teaspoon shortening.
2. In a microwave, melt Andes baking chips and 1 tablespoon shortening; stir until smooth. Pour into prepared pan. Refrigerate 10 minutes or until set.
3. In top of a double boiler or a metal bowl over barely simmering water, melt the white chips with remaining shortening; stir until smooth. Spread over chocolate layer; sprinkle with crushed peppermint candies. Cool. Refrigerate 2 hours or until firm.
4. Break into small pieces. Store in an airtight container.

Gooey Peanut Butter Bites

My sweet-and-salty bars start with the convenience of a white cake mix. The ooey-gooey filling is a rich, indulgent combination of cream cheese, peanut butter and white baking chips.

—LIBBY WALP CHICAGO, IL

PREP: 20 MIN. • **BAKE:** 40 MIN. + CHILLING
MAKES: 4 DOZEN

- 1 white cake mix (regular size)
- ½ cup butter, melted
- 1 egg
- ¼ cup white baking chips

FILLING

- 1 package (8 ounces) cream cheese, softened
- 1 cup creamy peanut butter
- ½ cup butter, melted
- 2 eggs
- 1 teaspoon vanilla extract
- 3¾ cups confectioners' sugar
- ½ cup white baking chips

1. Preheat oven to 350°. In a large bowl, combine cake mix, butter and egg; beat on low speed until combined. Stir in white baking chips. Press into a greased 13x9-in. baking pan.
2. In another bowl, beat cream cheese and peanut butter until smooth. Add the butter, eggs and vanilla; beat on low until combined. Add the confectioners' sugar; mix well. Pour over the crust; sprinkle with white baking chips.
3. Bake 40-45 minutes or until edges are golden brown. Cool completely on a wire rack. Refrigerate at least 2 hours. Cut into bars.

Baked Oatmeal Gift Jars

I love baked oatmeal on cold mornings, so I tried to think of a way I could share it as a holiday gift. This fresh-from-the-oven breakfast is guaranteed to warm up your gang on chilly winter days.

—JENNIFER BISTLINE CONFLUENCE, PA

PREP: 20 MIN. • **BAKE:** 25 MIN.
MAKES: 8 SERVINGS

- 3 cups old-fashioned oats
- 3 teaspoons baking powder
- 1 teaspoon ground cinnamon
- ½ teaspoon salt
- ⅓ cup packed brown sugar
- ⅓ cup sugar
- ½ cup chopped walnuts, optional
- ½ cup raisins, optional

ADDITIONAL INGREDIENTS

- 2 eggs
- 1 cup 2% milk
- ½ cup butter, melted
- 1 teaspoon vanilla extract

1. In a small bowl, mix oats, baking powder, cinnamon and salt. In a wide-mouth 1-qt. glass jar, layer the oat mixture, brown sugar, sugar and, if desired, walnuts and raisins in the order listed. Cover and store in a cool dry place up to 3 months. Makes: 1 batch (about 4 cups mix).
2. To prepare baked oatmeal: Preheat oven to 350°. In a large bowl, whisk eggs, milk, butter and vanilla until blended. Gradually add oatmeal mix, mixing well. Spread into a greased 13x9-in. baking dish.
3. Bake 25-30 minutes or until edges are golden brown. Serve warm.

"*Candied citrus strips were the inspiration for these petite, cream cheese-rich treats. The cherry pastries take a little extra time and effort to prepare, but they're well worth it!*"

—LILY JULOW LAWRENCEVILLE, GA

Cherry Citrus Pastries

PREP: 1 HOUR + CHILLING
BAKE: 15 MIN. + COOLING • **MAKES:** 3 DOZEN

- 2 **large grapefruit**
- ⅔ **cup water**
- ⅓ **cup sugar**

PASTRIES

- 2 **cups all-purpose flour**
- 2 **tablespoons sugar**
- 1 **cup cold butter, cubed**
- 1 **package (8 ounces) cream cheese, softened and cubed**
- ⅓ **cup cherry preserves**

1. Using a vegetable peeler, peel the grapefruit, making wide strips. With a sharp knife, carefully remove white pith from peel. Cut peel into ¼-in. strips. (Save fruit for another use.)
2. Place the strips in a small saucepan; add water to cover. Bring to a boil. Cover and cook 10 minutes; drain.
3. In same saucepan, combine ⅔ cup water, sugar and strips; bring to a boil. Reduce the heat; simmer, uncovered, 12-15 minutes or until the peels are transparent, stirring occasionally.
4. Using a slotted spoon, transfer strips to a wire rack placed over a baking pan. Let stand overnight. Meanwhile, in a large bowl, whisk flour and sugar. Cut in butter and cream cheese until mixture is crumbly. Turn onto a lightly floured surface; knead gently 8-10 times.
5. Roll dough into a 12x10-in. oval or rectangle. Starting with a shorter side, fold the dough into thirds, forming a 4x10-in. rectangle. Place the folded dough with the longer side facing you; repeat rolling and folding twice, always ending with a 4x10-in. rectangle. (If at any point the butter softens, chill after folding.) Wrap folded dough in plastic wrap; refrigerate overnight.
6. Preheat oven to 400°. On a lightly floured surface, roll the dough into a 12-in. square. Cut into 2-in. squares. Place 1 in. apart on ungreased baking sheets. Press a deep indentation in the center of each with the end of a wooden spoon handle. Fill each with a heaping ¼ teaspoon preserves.
7. Bake 12-14 minutes or until golden brown. Top with candied peel; remove from pans to wire racks to cool.

Rolling and Folding Pastry Dough

The cream cheese dough used for Cherry Citrus Pastries (recipe at left) requires a bit of kneading. When you finish that step, refer to these photos to roll and fold the dough as the recipe directs.

After wrapping the dough in plastic wrap and refrigerating it overnight (Step 5 below), the dough will be ready to cut into squares, fill with preserves and bake.

1. After kneading the pastry dough and turning it onto a lightly floured surface, roll the pastry dough into a 12x10-in. oval or rectangle.

2. Fold one of the two short sides of the dough toward the center of the oval or rectangle.

3. Bring the remaining short side of the dough toward the center, folding the dough into thirds and creating a 4x10-in. rectangle.

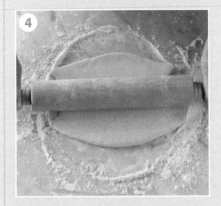

4. Position the folded dough with a long side facing you. Repeat the rolling and folding twice, always ending with a 4x10-in. rectangle.

5. After rolling and folding, wrap the rectangle in plastic wrap and refrigerate it overnight.

Homemade Mango Marshmallows

Homemade marshmallows are much better than bagged ones. I had yummy results when I flavored my recipe with mango nectar. Look for that ingredient in your store's hispanic food section.

—**DEIRDRE COX** KANSAS CITY, MO

PREP: 25 MIN. • **COOK:** 20 MIN. + COOLING
MAKES: 1½ POUNDS

- 2 **envelopes unflavored gelatin**
- 1¼ **cups chilled mango nectar, divided**
- 1½ **cups sugar**
- ¾ **cup light corn syrup**
- 1 **teaspoon almond extract**
- 2 **cups flaked coconut, toasted**

1. Line an 8-in.-square pan with foil; grease the foil with cooking spray. In a heatproof bowl of a stand mixer, sprinkle gelatin over ½ cup nectar.
2. In a large heavy saucepan, combine the sugar, corn syrup and remaining nectar. Bring to a boil, stirring occasionally. Cook, without stirring, over medium heat until a candy thermometer reads 240° (soft-ball stage).
3. Remove from heat; slowly drizzle into gelatin, beating on high speed. Continue beating until very stiff and doubled in volume, about 10 minutes. Immediately beat in extract. Spread into prepared pan. Cover and let cool at room temperature 6 hours or overnight.
4. Place coconut in a food processor; process until finely chopped. Using foil, lift candy out of pan. Using a lightly buttered kitchen scissors, cut into 1-in. pieces. Roll in coconut. Store in an airtight container in a cool dry place.
NOTE *To toast coconut, spread it in a 15x10x1-in. baking pan. Bake at 350° for 5-10 minutes or until golden brown, stirring frequently.*

Cherry Bounce

This delightful libation makes a special gift you can stir together ahead of time. On the jar, add a note with this dessert suggestion: Serve the drained cherries over ice cream.

—**MATT WARREN** MEQUON, WI

PREP: 5 MIN. • **COOK:** 25 MIN. + STANDING
MAKES: 5¼ CUPS

- 4½ **pounds fresh unpitted sweet cherries**
- 2¼ **cups sugar**
- ½ **teaspoon ground allspice**
- 1½ **cups spiced rum**
- 1½ **cups brandy**

1. Place cherries in a large saucepan. Bring to a boil. Reduce heat; simmer, uncovered, for 15-20 minutes or until soft. Strain the juice through a cheesecloth-lined colander; divide cherries among six 1-pint jars.
2. Return the juice to the saucepan; add the sugar and allspice. Bring to a boil. Reduce heat; simmer, uncovered, for 5 minutes. Transfer to a large bowl; cool completely.
3. Stir in the rum and brandy; pour the syrup into the jars over cherries. Cover and let stand for at least 1 month, stirring every week. Store in a cool dry place up to 3 months.

Red Velvet Candy Cane Fudge

My favorite cake, red velvet, inspired me to create this fudge. If you like, spoon the candy mixture into paper-lined mini muffin cups instead of spreading it in a pan.

—CRYSTAL SCHLUETER NORTHGLENN, CO

PREP: 25 MIN. + CHILLING
MAKES: 3¾ POUNDS

- **1 teaspoon butter**
- **2 packages (12 ounces each) white baking chips, divided**
- **⅔ cup semisweet chocolate chips**
- **3 teaspoons shortening, divided**
- **1 can (14 ounces) sweetened condensed milk**
- **1½ teaspoons red paste food coloring**
- **4 cups confectioners' sugar, divided**
- **6 ounces cream cheese, softened**
- **1 teaspoon vanilla extract**
- **¼ teaspoon peppermint extract**
- **3 tablespoons crushed peppermint candies**

1. Line a 13x9-in. pan with foil; grease foil with butter.
2. In a large microwave-safe bowl, combine 3¼ cups white baking chips, the semisweet chocolate chips and 2 teaspoons shortening. Microwave, uncovered, on high 1 minute; stir. Microwave at additional 15-second intervals, stirring until smooth. Stir in the sweetened condensed milk and red food coloring; gradually add 1 cup confectioners' sugar. Spread into the prepared pan.
3. In another large microwave-safe bowl, melt remaining white baking chips and shortening; stir until smooth. Beat in cream cheese and extracts. Gradually beat in the remaining confectioners' sugar until smooth. Spread over red layer; sprinkle with crushed candies. Refrigerate 2 hours or until firm.
4. Using the foil, lift the fudge out of the pan. Remove foil; cut fudge into 1-in. squares. Store between layers of waxed paper in an airtight container.

Strawberry Parfait Holiday Bark

One of my annual traditions is to put together holiday treat baskets for family and friends. When I spotted some dried berries at the supermarket, I thought of using them to make a fruit-filled bark.

—SUSAN BICKTA KUTZTOWN, PA

PREP: 10 MIN. + CHILLING
MAKES: ABOUT ¾ POUND

- **10 ounces white candy coating**
- **⅔ cup chopped walnuts, toasted**
- **⅔ cup freeze-dried strawberries, chopped**
- **½ cup miniature marshmallows**
- **½ cup coarsely chopped pretzels**

1. Line a 15x10x1-in. pan with parchment paper.
2. In a microwave, melt the candy coating; stir until smooth. Stir in the walnuts, strawberries, marshmallows and pretzels; spread into prepared pan. Cool. Refrigerate 1 hour or until set.
3. Break into pieces. Store in an airtight container.

NOTE *To toast nuts, spread them in a 15x10x1-in. baking pan. Bake at 350° for 5-10 minutes or until lightly browned, stirring occasionally. Or, spread in a dry nonstick skillet and heat over low heat until lightly browned, stirring occasionally.*

Crabby Snack Mix

I love boiled Maryland crabs and crab fries dipped in cheese. With those favorites in mind, I created a crunchy snack mix jazzed up with seafood seasoning. One handful never seems to be enough!

—**KARYN GORDON** CINNAMINSON, NJ

START TO FINISH: 10 MIN. • **MAKES:** 6 CUPS

- 2 **cups Corn Chex**
- 2 **cups Wheat Chex**
- 1 **cup cheddar-flavored snack crackers**
- 1 **cup sourdough pretzel nuggets**
- ¼ **cup unsalted butter, melted**
- 2 **tablespoons seafood seasoning**
- 1 **tablespoon celery seed**
- 1 **tablespoon lemon-pepper seasoning**
- ½ **teaspoon dill weed**

1. In a large microwave-safe bowl, combine the cereals, crackers and pretzels. In a small bowl, combine the butter, seafood seasoning, celery seed, lemon-pepper and dill weed. Pour over cereal mixture; toss to coat.

2. Microwave on high 3 minutes, stirring three times. Spread onto a baking sheet to cool. Store in an airtight container.

NOTE *This recipe was tested in a 1,100-watt microwave.*

Orange-Cinnamon Pecans

With a burst of citrus and a dash of spice, these glazed pecans taste like Christmas in a bowl. Holiday gatherings at our house just aren't the same without this treat.

—**CLEO GONSKE** REDDING, CA

PREP: 15 MIN. • **BAKE:** 30 MIN. + COOLING
MAKES: 3 CUPS

- 1 **cup sugar**
- ½ **cup orange juice**
- 2 **teaspoons ground cinnamon**
- ¼ **teaspoon ground nutmeg**
- 3 **cups pecan halves**
- 1 **teaspoon butter**
- 1 **teaspoon vanilla extract**

1. Preheat oven to 250°. Line a 15x10x1-in. baking pan with foil.

2. In a large heavy saucepan, combine the sugar, orange juice, cinnamon and nutmeg. Bring to a boil, stirring occasionally. Cook over medium heat 6-8 minutes or until a candy thermometer reads 236° (soft-ball stage), stirring occasionally.

3. Remove from the heat; stir in the pecans, butter and vanilla. Spread into prepared baking pan. Bake 30 minutes, stirring occasionally. Cool completely. Break apart; store in an airtight container up to 1 week.

Triple Chocolate Cookie Mix

Everyone likes a good old-fashioned cookie mix. Loaded with chips, this one goes over especially well with chocoholics!

—**PATRICIA SWART** GALLOWAY, NJ

PREP: 30 MIN. • **BAKE:** 15 MIN./BATCH
MAKES: 5 DOZEN

- 2¼ **cups all-purpose flour, divided**
- 1 **teaspoon baking powder**
- ½ **teaspoon salt**
- ½ **teaspoon baking soda**
- ½ **cup baking cocoa**
- 1 **cup packed brown sugar**
- ½ **cup sugar**
- ¾ **cup semisweet chocolate chips**
- ¾ **cup white baking chips**

ADDITIONAL INGREDIENTS
- ¾ **cup butter, melted and cooled**
- 3 **eggs**
- 3 **teaspoons vanilla extract**

1. In a small bowl, whisk 1¼ cups flour, baking powder, salt and baking soda. In another bowl, whisk the cocoa and remaining flour. In an airtight container, layer half of flour mixture and half of cocoa mixture; repeat. Layer the sugars and chips in the order listed. Cover and store in a cool dry place up to 3 months. Makes: 1 batch (about 5 cups).

2. To prepare cookies: Preheat oven to 350°. In a large bowl, beat butter, eggs and vanilla until well blended. Add the cookie mix; mix well.

3. Drop dough by tablespoonfuls 2 in. apart on ungreased baking sheets. Bake 12-14 minutes or until firm. Remove from pans to wire racks to cool. Store in an airtight container.

Basil Liqueur

After attending a class that I was teaching about herbs, a friend of mine gave me this liqueur recipe. Enjoy it as an after-dinner drink or as the base for a cocktail.

—**SUE GRONHOLZ** BEAVER DAM, WI

PREP: 10 MIN. + STANDING
MAKES: 2¾ CUPS

1½ cups vodka
1 cup loosely packed basil leaves, torn
1½ cups sugar
¾ cup water

1. Place the vodka and basil in a large glass or plastic container. Cover and let stand at room temperature for at least 6 weeks, stirring once a week.

2. In a small saucepan, bring sugar and water to a boil. Reduce heat; simmer, uncovered, for 5 minutes. Cool completely.

3. Strain vodka mixture, discarding basil. Return mixture to container; stir in sugar mixture. Pour into a glass bottle; seal tightly. Store in refrigerator up to 3 months. Serve chilled.

Spiced Almond Brittle

Sending homemade goodies to loved ones is always on my Christmas to-do list. When I couldn't decide between spiced nuts and brittle, I combined the two into one treat.
—**LESLIE DIXON** BOISE, ID

PREP: 15 MIN. • **COOK:** 15 MIN. + COOLING
MAKES: 1¼ POUNDS

- 1 **cup sugar**
- ½ **cup light corn syrup**
- ¼ **cup water**
- ¼ **teaspoon salt**
- 1½ **cups unblanched almonds**
- 2 **tablespoons butter**
- ½ **teaspoon pumpkin pie spice**
- ¼ **teaspoon cayenne pepper**
- ¼ **teaspoon dried rosemary, crushed**
- ⅛ **teaspoon ground nutmeg**
- 1 **teaspoon baking soda**

1. Line a 15x10x1-in. pan with parchment paper. (Do not spray or grease.)
2. In a large heavy saucepan, combine sugar, corn syrup, water and salt. Bring to a boil, stirring constantly to dissolve the sugar. Using a pastry brush dipped in water, wash down the sides of the pan to eliminate sugar crystals. Cook, without stirring, over medium heat until a candy thermometer reads 260° (hard-ball stage).
3. Stir in the almonds, butter and seasonings; cook until thermometer reads 300° (hard-crack stage), stirring frequently, about 8 minutes longer.
4. Remove from heat; stir in baking soda. (Mixture will foam.) Immediately pour onto prepared pan, spreading as thin as possible. Cool completely.
5. Break the brittle into pieces. Store between layers of waxed paper in an airtight container.

Holiday Helper

It's a good idea to test your candy thermometer before each use by bringing water to a boil; the thermometer should read 212°. Adjust your recipe temperature up or down based on your test.

until a toothpick inserted in the center comes out clean. Cool completely in the pan on a wire rack. Cut into bars. Store in an airtight container.

German Beer Cheese Spread

Bold and smooth, this flavor-packed cheese is wonderful with pretzels, crackers and pumpernickel bread. You could also serve the spread as a condiment to slather on bratwurst buns.
—**ANGELA SPENGLER** CLOVIS, NM

START TO FINISH: 15 MIN. • **MAKES:** 2½ CUPS

- 1 **pound sharp cheddar cheese, cut into ½-inch cubes**
- 1 **tablespoon Worcestershire sauce**
- 1½ **teaspoons prepared mustard**
- 1 **small garlic clove, minced**
- ¼ **teaspoon salt**
- ⅛ **teaspoon pepper**
- ⅔ **cup German beer or nonalcoholic beer**
    Assorted crackers

1. Place the cheese in a food processor; pulse until finely chopped, about 1 minute. Add the Worcestershire sauce, mustard, garlic, salt and pepper. Gradually add the beer, while continuing to process, until the mixture is smooth and spreadable, about 1½ minutes.
2. Transfer to a serving bowl or gift jars. Refrigerate, covered, up to 1 week. Serve with crackers.

Festive Almond Blondies

Short on time to spend in the kitchen? Whip up a simple dough for almond blondies and pop them in the oven. To add Christmas color, I sprinkle on red and green sugar before baking.
—**BETSY KING** DULUTH, MN

PREP: 20 MIN. • **BAKE:** 15 MIN. + COOLING • **MAKES:** 2 DOZEN

- ⅔ **cup butter, softened**
- 1 **cup packed brown sugar**
- 2 **eggs**
- 1 **teaspoon almond extract**
- 1⅔ **cups all-purpose flour**
- 1½ **teaspoons baking powder**
- ½ **teaspoon salt**
- ½ **cup unblanched almonds, finely chopped**
- ½ **teaspoon ground cinnamon**
- 2 **teaspoons each red and green colored sugars**

1. Preheat oven to 375°. In a large bowl, cream butter and brown sugar until light and fluffy. Beat in eggs and extract. In a small bowl, mix flour, baking powder and salt; gradually add to creamed mixture, mixing well.
2. Spread into a greased 13x9-in. baking pan. Sprinkle with the almonds, cinnamon and sugars. Bake 15-20 minutes or

Chocolate-Covered Peanut Butter & Pretzel Truffles

Rich chocolate, creamy peanut butter and salty pretzels create an irresistible truffle. It's a little bite of decadence and a special indulgence for the holiday season.

—**ASHLEY WISNIEWSKI** CHAMPAIGN, IL

PREP: 40 MIN. + CHILLING • **MAKES:** 3 DOZEN

1¾ cups creamy peanut butter, divided
⅓ cup confectioners' sugar
¼ cup packed brown sugar
2 tablespoons butter, softened
⅛ teaspoon salt
3¼ cups crushed pretzels, divided
3 cups (18 ounces) semisweet chocolate chips
3 tablespoons shortening

1. In a large bowl, beat 1½ cups peanut butter, confectioners' sugar, brown sugar, butter and salt until blended. Stir in 3 cups pretzels.

2. Shape pretzel mixture into 1-in. balls; transfer to waxed paper-lined baking sheets. Refrigerate at least 30 minutes or until firm.

3. In a microwave, melt the chocolate chips and shortening; stir until smooth. Dip truffles in chocolate; allow excess to drip off. Return to baking sheets.

4. Microwave remaining peanut butter on high for 30-45 seconds or until melted. Drizzle over truffles; sprinkle with remaining pretzels. Refrigerate until set. Store between layers of waxed paper in an airtight container in the refrigerator.

kitchen treats to share ❄

Basil Buttermilk Dressing

Why buy dressing from the store when it's so easy to whip up your own? Keep the mix on hand and simply add water, lemon juice and mayo to make it salad-ready.

—JENECE HOWARD ELKO, NV

START TO FINISH: 10 MIN.
MAKES: ABOUT 1 CUP PER BATCH

- 1 cup nonfat dry milk powder
- ¼ cup sugar
- 4 teaspoons dried minced onion
- 4 teaspoons dried basil
- 2 teaspoons ground mustard
- 1 teaspoon salt
- 1 teaspoon garlic powder

ADDITIONAL INGREDIENTS (FOR EACH BATCH)
- ½ cup cold water
- 1 teaspoon lemon juice
- ¾ cup mayonnaise

1. In a small bowl, combine the first seven ingredients. Store in an airtight container in a cool dry place for up to 1 year. Makes: 6 batches (1½ cups mix).
2. To prepare the dressing: In a small bowl, combine ¼ cup mix with the cold water and lemon juice. Whisk in the mayonnaise. Stir before serving. Refrigerate leftovers.

NOTE *Buttermilk blend powder may be substituted for the nonfat dry milk powder. Omit the lemon juice when preparing the salad dressing.*

Cheddar-Pecan Crisps

Lots of Christmas treats are sweet. For a change of pace, I fill holiday goodie bags with my cheese crackers. The recipe has a large yield, but you can freeze some of the dough. (See the tip box at top right.)

—HEATHER NECESSARY SHAMOKIN DAM, PA

PREP: 25 MIN. + CHILLING
BAKE: 15 MIN./BATCH • **MAKES:** 24 DOZEN

- 2 cups unsalted butter, softened
- 4 cups (16 ounces) shredded sharp cheddar cheese
- 4½ cups all-purpose flour
- 1 teaspoon salt
- ½ teaspoon garlic powder
- ½ teaspoon cayenne pepper
- 1 cup finely chopped pecans, toasted

1. In a large bowl, cream the butter and cheddar cheese until light and fluffy. In another bowl, whisk the flour, salt, garlic powder and cayenne pepper; gradually beat into creamed mixture. Stir in pecans.
2. Shape into eight 10-in.-long logs. Wrap in plastic wrap. Refrigerate 2 hours or until firm.
3. Preheat oven to 350°. Unwrap and cut dough crosswise into ¼-in. slices. Place 1 in. apart on ungreased baking sheets. Bake 12-14 minutes or until the edges are crisp and lightly browned. Cool on the pans 1 minute. Remove to wire racks to cool. Refrigerate in airtight containers.

NOTE *To toast nuts, spread them in a 15x10x1-in. baking pan. Bake at 350° for 5-10 minutes or until lightly browned, stirring occasionally. Or, spread in a dry nonstick skillet and heat over low heat until lightly browned, stirring occasionally.*

Holiday Helper

To bake a batch of the Cheddar-Pecan Crisps (recipe below left) later, freeze the wrapped logs in resealable plastic freezer bags. To use the logs, unwrap them and slice. If necessary, let them stand 15 minutes at room temperature before cutting. Bake as directed for an extra 1-2 minutes.

deck the
HALLS

Recycled Snowman Ornaments

Here's a frosty finish for empty gum or mint containers. If you like, buy new containers and leave the gum inside to use the snowmen as children's party favors. You could also replace the wiggle eyes and background circles with black buttons.

CRAFT LEVEL: QUICK & EASY

FINISHED SIZE: Excluding hanger, snowman ornament is 3¾ in. long x 3 in. wide.

MATERIALS (FOR ONE):
3-in.-wide circular gum or breath mint container
Card stock—scraps of white, black, orange and desired color for hat
Two ½-in. wiggle eyes
2¾-in. circle punch
⅝-in. circle punch
Standard hole punch
10-in. length of ⅛-in. white grosgrain ribbon
Permanent glue dots

DIRECTIONS (FOR ONE):
1. For the snowman's head, use the 2¾-in. punch to make a circle from white card stock.
2. For the hat, use scissors to cut a 1½-in.-high x 2¼-in.-wide triangle from desired card stock. Using the ⅝-in. punch, make a circle from white card stock and glue to the top of the triangle for the pompom. Align the bottom edge of hat on top of the head circle and glue in place.
3. For the eyes, use the ⅝-in. punch to make two circles from black card

stock. Glue a wiggle eye centered on each circle. Glue eyes centered on head circle below edge of hat.
4. For the carrot nose, use scissors to cut a 1¼-in.-high. x ¾-in.-wide triangle from orange card stock. Glue nose below eyes on head circle.
5. For the mouth, use the standard hole punch to make seven dots from black card stock. Glue in a half-circle shape below nose on head circle.
6. For the hanger, overlap the ends of the ribbon piece about ½ in. and glue in place, forming a loop. If needed, remove the wrapper on the circular container. Glue loop close to the edge on the back of the container.
7. Glue assembled snowman face centered on the back of the container, covering the glued end of hanger and aligning the hanger with the top of hat.

Owl Treat Holders

What a hoot! Tuck wrapped candy, a gift card or any small present you prefer inside this bright little bird. A folded rectangle of card stock forms the body—which is also the pouch—and ribbon handles allow it to hang on the tree.

CRAFT LEVEL: BEGINNER

FINISHED SIZE: Excluding handles, owl treat holder is 4 in. long x 4½ in. wide.

MATERIALS (FOR ONE):
6½- x 4½-in. rectangle of patterned card stock for body
Scraps of solid-color card stock—white, brown and desired colors for wings and eyes
Two 12 mm self-adhesive wiggle eyes
3-in., 1½-in. and 1-in. circle punches
1-in. square punch
Standard hole punch
12-in. length of ¼-in. coordinating grosgrain ribbon
Clear tape
Dry scrapbook adhesive
Glue stick
Desired wrapped candy or gift card for pouch

DIRECTIONS (FOR ONE):
1. Lay the card stock rectangle horizontally in front of you, patterned side down. Fold the left side and then right side toward the center, creating three sections with the center section measuring about 3 in. wide and shorter side sections overlapping about ½ in. when folded. Unfold and flatten, leaving the two vertical crease lines.
2. Fold up the bottom long edge about ½ in. Unfold and flatten, leaving the horizontal crease line. Below the horizontal crease, cut a ½-in. slit along each of the two vertical crease lines, creating three flaps at the bottom of the rectangle.
3. Fold up the bottom flap of each side section, then fold each side section of the rectangle back to the center so they overlap as before. Tape in place.
4. On remaining bottom flap, fold up both corners to create a small triangle, then fold up the entire flap to enclose the bottom of owl's body and form a pouch. Tape bottom flap in place.
5. For the hanger, use the hole punch to make a hole through the top corner on each side of the owl's body. Thread each end of the 12-in. ribbon through opposite holes and knot the ribbon ends. Pull out the ribbon loop slightly at both the back and front of owl, forming a double-handled hanger.
6. For the eyes, use the 1½-in. circle punch to make two circles from solid white card stock. Use the 1-in. circle punch to make two circles from desired solid-color card stock. Glue one small circle centered on top of each white circle. Glue a wiggle eye centered on each and set aside.
7. For the wings, use the 3-in. circle punch to make a circle from desired solid-color card stock. Cut the circle in half and set aside.
8. For the beak, use the square punch to make a square from solid brown card stock. Glue the brown square centered on front of the owl's body, positioning square at an angle to form a diamond shape for the beak.
9. Glue a half-circle on each side of the beak, positioning the half-circles at an angle to resemble wings.
10. Glue the eyes side by side on top, positioning them where the beak and wings meet. Let dry.
11. Fill pouch with desired wrapped candy or gift card.

Bottle Cap Snowman Ornaments

How refreshing—a project made with bottle caps! Simple patterns turn the little metal circles into dangling snowmen.

CRAFT LEVEL: BEGINNER

FINISHED SIZE: Excluding hanger, ornament is 4 in. long x 2 in. wide.

MATERIALS (FOR ONE):
Patterns on this page
Color photocopier (to photocopy
    patterns)
3 recyled or new bottle caps
⅛-in. circle punch
Three 8 mm silver jump rings
Needle-nose pliers
Rubber mallet
Dry scrapbook adhesive
Three 1-in. clear circle epoxy stickers
8-in. length of ⅜-in. ribbon for scarf
7-in. length of ¼-in. ribbon for hanger

DIRECTIONS (FOR ONE):

1. If using recycled bottle caps, remove the plastic inserts and clean bottle caps well before beginning.

2. Using punch, make two holes opposite each other on the curved edge of one bottle cap. Repeat on second bottle cap. On remaining bottle cap, make one hole.

3. Place bottle caps top side up on a work surface. Using the mallet, gently strike bottle caps in a circular motion until each flattens and the sides curl up.

4. Make a color photocopy of patterns and cut out each. Use adhesive to glue the face pattern to the top of one of the bottle caps with two holes, making sure the holes are positioned at the top and bottom of pattern.

5. Glue the buttons pattern to the second bottle cap with two holes. Glue the blank pattern to the remaining bottle cap. Press patterns firmly in place, smoothing out air bubbles.

6. Attach an epoxy sticker to the top of each bottle cap over the glued pattern.

7. Use pliers to twist jump rings open. Connect the hole on the blank bottle cap and one hole on the buttons bottle cap with a jump ring, using pliers to twist ring closed.

8. In same way, connect remaining hole on the buttons bottle cap and the bottom hole on the face bottle cap with a jump ring. Place remaining jump ring in the top hole on the face bottle cap and twist closed.

9. For scarf, wrap ⅜-in. ribbon around the jump rings between the top and middle bottle caps. Knot ribbon and trim ends at an angle.

10. For hanger, thread ¼-in. ribbon through top jump ring and tie a loop.

SNOWMAN PATTERNS

Acorn Wreath Napkin Ring

Bring a touch of outdoor beauty indoors with these rustic yet chic napkin rings. Use artificial acorns from the craft store or go on a nature hunt in your own backyard. Either way, you'll have charming table accents to enjoy during fall and winter.

CRAFT LEVEL: QUICK & EASY

FINISHED SIZE: Napkin ring is about 2½ in. across.

MATERIALS:

Miniature (2-in.-diameter) grapevine wreath
Artificial green wired stem with small white berries
Two natural or artificial acorns
Hot glue gun and glue sticks

DIRECTIONS:

1. While holding the grapevine wreath in one hand, use the other hand to wrap the wired berry stem around the wreath, leaving a small space between the wraps.
2. Tuck the ends of the wired berry stem into the wreath and secure stem to wreath with glue as needed.
3. Glue the acorns next to each other at the top of the wreath, pressing and holding the acorns to the wreath until securely attached. Let dry.
4. Slip the finished wreath over a folded napkin.

Felted Ball Decorations

These woolly spheres are simple to craft from yarn scraps or roving. Roll out a bunch and use them to create heartwarming decorations, such as a cozy wreath or versatile garland.

CRAFT LEVEL: BEGINNER

FINISHED SIZE: Varies.

MATERIALS (FOR BALLS):
Hollow plastic baseballs, golf balls and/or glass marbles
100% wool yarn and/or roving
Knee-high nylon stockings
Washer (dryer optional)
Liquid dish detergent
(FOR WREATH):
Low-temperature glue gun and glue sticks
Styrofoam wreath base
12-gauge wire
Wire cutters
(FOR GARLAND):
Tapestry needle
Thimble

DIRECTIONS:
BALLS
1. Wrap a ball with yarn and/or roving. Wrap even layers over ball until wrapping is about ½ in. thick all around.
2. Stretch stocking carefully and insert a wrapped ball, tying a knot to secure ball tightly in place.
3. Repeat Steps 1 and 2 for desired number of balls. (Each stocking can hold several, with a knot separating each ball.)
4. Wash all stockings with a few tablespoons of liquid dish detergent in washing machine using hot water. Repeat if felting is not firm to the touch after first wash.
5. Air-dry balls or place them in dryer on low heat to dry. Balls may be slightly embedded in stocking. With scissors, carefully work balls free and trim excess fuzz from surface.

WREATH
1. Make desired number of wool balls in a variety of sizes, including marble-size. Glue balls onto wreath base, stacking them randomly to add depth. Let dry.
2. For hanging loop, cut a 4-in. length of wire. Bend it in half and twist the ends together, forming a ½-in. loop. Insert twisted ends into back edge of base and fold the loop over so it is flush against base. Glue loop in place.

GARLAND
1. Make desired number of wool balls. Cut several 5-in. lengths of yarn. With needle and thimble, thread one piece through the edge of one ball. Thread same piece through the edge of another ball and tie yarn ends together, forming a loop that connects the balls.
2. Continue joining balls in the same way, forming a garland. On each end, use a yarn piece to make a loop for hanging.

Blue Star Ornament

Inspired by children's paper cutouts, Sandy Rollinger, of Apollo, Pennsylvania, shaped a starry accent that has eye-catching sparkle.

CRAFT LEVEL: BEGINNER

FINISHED SIZE: Excluding hanger, star is 3 in. across.

MATERIALS:
Sculpey UltraLight oven-bake clay
Toaster oven or standard oven
Craft knife
Foil-lined baking sheet or tray
Clay roller or rolling pin not used for food
Ruler
Toothpick
Cookie or clay cutters—3-in. star and ½-in. star
Blue metallic acrylic paint (Sandy used Jacquard Lumiere)
Small paintbrush
Glue (Sandy used Beach Adhesives Dazzle-Tac Glue)
Assorted small blue and gold beads
Satin varnish
10-in. length of silver thread

DIRECTIONS:
1. Condition clay and roll it to a ⅛-in. thickness.
2. Use 3-in. cutter to cut a star shape from clay. Use craft knife to remove excess clay from edges.
3. Use ½-in. cutter to cut a star from the center of clay star. Cut out five more small stars around center star.
4. Place large clay star on foil-lined tray. Use toothpick to make a small hole near one edge for hanger. Bake star according to clay manufacturer's instructions. Let cool.
5. Use paintbrush to apply paint to both sides of star. Let dry.
6. Apply glue to star and sprinkle beads on wet glue. Let dry.
7. Apply a coat of satin varnish following manufacturer's instructions. When dry, tie on thread for hanger.

Snowflake Wall Frames

Even if snowflakes are nowhere to be seen outdoors, you'll have a winter wonderland indoors when you display these frosted home accents. Choose whatever photo frames suit your decorating style.

CRAFT LEVEL: QUICK & EASY

FINISHED SIZE: Varies.

MATERIALS (FOR ALL):

Two photo frames with 5- x 7-in. openings

Photo frame with 8- x 10-in. opening

12-in.-square sheets of paper—two each of white, light blue and silver

1-in. and 3-in. snowflake punches

Three 24-in. lengths of 1½-in. light blue satin ribbon

Three small white pompoms and craft glue (optional)

DIRECTIONS (FOR ALL):

1. Lay all frames wrong side up on a flat surface. Remove the outside backing piece and the paper insert from each frame. Leave glass in frames. (If needed, wipe glass clean and replace in frames.)

2. Trace each paper insert onto light blue paper and cut out, creating two 5- x 7-in. background pieces and one 8- x 10-in. background piece. Set aside.

3. Use punches to make snowflakes of different sizes from white and silver paper. Set aside.

4. Lay paper snowflakes on the glass in each frame in desired arrangement. Position some snowflakes so that they extend past the edge of the frame opening, and trim off the excess paper.

5. When satisfied with snowflake arrangement, insert the appropriate-size blue background piece on top of the snowflakes in each frame. Carefully replace each frame's outside backing piece, securing snowflakes in place.

6. Thread a ribbon through the hanger on the back of each frame. Tie the ends of each ribbon in a bow to form loops for hanging. If desired, glue a white pompom to the center of each bow. Let dry.

7. Hang frames on wall using hooks or nails as desired.

Winter Candle Holder Set

With candlelight from silvery holders, the holiday season will shine even brighter. Sandy Rollinger, of Apollo, Pennsylvania, shared her shimmering designs trimmed with clay stars and ribbon.

CRAFT LEVEL: BEGINNER

FINISHED SIZE: Large holder shown is 6 in. high x 4 in. wide. Small holders shown are 2 in. high x 2 in. wide.

MATERIALS (FOR ALL):
Patterns on this page
Tracing paper
Toaster oven or standard oven
6-in.-high clear glass vase
Two 2-in.-high clear glass votive holders
Oven-bake clay (Sandy used Sculpey)—Whipped Cream
Clay texture sheet (Sandy used Sculpey Texture Maker)
Clay roller
Plastic mat
Craft knife
Ruler
Foil-lined baking sheet or tray
White tissue paper
1-in. sponge brush
Sparkle Mod Podge
Powdered pigment (Sandy used Jacquard Pearl-Ex Micro Pearl 650)
Small flat paintbrush
Silver-and-white ribbon—length of 2-in. ribbon to fit around vase and lengths of 1-in. ribbon to fit around all holders
Lengths of ¼-in. silver ribbon to fit around votive holders
1-in. rhinestone snowflake
Two ½-in. rhinestone stars
Craft glue (Sandy used Beacon Adhesives Fabri-Tac and Gem-Tac)

CANDLE HOLDER PATTERNS

LARGE STAR
Trace 1—tracing paper
Cut 1—oven-bake clay

SMALL STAR
Trace 1—tracing paper
Cut 2—oven-bake clay

DIRECTIONS (FOR ALL):

CLAY STARS
1. Trace star patterns onto tracing paper and cut out.
2. Condition the clay and roll it to a ⅛-in. thickness on the plastic mat.
3. Place texture sheet on top of clay. Use clay roller to press sheet into clay, adding texture to clay. Remove sheet.
4. Place cutout star patterns on textured clay. Use craft knife to cut one large star and two small stars from clay following pattern outlines.
5. Place clay stars on foil-lined baking sheet. Bake following clay manufacturer's instructions. Let cool.
6. Use paintbrush to apply powdered pigment to the front of stars. Let dry.

LARGE CANDLE HOLDER
1. Tear white tissue paper into small pieces. Use sponge brush to apply Sparkle Mod Podge to a small area on exterior of vase and adhere tissue pieces to vase. In the same way, add tissue to the entire exterior of vase. Let dry.
2. Cut a length of 2-in.-wide ribbon and 1-in.-wide ribbon to fit around vase. Apply Fabri-Tac around center of vase and adhere the wider ribbon piece around vase.
3. Apply Fabri-Tac around center of wider ribbon and adhere narrower ribbon around vase, positioning all ribbon ends in the same place on vase. Let dry.
4. Use Gem-Tac to adhere rhinestone snowflake to center of large clay snowflake. Glue clay snowflake to ribbons, covering the ribbon ends. Let dry.

SMALL CANDLE HOLDERS
Follow directions for large candle holder to decorate the votive holders, using the 1-in.-wide ribbon, ¼-in.-wide ribbon, small clay stars and rhinestone stars.

All-purpose thread to match fabrics
Tear-away stabilizer
⅞-in. buttons—two black and six white
Skein of bright blue six-strand embroidery floss
Embroidery needle
5¼-in. length of black jumbo rickrack
18- x 32-in. piece of lightweight quilt batting (Mary used Warm
   & Natural Needled Cotton batting)
Paper-backed fusible web
Quilter's marking pen or pencil
Rotary cutter and mat (optional)
Quilter's ruler
Standard sewing supplies

DIRECTIONS:

GENERAL INSTRUCTIONS

1. Either use quilter's marking pen or pencil to mark the fabrics before cutting them with a scissors or use rotary cutting tools to cut the pieces as directed in the instructions that follow. Cut strips crosswise from selvage to selvage unless directed otherwise.

2. Do all stitching with right sides of fabrics together, edges even, matching thread and an accurate ¼-in. seam. Press seams toward darker fabric unless directions say otherwise.

CUTTING

1. From blue stripe, cut one 20½- x 10½-in. rectangle with the stripes running lengthwise for the sky background of wall quilt.

2. From white solid, cut one 4½- x 10½-in. rectangle for snow under the snowman.

3. From medium blue dot, cut eight 2-in. squares and sixteen 1½- x 2-in. rectangles.

4. From light blue dot, cut eight 2-in. squares and sixteen 1½- x 2-in. rectangles.

5. From dark blue-and-white dot, cut four 3½- x 5½-in. rectangles and eight 3½- x 4½-in. rectangles.

Frosty Wall Quilt

You'll melt hearts when you display this colorful wintertime quilt. In Boyce, Virginia, Mary Ayres dressed a pieced wall hanging for the season with a whimsical appliqued snowman.

CRAFT LEVEL: INTERMEDIATE

FINISHED SIZE: Wall quilt is about 30 in. long x 16 in. wide.

MATERIALS:
Patterns on next page
Tracing paper
44-in.-wide 100% cotton fabrics—1 yd. of blue stripe for sky, binding and backing; ¼ yd. of white solid for snowman, snow and snowflake; ¼ yd. of dark blue-and-white dot for border; ⅛ yd. each of light and medium blue dot for border; and scraps each of gray print for hat, orange solid for nose, pink dot for cheeks, light green dot for scarf, lavender dot for hatband and red dot for heart

FIG. 1 Making pieced squares (make 4)

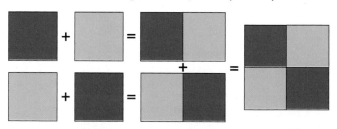

FIG. 2 Making pieced rectangles (make 8)

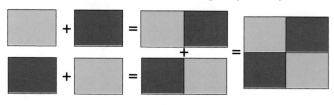

PIECING

1. Sew a long edge of the white solid rectangle to a short edge of the blue stripe background, making a 10½- x 24½-in. piece for the background.

2. Referring to Fig. 1 below left, sew two 2-in. medium and two 2-in. light blue dot squares together, making a four-patch block for a pieced border square. Repeat to make a total of four pieced squares for the corners of border.

3. Referring to Fig. 2 below left, sew two 1½- x 2-in. medium and two 1½- x 2-in. light blue dot rectangles together, making a pieced border rectangle. Repeat to make a total of eight pieced rectangles for the border.

BORDERS

1. Sew a short side of a 3½- x 4½-in. dark blue rectangle to opposite long sides of a pieced rectangle to make the top border piece. Repeat to make bottom border piece.

2. Referring to the photo at far left for position of pieced rectangles, sew the top and bottom borders to the short edges of the background piece. Open and press seams toward borders.

3. Referring to photo for position, lay out the following pieces for one side border: two pieced squares, two 3½- x 4½-in. dark blue rectangles, three pieced rectangles and two 3½- x 5½-in. dark blue rectangles. Sew edges together the same as for top and bottom borders, making one pieced side border. Make second side border in the same way.

4. Referring to photo for position of pieced rectangles, sew side borders to opposite long sides of the background. Open and press seams toward borders.

QUILTING

1. Place backing fabric wrong side up on a flat surface. Center batting on top of backing. Center pieced top on batting and smooth out all wrinkles. Baste layers together.

2. Hand- or machine-quilt as desired. Machine-stitch ⅛ in. from outer edges of pieced top. Remove the basting.

APPLIQUES

1. Use a photocopier to enlarge all patterns 200%. Trace them separately onto tracing paper.

2. Trace enlarged patterns separately onto paper side of fusible web. Cut apart the shapes, leaving a margin of paper around each.

(Continued on next page)

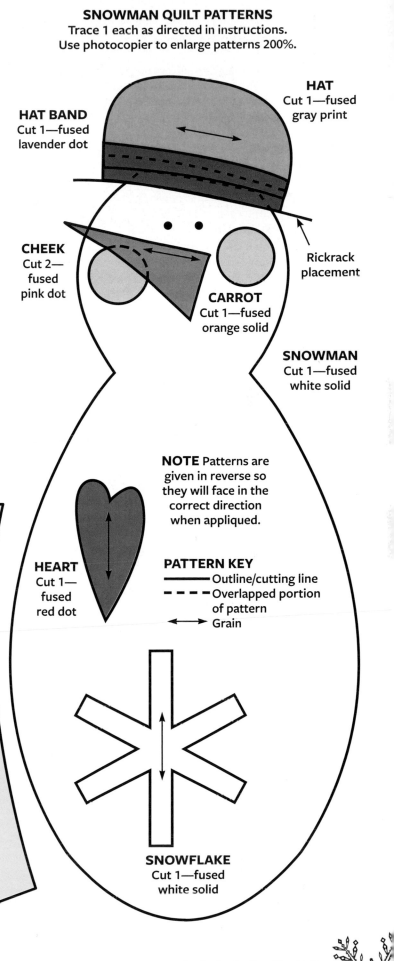

SNOWMAN QUILT PATTERNS
Trace 1 each as directed in instructions.
Use photocopier to enlarge patterns 200%.

HAT
Cut 1—fused
gray print

HAT BAND
Cut 1—fused
lavender dot

Rickrack
placement

CHEEK
Cut 2—
fused
pink dot

CARROT
Cut 1—fused
orange solid

SNOWMAN
Cut 1—fused
white solid

NOTE Patterns are given in reverse so they will face in the correct direction when appliqued.

HEART
Cut 1—
fused
red dot

PATTERN KEY
———— Outline/cutting line
– – – – Overlapped portion of pattern
⟷ Grain

SCARF
Cut 1—
fused
light green
dot

SNOWFLAKE
Cut 1—fused
white solid

3. Following web manufacturer's instructions, fuse the shapes to the wrong side of fabrics as directed on patterns. Let cool.

4. Cut out shapes following pattern outlines. Remove paper backing. Referring to photo for position, place shapes on the quilt top, overlapping pieces as shown on patterns. Fuse shapes to quilt top. Let cool.

EMBROIDERY

1. Separate six-strand embroidery floss and thread embroidery needle with two strands. Referring to photo for position, blanket-stitch around each applique shape. See Fig. 3 at right for stitch illustration.

2. Center and pin rickrack along bottom of hat band. Hand-sew rickrack to quilt top.

FIG. 3
Blanket stitch

BINDING

1. From blue stripe fabric, cut two 2-in.-wide strips the same length as the wall quilt.

2. With raw edges matching, sew a long edge of a binding strip to each side of wall quilt with a ½-in. seam. Fold ½ in. of strip to wrong side along remaining long edge.

3. Fold binding to back, encasing raw edges. Hand-sew fold of binding to back of quilt, covering seam.

4. Cut two 2-in.-wide strips that are 1 in. longer than the length of top and bottom edges of wall quilt.

5. Center and sew binding along top and bottom of wall quilt the same as before, leaving ½ in. of strip extending at each side.

6. Fold ends under, then fold ½ in. to wrong side along long edges. Fold and sew binding to back the same as before.

HANGING SLEEVE

1. Cut a 3- x 15-in. piece of fabric. Hem the short edges of fabric piece.

2. Fold hanging sleeve in half lengthwise with wrong sides together. Sew long edges together with a narrow seam to make a tube. Press tube flat and seam open.

3. Center and pin hanging sleeve along top back of wall quilt. Hand-sew folds of hanging sleeve to backing.

FINISHING

Referring to photo for position, sew two black buttons to snowman for eyes and sew white buttons around snowflake.

Paper Circle Trees

At the root of these pretty pines are plain foam cones. To spruce them up, just pin on punched circles and glue a trim on top.

CRAFT LEVEL: QUICK & EASY

FINISHED SIZE: Varies.

MATERIALS (FOR ONE):
3-5 circle punches of different sizes (see note)
Scraps of coordinating patterned and solid-color card stock
Styrofoam cone
Desired ornament or other trim for top of tree
Straight pins
Low-temperature glue gun and glue sticks

NOTE *Use small punches (such as ½- to 1½-in.) for small cones and use a variety, up to 3 in., for medium to large cones.*

DIRECTIONS (FOR ONE):

1. Use punches of different sizes to cut several circles from each different piece of card stock, keeping same-size circles together on your work surface.

2. Overlapping the circles slightly, pin a row of the smallest punched circles around the top of the cone, mixing patterns and solid colors throughout.

3. Continuing down the cone, pin several more rows of the smallest circles in the same way, overlapping the previous row slightly with each new row.

4. Increasing the size of the circles every few rows, continue pinning rows around the cone in the same way, using the largest circles for the bottom rows.

5. When bottom rows are complete, check for areas where the foam is exposed and fill in any gaps with small circles.

6. Glue an ornament or other trim to top of cone. Let dry.

Joy Votive Candle Cups

Share the spirit of the season with a trio of joyful candle holders. Mary Ayres, of Boyce, Virginia, made ordinary glass votive cups festive for Christmas using basic paper-crafting supplies. Want more ideas? Spell out "Noel" or "Yule"...or attach holiday shapes such as candy canes or wreaths instead of letters.

CRAFT LEVEL: QUICK & EASY

FINISHED SIZE: Each votive cup shown is 2¾ in. high x 2 in. wide.

MATERIALS:
Three clear glass votive holders with straight sides
Sheets or scraps of scrapbook paper in each of three coordinating patterns
Circle punches— 1⅜-in.,1-in. and ¹⁄₁₆-in.
⅜-in. ribbon—10-in. length each of three coordinating colors
Card stock—blue, lime green, purple, red, turquoise and white
Black fine-line permanent marker
Round mini brads—one each of blue, lime green and purple
Glue (Mary used Beacon Adhesives Zip-Dry Glue)
Ruler
Computer with printer (optional)

DIRECTIONS:
1. From each of the three patterned scrapbook papers, cut a rectangular piece to fit around votive holders.
2. Use ruler and black marker to draw a border line ⅛-in. from the long edges on each rectangle.
3. Using circle punch, make a 1⅜-in. circle from each of blue, red and purple card stock.
4. Use computer or black marker to print "J" on lime green card stock, "O" on white card stock and "Y" on turquoise card stock.
5. With the letters centered, punch out the card stock letters using the 1-in. circle punch.
6. Use black marker to draw a border line about ⅛ in. from the outer edge of each letter circle.
7. Glue each letter circle to a larger circle as shown in the photo below, leaving a small space above each letter circle for a brad. Let dry.
8. Use ¹⁄₁₆-in. circle punch to make a hole through the top of each large circle. Through each patterned paper rectangle, make a ¹⁄₁₆-in. hole that is centered along one long edge and about ⅜ in. from the long edge.
9. Insert a brad through the punched hole of a large circle and then through the hole on one of the patterned paper rectangles. Open and bend the ends of brad flat on back of paper. Position brad ends so they are vertical, allowing the paper to wrap smoothly around the votive holder. Add brads to remaining circles and rectangles in the same way.
10. Wrap and glue a completed rectangle right side up around each votive holder. Let dry.
11. Wrap a ribbon piece around the bottom of a votive holder. Tie the ends in a knot under the letter. Use scissors to trim the ends as desired. Add ribbon to the remaining votive holders in the same way.
12. Rotate the letter on each votive holder slightly so the letter is positioned at an angle, and glue in place. Let dry.

Folk Art Ornaments

Recall years past with these Americana trims from Cindy Lund, of Sandy, Utah. They're fun and easy to make with bright felt, embroidery floss, ribbon and basic craft supplies. Hang the ornaments on the tree or attach them to gift boxes.

CRAFT LEVEL: BEGINNER

FINISHED SIZE: Excluding hangers, ornaments are 3 in. across.

MATERIALS (FOR ALL):
Patterns on next page
Tracing paper
Ruler
Felt—one 9- x 12-in. sheet each of dark red, dark green, gold and off-white
Paper-backed fusible web
Embroidery needle
Six-strand embroidery floss—dark green, gold and dark red
Three 4-in. lengths of ⅜-in. gold grosgrain ribbon
Iron and ironing surface
Tacky craft glue

DIRECTIONS (FOR ALL):
DOVE ORNAMENT
1. Cut a 4-in. square each of green, white and red felt.
2. From fusible web, cut two pieces that are slightly smaller than the felt squares. Following manufacturer's instructions, fuse a web piece to the back of the green and white felt squares. Let cool.
3. Trace dove, heart and star patterns separately onto tracing paper.
4. Center heart pattern on white felt square and center dove pattern on green felt square. Cut out heart and dove on pattern outlines without cutting into the surrounding square.
5. Remove the paper backing from the felt squares. Place the white felt square right side up on top of the red felt square with edges matching. Fuse squares together. Let cool.
6. In the same way, fuse the green felt square onto the white felt square, positioning the heart in the center of the dove.
7. Trace circle pattern onto tracing paper and cut out. Center pattern on top of fused felt. Cut out circle, cutting through all layers of felt.

8. Thread embroidery needle with gold six-strand floss. Blanket-stitch around outside edge of circle. See Fig. 1 below right for stitch illustration.

9. Fold gold ribbon piece in half to form a loop. Hand-sew ends of loop to top back of ornament.

10. Using star pattern, cut out a gold felt star and glue it over the ends of the loop on back of ornament. Let dry.

TREE ORNAMENT

1. Cut a 4-in. square each of gold, green and white felt.

2. From fusible web, cut two pieces that are slightly smaller than the felt squares. Following manufacturer's instructions, fuse a web piece to the back of the green and white felt squares. Let cool.

3. Trace star, tree and heart patterns separately onto tracing paper.

4. Center star pattern on green felt square and center tree pattern on white felt square. Cut out star and tree on pattern outlines without cutting into the surrounding square.

5. Remove the paper backing from the felt squares. Place the green felt square right side up on top of the gold felt square with edges matching. Fuse squares together. Let cool.

6. In the same way, fuse the white felt square onto the green felt square,

positioning the star in the center of the tree.

7. Trace circle pattern onto tracing paper and cut out. Center pattern on top of fused felt. Cut out circle, cutting through all layers of felt.

8. Thread embroidery needle with red six-strand floss. Blanket-stitch around outside edge of circle. See Fig. 1 below right for stitch illustration.

9. Fold gold ribbon piece in half to form a loop. Hand-sew ends of loop to top back of ornament.

10. Using heart pattern, cut out a red felt heart and glue it over the ends of loop on back of ornament. Let dry.

STOCKING ORNAMENT

1. Cut a 4-in. square each of gold, white and red felt.

2. From fusible web, cut two pieces that are slightly smaller than the felt squares. Following manufacturer's instructions, fuse a web piece to the back of the white and red felt squares. Let cool.

3. Trace star, stocking and heart patterns separately onto tracing paper.

4. Center stocking pattern on red felt square. Cut out stocking on pattern outlines without cutting into the surrounding square.

5. Lay red square on white felt square with edges matching. Using stocking

cutout as a guide, place star pattern on white square. Cut out star the same as for stocking.

6. Remove the paper backing from the felt squares. Place the white felt square right side up on top of the gold felt square with edges matching. Fuse squares together. Let cool.

7. In same way, fuse the red felt square onto the white felt square, positioning the star near the top of stocking.

8. Trace circle pattern onto tracing paper and cut out. Center pattern on top of fused felt. Cut out circle, cutting through all layers of felt.

9. Thread embroidery needle with green six-strand floss. Blanket-stitch around outside edge of circle. See Fig. 1 below for stitch illustration.

10. Fold gold ribbon piece in half to form a loop. Hand-sew ends of loop to top back of ornament.

11. Using heart pattern, cut out a red felt heart and glue it over the ends of loop on back of ornament. Let dry.

FIG. 1
Blanket stitch

ORNAMENT PATTERNS
Trace 1 each—tracing paper
Cut 1 each as directed in instructions

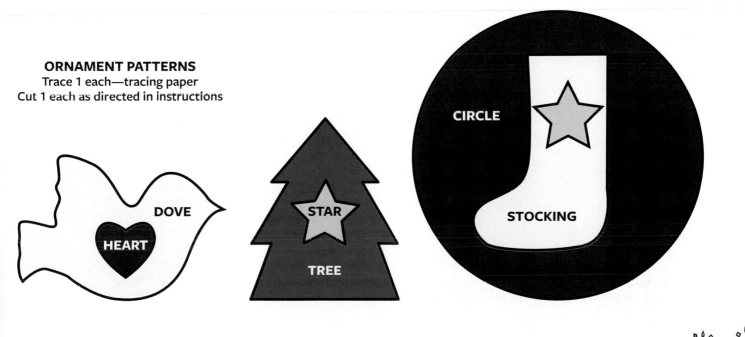

DOVE
HEART
STAR
TREE
CIRCLE
STOCKING

Wine Cork Tree

Raise your glass to a simply sophisticated project featuring wine bottle corks. Just glue them together in the shape of a tree, then add a ribbon hanger for a distinctive decoration you can display wherever your home needs a holiday touch.

CRAFT LEVEL: BEGINNER

FINISHED SIZE: Excluding loop, cork tree is 7 in. high x 5⅜ in. wide.

MATERIALS:
12 wine corks
Low-temperature glue gun and glue sticks
Craft knife
18-in. length and 8-in. length of 1-in. floral ribbon

DIRECTIONS:
1. Using craft knife, cut two wine corks in half crosswise. (For easier cutting, start on one side and rotate cork in a circular motion underneath the knife blade instead of cutting straight through cork.) Discard one piece and set remaining pieces aside.
2. For first (bottom) row of tree, glue three uncut wine corks end-to-end and set aside to dry. In the same way, glue together 2½ corks for the second row, two corks for the third row and 1½ corks for the fourth row.
3. On top of the row of three corks, center and glue the row of 2½ corks. In the same way, glue the third row to the second row and then the fourth row to the third row, making sure the assembled tree piece will lie flat. In same way, glue one cork to the fourth row and ½ cork to the top of the tree for the final row.
4. Using craft knife, cut about ⅓ from the end of the remaining unglued wine cork. Glue the larger cut piece vertically to the center bottom edge of the tree for the trunk. Let dry.
5. Tie longer ribbon piece into a bow and glue to the top of tree. Trim ends of bow as desired.
6. For the hanger, form the remaining ribbon into a loop and glue the ends behind the bow at the top of tree. Let dry. Hang as desired.

Christmas Kissing Ball

Who needs mistletoe? This herb- and holly-adorned ball is sure to cultivate kisses!

CRAFT LEVEL: QUICK & EASY

FINISHED SIZE: Varies.

MATERIALS:
4-in. moss-covered or green Styrofoam ball
Three 16-in. lengths of 20-gauge craft wire
Wire cutters
Fresh or artificial holly, boxwood and rosemary
Red artificial berries
Greening pins
1 yd. of gold ribbon

NOTE *Greening pins are available in the floral section of craft stores. Fresh holly will last for about a week at room temperature. Refrigerate ball or mist it with water periodically to keep it longer.*

DIRECTIONS:
1. Insert the three pieces of craft wire into the top center of the moss-covered or green Styrofoam ball, extending the pieces out of the bottom of the ball by about 1 in.
2. At the bottom, individually bend each wire end to make a U shape. Push the bent wire ends into the bottom of the ball to secure. At the top, twist the wire ends together to form a small loop for hanging. Cut away any excess wire.
3. Cut or break the holly into pieces measuring about 3 in. long and secure them to the ball with pins. Add the boxwood and rosemary in the same way until entire ball is covered. Add red berries where desired.
4. Thread a piece of ribbon through the wire loop at the top of the ball and knot the ends for a hanging loop. Tie another piece into a bow at the base of the hanger. In the same way, add a bow to the bottom of the kissing ball.

Cross-Stitched Hobby Trees

If you're passionate about sewing or quilting, you'll love these trees from Ronda Bryce, of North Augusta, South Carolina. Frame them or use them to decorate scrapbooks of your holiday designs.

CRAFT LEVEL: BEGINNER

FINISHED SIZE: Quilting tree design area is 78 stitches high x 48 stitches wide and measures 5½ in. high x 3⅜ in. wide. Sewing tree design area is 78 stitches high x 52 stitches wide and measures 5½ in. high x 3⅝ in. wide.

MATERIALS (FOR EACH):
Charts on next page
12-in. square of white 14–count Aida cloth
DMC six-strand embroidery floss in the colors listed on the color keys
Size 24 tapestry needle
Desired 5- x 7-in. photo mat, scrapbook and fabric glue (optional)

DIRECTIONS (FOR EACH):
GENERAL INSTRUCTIONS
1. Each square on the chart represents one set of fabric threads surrounded by four holes. Each stitch is worked over one set of threads with the needle passing through the holes.
2. The color and/or symbol inside each square on the chart, along with the color key, tells which color of six-strand embroidery floss to use to make cross-stitches. Wide lines on the chart show where to make backstitches. Dashed lines show where to make running stitches. See Figs. 1-3 on next page for stitch illustrations.
3. Use 18-in. lengths of floss. Longer strands tend to tangle and fray. Separate floss and thread needle with two strands for cross-stitches. Use one strand for backstitches and running stitches.

CROSS-STITCHING
1. Zigzag or overcast the edges of cloth to prevent fraying. To find the center, fold cloth in half crosswise, then fold it in half lengthwise and mark where the folds intersect.
2. Draw lines across the chart, connecting opposite arrows. Mark where the lines intersect. Begin stitching here for a centered design.
3. To begin stitching, leave a 1-in. tail of floss on back of work and hold tail in place while working the first few stitches over it. To end stitching, run needle under a few stitches on back before clipping floss close to work.
4. When all stitching is complete, and only if necessary, gently wash the stitched piece in lukewarm water. Press right side down on a terry towel to dry.

FINISHING
If desired, center photo mat over the stitched piece. Trim stitched piece as needed to fit on back of mat. Center and glue stitched piece and mat to front of scrapbook. Let dry.

QUILTING CHRISTMAS TREE

COLOR KEY

		DMC
☐	Very Light Moss Green	165
⊞	Very Light Jade	564
▣	Very Dark Olive Green	730
⊟	Very Light Yellow Green	772
☒	Very Dark Hunter Green	895
◉	Medium Dark Rose	899
◎	Light Parrot Green	907
◼	Black Avocado Green	934
◪	Very Light Dusty Rose	3716
▤	Dark Mocha Brown	3781
◆	Light Mocha Brown	3882
▢	Ultra Dark Beige Gray	3790
◉	Ultra Very Dark Turquoise	3808
◕	Dark Raspberry	3831
▯	Dark Bright Green	3850
⊡	Winter White	3865
▨	Metallic Gold	5282

BACKSTITCH

▬	Black	310
▬	Metallic Gold	5282

RUNNING STITCH

▬	Dark Mocha Brown	3781

SEWING CHRISTMAS TREE

COLOR KEY

		DMC
☑	Ecru	
▣	Christmas Green	699
▨	Light Christmas Green	701
◉	Very Light Baby Blue	775
◻	Garnet	816
◎	Medium Dark Rose	899
▣	Dark Mocha Brown	3781
◆	Light Mocha Brown	3882
▢	Ultra Dark Beige Gray	3790
⊞	Dark Straw	3820
⊟	Light Straw	3822
⊡	Winter White	3865

BACKSTITCH

▬	Black	310
▬	Dark Mocha Brown	3781
▬	Dark Straw	3820
▬	Metallic Silver	5283

RUNNING STITCH

▬	Dark Mocha Brown	3781

FIG. 1 Cross-stitch

FIG. 2 Backstitch

FIG. 3 Running stitch

QUILTING CHRISTMAS TREE CHART

SEWING CHRISTMAS TREE CHART

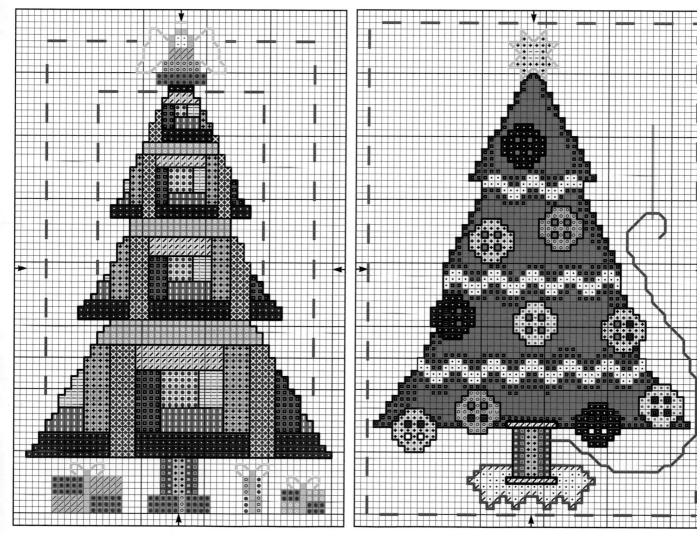

Quilted Floor Pillow

Big and cozy, this oversized pillow is sure to beckon your holiday guests—even if there are plenty of chairs to go around! Jane Craig, of Big Bend, Wisconsin, created the festive design.

CRAFT LEVEL: INTERMEDIATE

FINISHED SIZE: Pillow is about 33 in. square.

MATERIALS:

44-in.-wide 100% cotton fabrics—¾ yd. of red floral print for blocks; 2 yds. of green print for sashing, outer flange and envelope pillow back; and ¼ yd. of small red print for binding
All-purpose thread to match fabrics
32-in. square of fabric for backing
32-in. square of lightweight quilt batting
Rotary cutting tools
Quilter's ruler
27-in.-square pillow form
Standard sewing supplies

DIRECTIONS:

GENERAL INSTRUCTIONS

Use rotary cutter and quilter's ruler to cut all fabrics. Do all piecing with right sides of fabrics together, edges matching and an accurate ¼-in. seam.

CUTTING

1. Wash all fabrics, washing each color separately. If rinse water is discolored, wash again until water runs clear. Dry and press all fabrics.
2. Refer to Fig. 1 at far right as a guide when cutting. From red floral print, cut thirteen 6-in. squares (A). Cut two 9-in. squares, then cut these squares in half twice diagonally to make eight triangles for sides (B). Cut two 4¾-in. squares, then cut these squares in half diagonally to make four triangles for corners (C).
3. From green print, cut thirty-six 1½- x 6-in. rectangles for sashing (D) and twelve 1½-in. squares for corners (E). Cut three 2⅝-in. squares, then cut these squares in half diagonally twice to make 12 triangles for sides (F). Cut eight 3- x 44-in. strips and eight 3-in. squares for outer flange on front and back of pillow. For envelope pillow back, cut two 21½- x 27½-in. rectangles.
4. From small red print, cut four 2½- x 44-in. binding strips.

PIECING

1. Referring to Fig. 1 and Layout Diagram at right, lay out pieces A through F right side up on a flat surface.
2. Sew a small triangle (F) to opposite short ends of one sashing rectangle (D). Press seams in one direction. Sew assembled sashing strip to the long edge of a corner triangle (C). Press seam toward sashing strip.

3. Sew a side triangle (B), sashing rectangle (D), square (A), sashing rectangle (D) and side triangle (B) together as shown. Press seams in opposite direction. Sew assembled row to bottom of previous row.

4. In the same way, sew remaining pieces and rows together to complete the pillow top.

QUILTING

1. Place backing fabric on a flat surface. Center batting on top of backing, then center pieced pillow top right side up on top of batting. Baste layers together as needed to hold.

2. Quilt as desired. Trim excess batting and backing fabric, squaring the top.

PILLOW BACK

1. Press one long edge of each $21\frac{1}{2}$- x $27\frac{1}{2}$-in. pillow back piece $\frac{1}{4}$ in. to wrong side. Fold and press 1 in. to wrong side and sew close to first fold with matching thread for hem.

2. Place pillow back pieces right side up on back of pieced and quilted pillow top with outside edges matching and hemmed edges of pillow back pieces overlapping.

3. Pin to hold. Sew around outside edges with $\frac{1}{4}$-in. seam.

FLANGE

1. Cut the eight 3-in.-wide pieces of green print equal to the length of sides of the pillow top for the flange.

2. Pin a flange piece to both the front and back of one side of the pillow top with raw edges matching. (Pillow top will be sandwiched between the flange pieces.) Sew the edge with a $\frac{1}{4}$-in. seam. Open and press. Repeat on the opposite side of pillow top.

3. Sew a 3-in. square to opposite short ends of each remaining flange piece. Pin and sew a pieced flange strip to front and back of top edge of pillow top as before. Repeat on bottom edge of pillow top. Open and press.

4. Baste flange edges together with wrong sides together and edges matching.

BINDING

1. Sew short ends of binding strips together diagonally to make one long strip. Trim and press seams open.

2. Press one short end diagonally $\frac{1}{4}$ in. to wrong side. Press strip in half lengthwise with wrong sides together.

3. Sew binding strip to right side of pillow flange with edges matching and a $\frac{1}{4}$-in. seam, mitering corners.

4. Fold the binding to the back, encasing the raw edges. Hand-sew the fold of binding to the back of flange, covering the seam. Insert the pillow form.

LAYOUT DIAGRAM KEY
◆ = red 6-in. squares (A)
▼ = red large triangles (B)
▼ = red small triangles (C)
▬ = green 1½- x 6-in. rectangles (D)
◆ = green 1½-in. squares (E)
▼ = green small triangles (F)

FIG. 1 Piecing diagonal rows

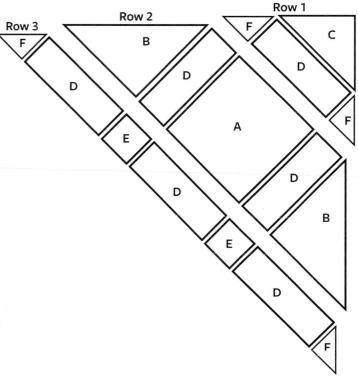

LAYOUT DIAGRAM

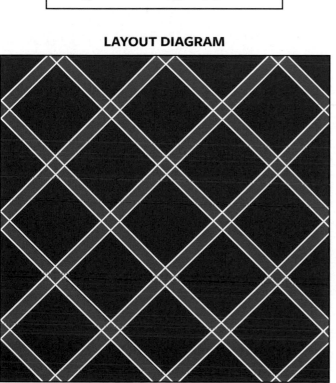

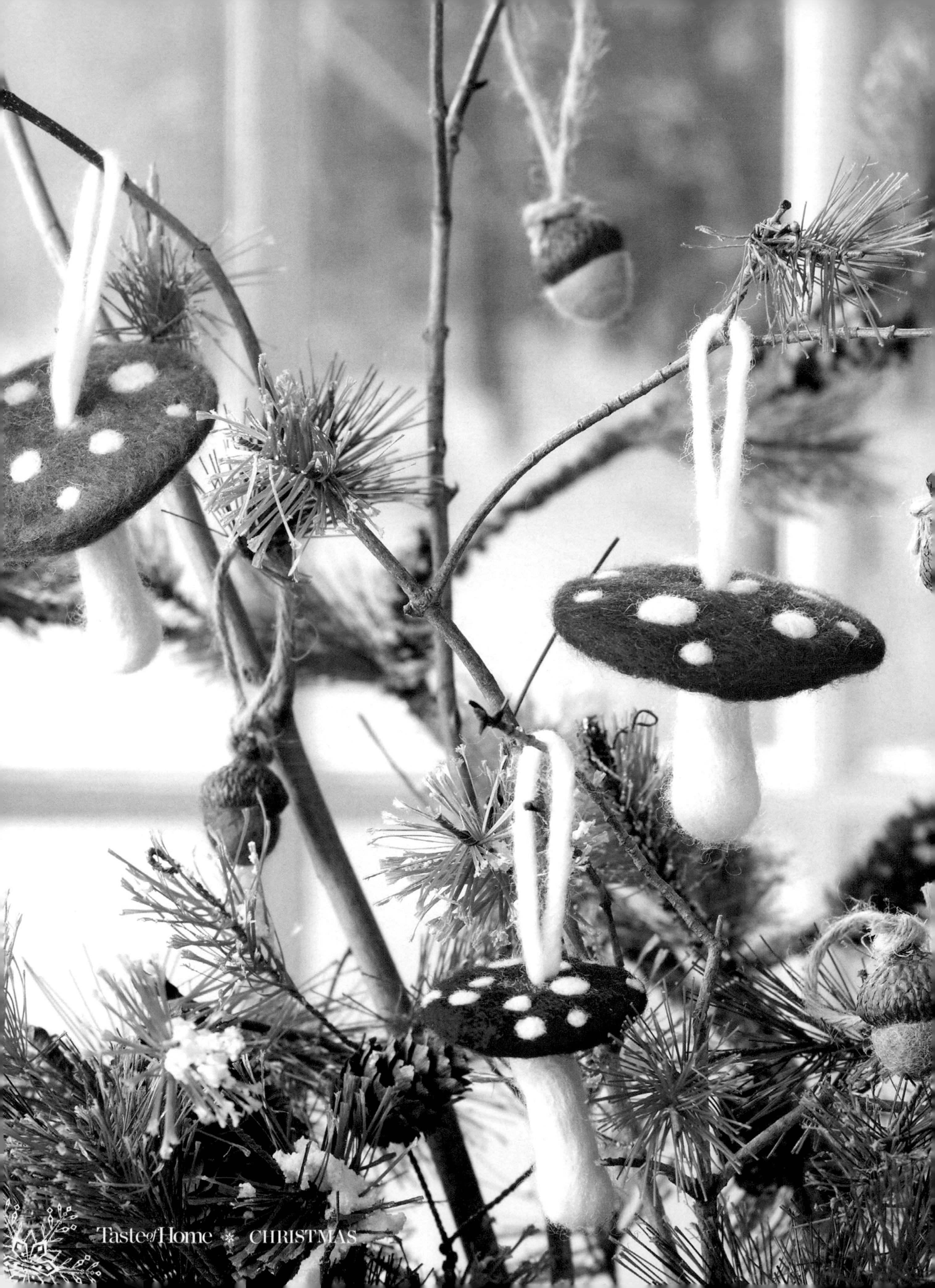

Needle-Felted Mushrooms & Acorns

Christmas comes to the forest! Bright mushrooms and acorns make an unusual but charming addition to seasonal decor.

CRAFT LEVEL:
ACORNS: BEGINNER
MUSHROOMS: INTERMEDIATE

FINISHED SIZE: Varies.

MATERIALS (FOR MUSHROOMS):
1 oz. white wool roving
1 oz. combination of colored wool roving
Medium- to fine-gauge felting needle
Two circle cookie cutters, ½ in. apart in diameter
Dense foam piece, at least 6 in. square and 2 in. thick, for work surface
Ruler
(FOR ACORNS):
Natural acorn caps
1 oz. combination of colored wool roving
Medium- to fine-gauge felting needle
Dense foam piece, at least 6 in. square and 2 in. thick
Clear-drying craft glue
Ruler
Jute twine (optional)

DIRECTIONS:

GENERAL INSTRUCTIONS
When poking wool roving with needle, work over the foam as a work surface.

MUSHROOMS
Follow directions in box below.

ACORNS

1. Roll a strip of roving measuring 8 to 12 in. long and ½ in. wide very tightly from one end. Wrap strip around itself in all directions to form a ball.
2. Holding ball tightly over foam, carefully poke at ball repeatedly to felt in place until ball is solid but spongy. (Or felt ball using method in tip box at right.) Glue into acorn cap. If desired, attach twine for a hanger.

Holiday Helper

To speed up the felting process, use the heat and agitation of your washing machine. Tie the loosely felted balls into knee-high nylon stockings (approximately 10 balls per stocking), knotting between balls. Secure the stockings in a pillowcase and run it through the hottest cycle with a few squirts of dishwashing liquid. Remove the balls from the stockings to air-dry.

Making Mushrooms

1. For the mushroom cap, place the large cookie cutter on the foam piece. Fill cookie cutter with three or four crisscrossing layers of colored roving. Poke repeatedly with the needle, flipping wool a few times, until it forms a solid but spongy disk. Remove cookie cutter.
2. Center the small cookie cutter on the felted disk and fill cookie cutter with two crisscrossing layers of white roving. Poke repeatedly with needle until white roving is felted in place. Remove cookie cutter.
3. Shape the disk's edges by gently poking the needle around it to tuck in loose fibers. Trim any remaining fuzzy fibers with scissors.
4. For each dot, pinch a bit of white wool between your fingers and rub it into a loose ball. Place ball on disk and poke repeatedly with needle until felted in place. In the same way, randomly attach dots of various sizes to disk.
5. For the stem, fold a 12- x ½-in. piece of white roving in half and in half again. (For an even smaller stem, fold again.)
6. Roll the folded roving between your palms to loosely mesh the fibers in place.
7. Poke stem repeatedly with the needle all around the sides, rotating the stem as you go. Continue until a solid but spongy stem is formed.
8. Center one end of stem on underside of disk. Poke repeatedly at the end of stem into disk until fibers felt together. If desired, attach a strand of roving for hanging.

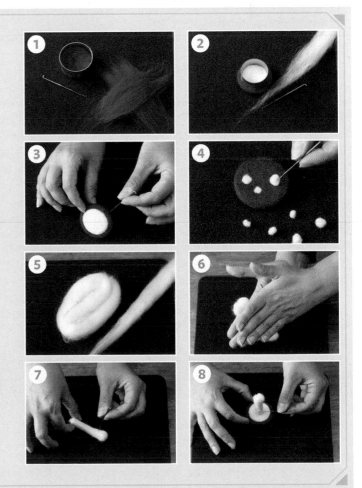

Bird on a Snowman Ornament

A bird's-eye view makes this wintry trim extra fun. In Petaluma, California, Loretta Mateik used purchased wood shapes and bright craft paints to form a whimsical snowman and feathered friend.

CRAFT LEVEL: BEGINNER

FINISHED SIZE: Excluding hanger, snowman ornament is 4 in. high x 4 in. wide.

MATERIALS:

¹⁄₁₆-in.-thick purchased wood shapes (Loretta used Woodsies)—2½-in. circle, 3¼-in. oval, 1½-in. teardrop and 2½-in. teardrop
⅛-in.-thick x ¾-in.-high wood bird shape
Drill with ¹⁄₃₂-in. bit
Water container
Paper towels
Foam plate or palette
Acrylic craft paints (Loretta used DecoArt Americana acrylic craft paints)—Antique Gold, Country Red, Evergreen, French Grey Blue, Hauser Medium Green, Lamp Black, Light Buttermilk, Rookwood Red and Tangelo Orange
Paintbrushes—small flat and liner
Toothpick
Cotton swab
Textured snow medium
8-in. length of ¹⁄₁₆-in. white ribbon
Wood or craft glue

DIRECTIONS:

GENERAL INSTRUCTIONS

Keep paper towels and a container of water handy to clean paintbrushes. Place small amounts of paint onto foam plate or palette as needed. Add coats of paint as needed for complete coverage, letting paint dry after every application.

PAINTING

1. Drill a hole through the 2½-in. wood circle, positioning the hole near the edge.
2. Use small flat brush and Light Buttermilk to paint circle for head.
3. Use small flat brush and Tangelo Orange to paint small teardrop for nose.

4. Use small flat brush and Hauser Medium Green to paint the oval and remaining teardrop for scarf.
5. Use small flat brush and Country Red to paint the bird.
6. Use small flat brush and French Grey Blue to shade the edges of the circle head.
7. Use small flat brush and Rookwood Red to shade the edges of the nose.
8. Dip toothpick into Lamp Black and add two small dots to the circle for the snowman's eyes. In the same way, add a tiny dot to bird for eye.
9. Use liner and Lamp Black to add eyebrows to the head. In the same way, add a curved line to the bird's body for the wing.
10. Dip cotton swab into Country Red and remove excess paint on a paper towel. With a nearly dry cotton swab and a circular motion, add the cheeks to snowman.
11. Use liner and Antique Gold to paint the beak on the bird.
12. Use small flat brush and Antique Gold to paint wide stripes on the oval

scarf. In the same way, paint wide stripes on the large teardrop scarf.
13. Use liner and Rookwood Red to add narrow stripes to the center and sides of each Antique Gold stripe.
14. Use liner and Antique Gold to add dashed lines between the painted stripes on the oval and large teardrop.
15. Use small flat brush and Evergreen to shade the edges of the oval and large teardrop.

ASSEMBLY

1. Glue oval scarf to the bottom of the snowman's head. Glue the teardrop shape to the left side of the oval. Let dry.
2. Glue the nose to the snowman's head. Let dry.
3. Glue the bird to the tip of the nose. Let dry.
4. Thread the 8-in. white ribbon through the drilled hole in snowman's head. Tie the ends of ribbon in a knot for the hanging loop.
5. Apply textured snow to the tip of snowman's nose. Let dry.

Mosaic Photo Frame

Bit by bit, you can transform an unfinished wood frame into the pieced design from Mary Ayres, of Boyce, Virginia. Patterned paper behind the clear quartz adds lovely green color and dimension to the mosaic. If you like, replace the framed holiday message with a special snapshot.

CRAFT LEVEL: BEGINNER

FINISHED SIZE: Photo frame is 8 in. square.

MATERIALS:

8-in.-square unfinished wood photo frame
Clear quartz pieces (enough to cover front of frame)
Scrapbook paper (Mary used Basic Grey papers)—green print for background under quartz pieces and Christmas greeting print for opening of frame
White sanded tile grout
Mosaic glue
Paper towels
Water basin
Foam plate or palette
Acrylic craft paint for sides and back of frame (Mary used DecoArt)— Dazzling Metallic Glorious Gold
1-in. sponge brush
Small household sponge
Disposable gloves
Jumbo craft stick
Soft cloth
Ruler

DIRECTIONS:

1. From green print scrapbook paper, cut a piece that will cover the wood front of the frame.

2. Apply glue to entire back of green print paper piece and adhere paper to wood front of frame.

3. When frame is dry, lay frame flat in front of you with right side up. Arrange clear quartz pieces on the front of frame as desired, leaving a small space between all quartz pieces. When satisfied with the mosaic arrangement, glue quartz pieces in place. Let dry for 24 to 36 hours.

4. Prepare the white sanded tile grout following the grout manufacturer's instructions.

5. Use the jumbo craft stick to spread the prepared grout over the quartz pieces on frame and into the openings between all pieces. Let the grout set for 10 to 15 minutes.

6. Dampen small household sponge. Wearing disposable gloves, use damp sponge to wipe off all excess grout from the top of quartz pieces and from the sides of frame. Let dry.

7. Use soft cloth to polish the quartz pieces on frame.

8. For painting, keep paper towels and a container of water handy to clean the sponge brush as needed. Place a small amount of Glorious Gold acrylic craft paint onto the foam plate or palette. Use sponge brush and Glorious Gold to paint the back and sides of frame, adding more paint to plate or palette as needed. Let dry.

9. Add coats of Glorious Gold paint to back and sides of frame if needed for complete coverage, letting paint dry after every application.

10. Cut the greeting print scrapbook paper to fit the opening of frame and insert paper into frame.

7. Turn tree right side out and firmly stuff with fiberfill. If desired, cut a square of cardboard that is slightly smaller than the base and insert square into bottom of tree for added stability. Hand-stitch the open seam closed.

8. If desired, sew buttons on tree to resemble ornaments.

TREE PATTERNS
Trace 1 each—
tracing paper
Cut 4 each—
fabric scraps

Use photocopier to enlarge patterns 200%.

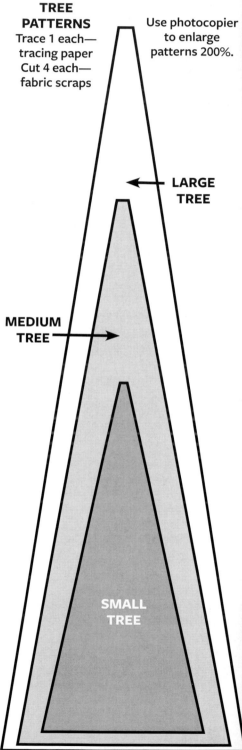

LARGE TREE

MEDIUM TREE

SMALL TREE

Scrappy Fabric Trees

Stuff plenty of extra cheer into the yuletide season with a forest of sewn evergreens. You're sure to enjoy experimenting with different combinations of fabric prints and coordinating embellishments.

CRAFT LEVEL: BEGINNER

FINISHED SIZE: Large tree is 14 in. high x 4½ in. wide, medium tree is 9 in. high x 3¾ in. wide and small tree is 5½ in. high x 2½ in. wide.

MATERIALS (FOR EACH):
Patterns on this page
Tracing paper
Desired fabric scraps
Coordinating all-purpose thread
Polyester fiberfill
Standard sewing supplies
Thin cardboard scrap and assorted
    buttons (optional)

DIRECTIONS (FOR EACH):

1. Prewash all fabrics and use iron to press. Do all stitching with edges matching, a ¼-in. seam allowance and coordinating all-purpose thread.

2. Trace an enlarged tree pattern. Cut four trees of the same size from fabric.

3. Pin two fabric trees with right sides together. Beginning ¼ in. from base, sew one long side to join the pieces.

4. Continue sewing fabric trees together in the same way until all pieces are joined into a dimensional pyramid shape. Leave wrong side out.

5. From fabric, cut a 3¼-in. square for base of small tree, a 4-in. square for base of medium tree or a 5-in. square for base of large tree.

6. With right sides together, sew one edge of square base to bottom edge of one side on the pyramid. In the same way, sew base to two more of the side pieces, leaving one side unstitched.

Yarn Mini Wreath Garland

Going in circles is as fun as can be when you make this charming holiday garland. Use covered wire and your excess yarn to form the little rings. Need a quicker project? Create only one wreath as an ornament for the Christmas tree.

CRAFT LEVEL: BEGINNER

FINISHED SIZE: Varies.

MATERIALS:
- **Skeins or balls of yarn in different solid colors**
- **Roll of covered floral wire**
- **Wire cutters**
- **Ruler**
- **Low-temperature glue gun with glue sticks**
- **1- to 2-in.-wide ribbon of desired length for garland**

Jingle bell ornaments, artificial pine boughs or desired decorations for wreaths (optional)

DIRECTIONS:

1. Using wire cutters, cut an 8- to 12-in. length of floral wire (the longer the wire, the larger the mini wreath will be). Straighten the wire.

2. Align the ends of yarn from 2-3 skeins or balls. Holding the aligned ends together, tie them about 1 in. from one end of the wire.

3. Leaving ¼ in. of wire uncovered at each end of the wire, wrap the yarn strands together around the wire, covering the yarn ends first and then wrapping the length of the wire 4-5 times back and forth.

4. When the wire is covered in a thick layer of wrapped yarn, cut the yarn, leaving about a 3-ft.-long tail.

5. Bend the yarn-covered wire into a circle, positioning the uncovered ¼-in. wire ends so that they overlap and touch. Glue the wire ends together to hold the circle in place. Let dry.

6. Wrap the remaining 3-ft. tail of yarn around the uncovered glued ends of wire to conceal them, leaving about a 6-in.-long tail of yarn for hanger.

7. Knot the remaining 6-in. tail to form a loop for hanging. Pass the loop through the previously wrapped yarn layers to secure it in place on the outer edge of wreath. Trim excess yarn from the knotted end.

8. If desired, trim wreath with small jingle bell ornaments, artificial pine boughs or other decorations.

9. Repeat Steps 1-8 to make as many mini wreaths as desired for garland.

10. To make the garland, string desired number of mini wreaths onto ribbon, leaving a few inches of ribbon on each end for hanging.

Holiday Dining Chairs

Take the dining room from everyday to formal with a few simple supplies. Guests will love sitting at your dressed-up table!

CRAFT LEVEL: BEGINNER

FINISHED SIZE: Varies.

MATERIALS (FOR WRAPPED FABRIC CHAIR):
Lightweight silk or desired fabric
Flexible tape measure and quilter's ruler
Rotary cutter and cutting mat
⅝-in.-wide peel-n-stick fabric fuse tape
 or sewing machine and standard
 sewing supplies
Iron and ironing board
Safety pins
2-in.-wide satin ribbon
Desired paper flower embellishment
Hot glue gun and glue sticks
(FOR ORNAMENT CHAIR):
2½-in.-wide wired ribbon
⅛-in.-wide satin ribbon
2½-in.-wide ornament
Straight pins or safety pins
Flexible tape measure

DIRECTIONS:
WRAPPED FABRIC CHAIR

1. Using tape measure, measure height of the chair back from top edge to seat base. Double the measurement and make note of this number.

2. In the same way, measure from side to side across chair back, starting at the seat base on one side and ending at the seat base on the other side. Add 12 in. to the measurement and make note of this number.

3. Add 2 in. to both noted numbers to allow for hem. Using these numbers as the length and width measurements, cut a fabric piece for chair.

4. Using iron, press a 1-in. hem on all sides of fabric piece.

5. Either use peel-n-stick fabric fuse tape between hem layers to secure the hems in place, or sew hems with a straight stitch about ½ in. from edge.

6. To cover chair, fold fabric piece in half lengthwise with wrong sides together. Place the folded fabric over chair back so that the chair back is sandwiched between the folded fabric layers. Pull each side of fabric forward, crisscrossing fabric to form a V shape where fabric edges meet. Use a safety pin to secure fabric.

7. Use 2-in.-wide satin ribbon to make a bow, shaping the bow and trimming the ends as desired. Glue paper flower to the center of bow.

8. Attach bow with a safety pin to the fabric on back of chair, positioning bow where fabric edges meet in a V shape.

ORNAMENT CHAIR

1. Wrap tape measure around the center of the chair back to determine the chair's circumference. Add 24 in. to this measurement and cut a length of wired ribbon that equals this measurement.

2. Wrap cut ribbon snugly around chair back. Tie a knot to secure ribbon in place on back of chair. Trim ribbon ends in inverted V shapes.

3. Cut a 9-in. length of wired ribbon. Wrap loosely around tied knot to cover it, overlapping ribbon ends about 1 in. in back of knot. Secure with pins.

4. Cut an 8-in. length of ⅛-in.-wide satin ribbon. Loop ribbon through metal hoop on ornament and knot ends. Use pins to secure knotted end of ribbon centered behind knot on chair ribbon, allowing ornament to hang from chair ribbon.

gifts to
GIVE

Ribbon-Trimmed Kitchen Towels

What's cookin'? Easy accents for the kitchen! Simply buy inexpensive plain towels and brighten them up by sewing a fun and cheery border on the bottom. It's a great use for scraps of ribbon.

CRAFT LEVEL: QUICK & EASY

FINISHED SIZE: Varies.

MATERIALS:
Kitchen towels
1½-in.-wide coordinating ribbon without wire
Coordinating all-purpose thread
Thermoweb Peel-n-Stick fabric fuse tape (optional)
Standard sewing supplies

DIRECTIONS:
1. Wash, dry and iron all towels.
2. Measure the width of one towel. Add ½ in. to this measurement and make note of the new number.
3. Cut a piece of ribbon so that the length equals the new number. Press the ribbon flat. Fold each end of ribbon under about ¼ in. and press in place. Fold under again about ¼ in. and press in place. If desired, use fabric fuse tape to secure the folds.
4. Place the ribbon right side up across the width of towel, positioning ribbon about ½ in. from the bottom of towel and ¼ in. from each side edge. Either pin ribbon in place or center a strip of fabric fuse tape across the back of ribbon to secure it in place.
5. Using coordinating thread, topstitch in a straight line about ¼ in. from each long edge of ribbon.
6. Repeat Steps 2-5 for each remaining towel.

Green Cable-Knit Scarf

This chunky accessory is the perfect way to bundle up in winter. Designed by Catherine Perrigo, of Bridgeport, New York, the knit scarf is both fashionable and functional. Use yarn in a gorgeous shade of medium green (like the one shown below right) or choose whatever color suits your style. Can't decide? Make more than one!

CRAFT LEVEL: INTERMEDIATE

FINISHED SIZE: Excluding the fringe, scarf is about 62 in. long x 6½ in. wide. Slight variation in gauge may change finished size a bit.

MATERIALS:
12 oz. bulky-weight yarn (scarf shown was created with Lion Brand Wool-Ease Thick & Quick yarn)
Size 15 knitting needles (or size needed to obtain correct gauge)
Cable needle
Measuring tape

GAUGE: Working in seed stitch, 5 sts and 7 rows = 2 in.

SPECIAL STITCHES:
• **SS = seed stitch**
Row 1: K1, p1; Row 2: P the k sts and k the p sts. Repeat Row 2.
• **C4F = cable 4 sts front**
Sl next 2 sts onto cable needle and hold in front of work, k the next 2 sts, then k the 2 sts from the cable needle.
• **C4B = cable 4 sts back**
Sl next 2 sts onto cable needle and hold in back of work, k the next 2 sts, then k the 2 sts from the cable needle.

DIRECTIONS:
SCARF
1. Cast on 18 sts.
2. Row 1 (WS): K1, p1, k2, p10, k2, p1, k1: 18 sts.
3. Row 2: K1, p1, k1, p1, k2, [C4F] twice, p1, k1, p1, k1: 18 sts.
4. Row 3: K1, p1, k2, p10, k2, p1, k1: 18 sts.
5. Row 4: K1, p1, k1, p1, [C4B] twice, k2, p1, k1, p1, k1: 18 sts.
6. Rows 5-208: Repeat Rows 1-4 fifty-two times. Bind off on WS in pattern of Row 1.

FRINGE
1. Cut twenty 24-in. strands of yarn.
2. Holding 2 strands together as one, fold them in half and pull loop through the sts on one narrow end of scarf.
3. Thread loose ends through the loop and pull to tighten, creating one section of fringe.
4. Repeat Steps 2-3 five more times across each narrow end of the scarf, creating fringe across each end.

Recycled Sweater Coffee Sleeves

What a cozy idea! Cut pieces from colorful sweaters to make cute wraps for coffee mugs. The simple sleeves open and close with Velcro. If you like, use felt instead of a sweater for the personalized label—or skip that detail completely for an easier project.

CRAFT LEVEL: BEGINNER

FINISHED SIZE: Open sleeve is about 11 in. long. x 3 in. high.

MATERIALS (FOR ONE):
Patterns on this page
4- x 12-in. or larger piece of a clean bright-colored sweater
2½- x 4-in. or larger piece of a clean light-colored sweater
3-in.-long strip of ¾-in. sew-on Velcro
HeatnBond light paper-backed iron-on adhesive
Coordinating embroidery floss
Tapestry needle
Standard sewing supplies
1-in.-high or smaller letter stencils (optional)

DIRECTIONS (FOR ONE):
COFFEE SLEEVE

1. Press sweater pieces flat if needed. Trace sleeve pattern on back of the bright-colored sweater piece and cut out.

2. Either hand-stitch or use a sewing machine to sew the Velcro on each short end of the cutout sleeve as shown on pattern, positioning the Velcro so that it sticks together when overlapped. Trim ends of Velcro even with edges of sleeve if needed. Set sleeve aside.

PERSONALIZED LABEL

1. Trace label pattern on back of the light-colored sweater piece and cut out.

2. Trace label pattern on paper-backed iron-on adhesive and cut out. Following adhesive manufacturer's instructions and with edges even, fuse adhesive on back of the cutout sweater label. Leave paper backing on until directions state otherwise.

3. Using stencils if desired, write desired name or word with pencil on center front of the cutout sweater label, writing lightly so it will not show under the stitching.

4. Using tapestry needle and embroidery floss, backstitch on top of the written name or word, outlining the letters. If desired, use Smyrna cross-stitches as dots

or to embellish letters. See Figs. 1-3 below left for stitch illustrations.

5. When finished stitching desired letters, remove paper backing, making sure to remove it from underneath the stitching as well.

6. Lay the open coffee sleeve horizontally in front of you with right side up (sleeve should curve downward to be in the correct position). Lay the label right side up on front of sleeve as shown on pattern.

7. Following adhesive manufacturer's instructions, use an iron and pressing cloth to fuse the label in place on sleeve.

8. Using tapestry needle and embroidery floss, sew a running stitch all the way around the label about ¼ in. from the edge.

9. To use sleeve, wrap sleeve around coffee mug or cup and secure the Velcro on edges to close.

FIG. 1
Backstitch

FIG. 2 Smyrna cross-stitch

FIG. 3 Running stitch

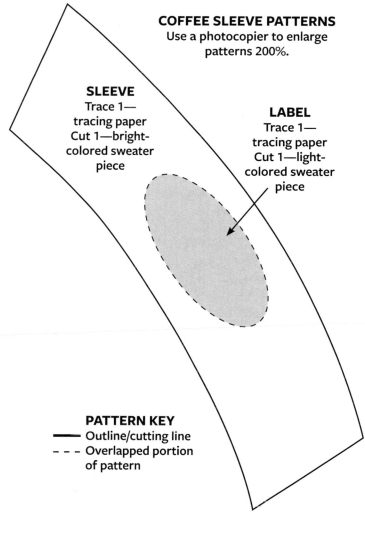

COFFEE SLEEVE PATTERNS
Use a photocopier to enlarge patterns 200%.

SLEEVE
Trace 1—tracing paper
Cut 1—bright-colored sweater piece

LABEL
Trace 1—tracing paper
Cut 1—light-colored sweater piece

PATTERN KEY
— Outline/cutting line
- - - Overlapped portion of pattern

Joy Fabric Gift Bag

Eco-friendly and fun, a fabric gift bag is the wrap that keeps on giving. This one comes from Doris Deutmeyer, of Dyersville, Iowa.

CRAFT LEVEL: BEGINNER

FINISHED SIZE: Excluding handles, gift bag is 8 in. high x 8 in. wide x 4 in. deep.

MATERIALS:
Rotary cutter, ruler and mat
⅜ yd. fabric for bag
Coordinating fabric scraps for "Joy," ornament and pine branch appliques
⅜ yd. heavy fusible interfacing (Doris used Pellon 809 Decor Bond)
Coordinating all-purpose thread
2¼-in. square of scrap card stock
10-in. square of fusible web (Doris used Therm O Web HeatnBond UltraHold)
Four ¼-in. eyelets and eyelet tools
Two 12-in. lengths of cording or ribbon for handles
3½- x 7½-in. rectangle of cardboard
Sewing machine or serger
Standard sewing supplies

DIRECTIONS:
FABRIC BAG

1. Using rotary cutter, ruler and mat, cut two 12½-in. squares each of bag fabric and fusible interfacing.

2. Following manufacturer's instructions, fuse interfacing to the wrong side of each fabric square. Trim each bonded fabric square to 12 in.

3. Edge-stitch or serge one side of each bonded fabric square (this will become the opening).

4. With right sides together, stitch or serge a ¼-in. seam on the other three sides of each fabric square.

5. Turn right side out. At top edge, fold 2¼ in. to inside; press.

6. Turn bag inside out. Align the card stock square with the outside edge and bottom of bag. Use pencil to trace the square at each bottom corner, front and back. See Diagram 1 below right.

7. Flatten corners to make triangular points. Align the bottom seam and side seams. Stitch on the lines of the

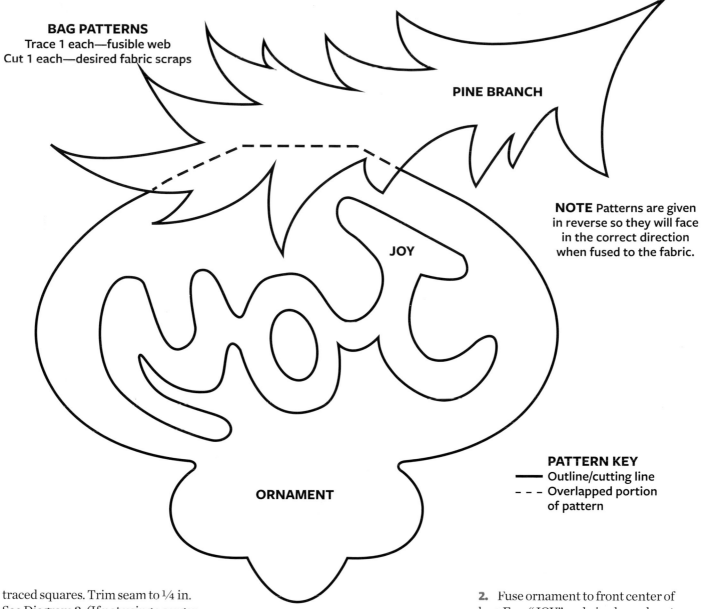

BAG PATTERNS
Trace 1 each—fusible web
Cut 1 each—desired fabric scraps

PINE BRANCH

JOY

NOTE Patterns are given in reverse so they will face in the correct direction when fused to the fabric.

PATTERN KEY
—— Outline/cutting line
- - - Overlapped portion of pattern

ORNAMENT

traced squares. Trim seam to ¼ in. See Diagram 2. (If not using a serger, finish all edges with a zigzag stitch or trim with pinking shears.)

8. Turn the bag right side out. On the front of bag, measure 2 in. from the side seams. Finger-press a fold in place, then steam press. Repeat for bottom and then back of bag. (Press carefully so bag lies flat.)

APPLIQUES

1. Trace the ornament, "Joy" and pine branch patterns onto fusible web. Following the web manufacturer's instructions, fuse traced patterns to desired fabric scraps. Cut out each fabric piece on traced lines.

2. Fuse ornament to front center of bag. Fuse "JOY" and pine branch onto ornament and bag, overlapping pieces where shown in photo.

HANDLES AND FINISHING

1. Cut two 1- x 4-in. pieces of fusible web. To secure the folded opening, place strips under top fold on both the front and back of bag and fuse together.

2. On bag front, insert and secure two eyelets, placing them ¾ in. from the top edge and 1¾ in. from opposite sides. Repeat on bag back.

3. From bag front, insert end of a cord or ribbon piece into one eyelet and knot the end inside bag. Repeat with the opposite end and other eyelet. Add handle on bag back in same way.

4. Place cardboard rectangle in bottom of bag.

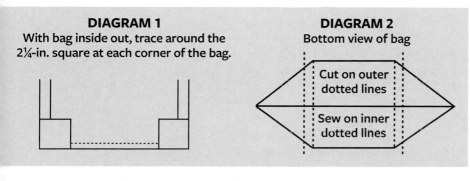

DIAGRAM 1
With bag inside out, trace around the 2¼-in. square at each corner of the bag.

DIAGRAM 2
Bottom view of bag

Cut on outer dotted lines

Sew on inner dotted lines

Felt Santa Purse

Any little girl will adore this Kris Kringle purse shared by Mary Ayres, of Boyce, Virginia. It makes an even more special gift with a few treats tucked inside.

CRAFT LEVEL: BEGINNER

FINISHED SIZE: Excluding strap, Santa purse is about 9 in. long x 8 in. wide.

MATERIALS:

Patterns on next page
Tracing paper
Size 8 black pearl cotton
Wool felt—¼ yd. of white for purse and inside of strap, ⅛ yd. of red for hat brim and outside of strap, and scrap of flesh-tone for face
Embroidery needle
Approximately 45 white sew-through buttons in assorted sizes for hat brim
Two ⅝-in. pink sew-through buttons for cheeks
One ⅝-in. red sew-through button for purse strap
Two ⅜-in. black snaps for eyes
White all-purpose thread
Off-white cotton cord for pompom
1¼- x 5-in. piece of cardboard
Standard sewing supplies

DIRECTIONS:

PREPARATION

1. Wet white, red and flesh-tone wool felt with water separately. Dry each separately in dryer to give the felt a crinkly aged look.

2. Trace enlarged patterns onto tracing paper with pencil as directed on patterns.

3. Cut pattern pieces from felt as directed on patterns.

ASSEMBLY

1. Pin red hat and flesh-tone face pieces to right side of one purse piece as shown on pattern.

2. Thread embroidery needle with a single strand of black pearl cotton. Blanket-stitch across the top and bottom of red hat piece and around edge of flesh-tone face. See Fig. 1 above right for stitch illustration.

3. With pencil, transfer inside design lines of hat and mustache to front of purse. Blanket-stitch along marked lines.

4. Using white all-purpose thread, hand-sew the black snaps and pink buttons to face where shown on pattern. Hand-sew white buttons to hat brim, leaving about ¼ in. along each side edge of the brim uncovered for adding blanket stitches.

FIG. 1 Blanket stitch

5. Pin front and back purse pieces together with wrong sides together. Blanket-stitch around edge of purse, leaving the top edge open.

6. For strap, cut a 1- x 14-in. strip each of white and red felt. Pin the strips together with edges matching. Blanket-stitch around edges.

7. With the red side out, pin opposite ends of the strap to opposite top edges of the purse. Hand-sew the white side of the strap ends to purse. With black pearl cotton, hand-sew red button to one strap end.

PURSE PATTERNS
Use a photocopier to enlarge patterns 200%.

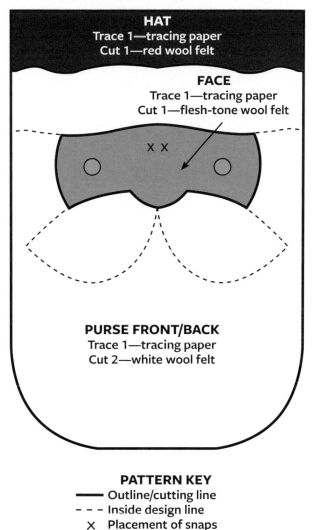

HAT
Trace 1—tracing paper
Cut 1—red wool felt

FACE
Trace 1—tracing paper
Cut 1—flesh-tone wool felt

× ×

PURSE FRONT/BACK
Trace 1—tracing paper
Cut 2—white wool felt

PATTERN KEY
—— Outline/cutting line
- - - Inside design line
× Placement of snaps
● Placement of pink buttons

POMPOM
1. For the tie, cut a 10-in. length of cord. Center tie along the 5-in. length of the cardboard strip.
2. Working back and forth along the length of the cardboard strip, wrap cord around the tie and width of the strip about 30 times so that each wrap is smooth but not tight and lies against the previous wrap.
3. Carefully bend the cardboard strip lengthwise and remove the cardboard without removing the tie. Knot the ends of the tie with a double knot, pulling the ends tight to make a donut shape.
4. Without cutting the ends of the tie, cut loops along the outermost edge of donut shape. Fluff ends to untwist the cord. Trim ends even.
5. Hand-sew the pompom to the purse strap, placing it at the end without the button.

Scrappy Ribbon Flowers
Wondering what to do with scraps of ribbon or fabric? Turn them into simple flowers you can use in place of standard bows on gift boxes. Or, attach a pin back or hair clip for a wearable accent.

CRAFT LEVEL: QUICK & EASY

FINISHED SIZE: Varies.

MATERIALS (FOR ONE):
1-in.-wide ribbon or fabric strip
Extra-large circle glue dot (1 to 2 in.)
Additional smaller glue dots
Scrap of card stock

DIRECTIONS (FOR ONE):
1. Adhere an extra-large circle glue dot onto card stock; cut out around the glue dot.
2. Fold ribbon or fabric strip in half to measure about ½ in. wide. Adhere one end to outer edge of extra-large glue dot.
3. Keeping the folded edge up, adhere the open edge to the glue dot, spiraling inward toward the center and using small glue dots to secure the edge as needed.
4. At the center, trim the remaining end to about 1 in. and make a loop. Use small glue dots to secure loop in the center.

Decorative Gift Jars

Go ahead—lift the lid on this easy idea shared by Loretta Mateik, of Petaluma, California. You'll discover merry wrappers that can decorate gifts of jam, salsa or other treats from your kitchen. Loretta used jelly jars, but this project will work with jars of other sizes, too.

CRAFT LEVEL: QUICK & EASY

FINISHED SIZE: Each jar shown is about 4 in. high x 2⅝ in. wide.

MATERIALS (FOR ALL):
- Three glass jars with lids and bands (Loretta used jelly jars)
- Card stock—one sheet each of a print and a coordinating solid for each jar wrapper, plus scraps each of green, gold and white solid
- Tree, snowflake and star punches (optional)
- Coordinating chalk or colored pencils
- Black fine-line marker
- 14-in. length of coordinating ribbon for each jar (or length needed to tie around jar)
- Two metal eyelets and eyelet tools
- Pop-ups or glue dots
- Paper glue
- Double-stick tape
- Measuring tape
- Computer and printer (optional)

DIRECTIONS:

EACH JAR

1. Measure around jar and add 1 in. to that measurement. Measure the height of jar from just below the rim to about ⅜ in. from the bottom. Cut a rectangular piece of solid card stock equal to these measurements.
2. Cut a piece of patterned card stock that has the same length as the solid piece but is about ¼ in. narrower.
3. Glue the patterned piece of card stock to the solid piece, leaving a margin of solid paper showing along both long edges.
4. Using double-stick tape, adhere layered card stock to outside of jar. Overlap the narrow ends and use double-stick tape to secure them.
5. Using a computer or marker, print a greeting on paper and cut it in a circle to fit on jar lid. Glue circle to lid.

TREE JAR

1. Wrap the jar with a length of coordinating ribbon. Knot the ribbon in back of jar.
2. Cut a tree shape from green solid card stock using a scissors or a punch.
3. Attach the tree to the ribbon on front of jar using a pop-up or glue dot.

STAR JAR

1. Cut a star shape from gold solid card stock using a scissors or a punch.
2. Use marker to write contents of jar on star.
3. Rub edges of star with chalk or colored pencil to shade.
4. Using eyelet tools, attach the metal eyelets to opposite sides of star and thread ribbon through the eyelets. Wrap the ribbon around the jar and knot the ends in back.

SNOWFLAKE JAR

1. Wrap the jar with a length of coordinating ribbon. Knot the ribbon in back of jar.
2. Cut a snowflake shape from white solid card stock using a scissors or a punch.
3. Use marker to write contents of jar on snowflake.
4. Rub edges of snowflake with chalk or colored pencil to shade.
5. Attach snowflake to ribbon on front of jar using a pop-up or glue dot.

Santa Claus Card

What a special delivery! Sandy Rollinger, of Apollo, Pennsylvania, created an elfish greeting card to send Christmas wishes in an especially merry way. Her design calls for readily available craft supplies. You'll be able to make one—or a bunch—of your own Kris Kringles in a flash.

CRAFT LEVEL: QUICK & EASY

FINISHED SIZE: Card is 6½ in. wide x 5 in. high.

MATERIALS (FOR ONE):
Card stock—8½- x 11-in. sheet of red and scraps each of flesh-tone, green and white
Paper crimper
8½- x 11-in. sheet or scrap of Christmas-print scrapbook paper (Sandy used a print of Christmas words and phrases)
Small beads—one red bead for berry and one white bead for hat
Clear micro beads for beard
Black fine-line permanent marker
Ruler
Toothpick
Glue (Sandy used Beacon Adhesives Zip-Dry Glue)
Paper cutter (optional)
Compass or circle punches (optional)—1½-in. punch and ½-in. punch

NOTE *If sending the card through the mail, have the post office hand-stamp the card.*

DIRECTIONS (FOR ONE):

1. Cut a 6½- x 10-in. piece from red card stock. Fold in half crosswise to make a 6½- x 5-in. card.

2. Cut a 4⅜- x 6-in. piece of Christmas paper. Lay card on a flat surface with the fold at the top. Glue the Christmas paper piece right side up on the front of the card.

3. Cut a 2-in. square from red card stock. Run square piece through paper crimper. Center and glue square on front of the card.

4. Cut a 1½- x 1¼-in. rectangle from green card stock. Center and glue green rectangle vertically on the red square on card.

5. Using compass or circle punch, cut a 1½-in. circle from white card stock for Santa's head and beard. Cut a small triangle from red card stock for hat and glue it to the top of the white circle.

6. Using compass or circle punch, cut a ½-in. circle from flesh-tone card stock for face. Glue face to the center of the head.

7. Cut a ¼-in.-wide x 1½-in.-long strip from white card stock for brim on hat. Run the strip lengthwise through paper crimper. Glue strip to bottom edge of hat.

8. Cut two ⅜-in. diamond shapes from green card stock for leaves. Glue leaves to right side of hat brim.

9. Glue white bead to tip of hat and glue red bead to center of leaves. Using toothpick, spread glue over Santa's beard. While glue is still wet, sprinkle on micro beads. Let dry.

10. Use black marker to add two tiny dots for eyes. Glue Santa head to green rectangle on card. Let dry.

Wishing
you good
fortune in
the new year.

Good Fortune Box

Make friends or neighbors smile with felt fortune cookies in a takeout box. It's a sweet Christmas treat with no calories!

CRAFT LEVEL: QUICK & EASY

FINISHED SIZE: Excluding handle, closed box is 4 in. high.

MATERIALS:
Marker or computer with printer
9- x 12-in. sheets of felt—brown, dark pink, light pink and tan
Compass and fabric marker
Scraps of card stock—dark pink and brown sparkle
Sheet or scraps of white paper
Glue stick
Dimensional glue dot
4-in.-high white sparkle takeout box
⅝-in. star punch
Low-temperature glue gun and glue sticks
Ruler

DIRECTIONS:

TAKEOUT BOX LABEL

1. Using a computer or marker, print a greeting on white paper. Centering the greeting, cut out a 2-in. square.
2. From pink card stock, cut a 2⅜- x 2⅜-in. square. From brown card stock, cut a 2¾- x 2¾-in. square and make a star with paper punch.
3. Center white square on pink square and attach with glue stick. Center glued squares on brown square and attach in same way.
4. Using glue stick, attach assembled label to takeout box. Let dry.
5. Use glue dot to attach star to label.

FELT FORTUNE COOKIES

1. With compass and fabric marker, draw 3-in.-diameter circles on felt and cut out. Print fortunes on white paper and cut out each in a 2- x ½-in. strip.
2. Center a strip on a circle. Fold circle in half over strip and use glue gun to secure the felt in the center whcre felt edges meet. Fold the open ends back until they touch, forming a U-shaped cookie. Use glue gun to secure.
3. Repeat Step 2 as desired. When dry, place cookies in takeout box.

Peppermint Bath Salts

How refreshing—bath time with a burst of cool peppermint. Pack these fragrant salts in a jar tied with a candy-inspired cord.

CRAFT LEVEL: QUICK & EASY

FINISHED SIZE: Makes about 2 cups bath salts.

MATERIALS:
1 cup Epsom salts
½ cup sea salt
½ cup baking soda
10-20 drops peppermint essential oil
Desired glass jar with lid
Decorative cord

DIRECTIONS:

1. In a large measuring cup or mixing bowl, combine the Epsom salts, sea salt, baking soda and peppermint essential oil. Stir well.
2. Place bath salts in lidded jar. Wrap decorative cord around top of jar and tie a bow. Trim ends of bow as desired.

Christmas Home Cards

Open the door to Christmas cheer with these charming holiday houses from Mary Ayres, of Boyce, Virginia. They're so cute, you may want to make a bunch and display them as a village!

CRAFT LEVEL: BEGINNER

FINISHED SIZE: Tall house card is about 5½ in. high x 4¼ in. wide. Wide house card is about 4¼ in. high x 5½ in. wide.

MATERIALS NEEDED (FOR BOTH):
Patterns on next page
Tracing paper
Scraps of heavy-weight patterned papers—yellow, textured red, damask red, lime green, bright green, coordinating stripe and white
Ink pads—blue, green, red and yellow

Two 8½- x 11-in. sheets of white card stock
Four gold brads
Four 12-in. lengths of red pearl cotton
Black markers—fine-line and medium-point
Iridescent glitter
Small paintbrush and craft glue for paper
Ruler
Scallop-edge scissors
Circle punches—¹⁄₁₆-in., ⅛-in., ¼-in. and ¾-in.
Scoring blade

DIRECTIONS (FOR BOTH):
GENERAL INSTRUCTIONS
Before gluing the cutout paper pieces together, shade the outside edges of each piece (excluding the tags) with the following ink colors: Rub red ink on red paper pieces, yellow ink on yellow pieces, green ink on green pieces and blue ink on white and striped pieces.

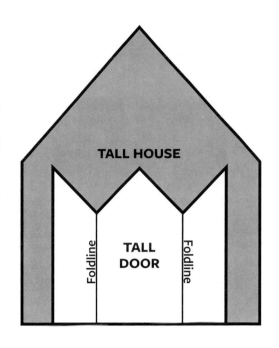

CARD PATTERNS
Use a photocopier to enlarge
patterns 200%.
Trace 1 each—tracing paper
Cut 1 each as directed

TALL HOUSE CARD

1. Trace enlarged tall house and tall door patterns separately onto tracing paper with pencil. Cut out shapes.

2. Cut an 8½- x 5½-in. rectangle from white card stock. Score a line crosswise across the center of the white rectangle and fold it in half to make a 5½-in.-high x 4¼-in.-wide card.

3. Cut a 5½- x 4¼-in. piece of textured red paper. With edges matching, glue paper to the front of card. With the fold of the card at the left, place tall house pattern on top of card and trim the top of card following the roofline on pattern.

4. For roof trim, cut two ½- x 4-in. strips of white paper. Trim one long edge of each strip with scallop scissors to make ⅜-in.-wide strips. Glue strips to top edges of roof. Trim short ends of roof trim even with edges of card.

5. Place door pattern on wrong side of striped paper and cut out door. With the striped pattern on the outside, fold sides of door in where foldlines are shown on pattern.

6. Cut the traced door pattern along foldlines to create pattern for inner door. From yellow paper, cut one inner door, two ¾- x 2¼-in. rectangles for side windows and one 1-in. square for dormer window. Glue inner door right side up to inside center of door. Let dry.

7. Referring to photo above left, use fine-line marker to add design lines to windows. Use medium-point marker to write "holiday hugs to you" on inner door. Open sides of door and use fine-line marker to outline inside door section.

8. For doorknobs, use ⅛-in. circle punch to make a hole in each side of door. Insert a brad into each hole and bend prongs on the inside.

9. For wreath, use punch to make a ¾-in. circle from bright green paper. Punch a ¼-in. hole in the center of the circle to make a wreath. Glue wreath to center of square window.

10. For tag, cut a 1¼- x ½-in. rectangle from white card stock. At one short end, cut off corners to create a tag shape. Use fine-line marker to write "Please Enter" and to add a border around the edge. Use ¹⁄₁₆-in. punch to make a hole at the tapered end.

11. Referring to photo for position, glue assembled door and windows to front of card.

12. Wrap a length of red pearl cotton around brads on door and add the tag. Tie ends in a bow to close doors. Trim ends of bow as desired. Tie an overhand knot close to each end.

13. Tie another length of red pearl cotton into a small bow. Trim ends as desired. Glue bow to top of wreath.

14. Use paintbrush to apply a thin layer of glue to roof trim and windowpanes. While glue is still wet, sprinkle on glitter. Let dry. Tap off excess glitter when dry.

WIDE HOUSE CARD

1. Trace enlarged wide house and wide door patterns separately onto tracing paper with pencil. Cut out shapes.

2. Cut an 11- x 4¼-in. rectangle from white card stock. Score a line crosswise across the center of the white rectangle and fold it in half to make a 4¼-in.-high x 5½-in.-wide card.

3. Cut a 4¼- x 5½-in. piece of lime green paper. With edges matching, glue paper to the front of the card. With the fold of the card at the left, place wide house pattern on top of card and trim the top of card following roofline on pattern.

4. For roof trim, follow Step 4 for Tall House Card.

5. For door and windows, follow Steps 5-8 for Tall House Card, using damask red paper instead of striped paper and cutting 1- x 1½-in. rectangles for side windows.

6. For wreath and tag, follow Steps 9-13 for Tall House Card.

7. To finish, follow Step 14 for Tall House Card.

Mommy & Me Hobby Aprons

Designed by Diane Coates, of West Allis, Wisconsin, these simple aprons will go to work in your kitchen, vegetable garden, flower bed, craft room...wherever you and a young helper want to team up. The apron pocket sizes can be customized to suit the supplies you need, and whimsical fabric prints will make any task fun.

CRAFT LEVEL: BEGINNER

FINISHED SIZE: Adult apron is about 17½ in. wide x 15¾ in. long. Child apron is about 12½ in. wide x 10 in. long.

MATERIALS:
Fabric marking pen and quilter's ruler
Iron and pressing cloth

100% cotton solid duck cloth for base
  (½ yd. for child apron and ⅝ yd. for adult apron)
100% cotton print fabric for pocket
  (½ yd. for child apron and ⅝ yd. for adult apron)
1- to 2-yd. length of ⅜-in.-wide coordinating grosgrain ribbon for waist tie of each apron
Standard sewing supplies

DIRECTIONS:

CUTTING

1. From solid duck cloth, cut a 15- x 13-in. base piece for child apron and a 20- x 19-in. base piece for adult apron.

2. From print cotton fabric, cut a 15-in.-square pocket piece for child apron and a 20-in.-square pocket piece for adult apron.

APRON

1. Fold pocket fabric piece in half with wrong sides together. Press in place with iron.

2. Pin the pocket to right side of coordinating duck cloth piece. Place raw edges of pocket along bottom and sides of duck cloth piece. (The folded pocket edge should lie horizontally in the center of duck cloth with the side and bottom edges matching.)

3. On sides and bottom only, turn all fabric layers under ½ in.; press in place. Turn under again ⅝ in. and press in place. If desired, miter corners. Pin all folds in place, then stitch along pinned folded edges.

4. On the top edge of each apron, turn under ½ in. and press in place. Turn under again 1⅛ in. and press in place. Pin the folds in place, then stitch about 1 in. from top folded edge, forming the casing for the tie.

POCKETS AND TIE

1. Use a quilter's ruler and fabric marking pen to draw vertical and horizontal lines on the pocket piece, dividing pocket into smaller segments as desired.

2. Use a straight stitch to sew on the vertical and horizontal marked lines.

3. Thread a 1- to 2-yd. length of ribbon through the casing for the waist tie. Cut the ends of tie on an angle to help prevent fraying.

Christmas Light Charms

Holiday parties shine even brighter with the beaded light bulb charms from Nancy Valentine Baker, of Paupack, Pennsylvania. Add one to each stemmed glass so your guests can easily identify their own.

CRAFT LEVEL: BEGINNER

FINISHED SIZE: Excluding the gold loop, each beaded charm is about 1¼ in. long x ⅝ in. wide.

MATERIALS (FOR ONE):
Beading chart on this page
14-in. length of 28-gauge gold wire
Nineteen 4 mm round transparent beads
   (aqua, green, pink, purple or red)
Six 3 mm round gold metallic beads
Gold wire earring hoop
Wire cutters

DIRECTIONS (FOR ONE):

1. Referring to the beading chart, fold the gold wire in half and center a 4 mm bead on it to start the first row at the bottom of the light bulb.

2. Add two more 4 mm beads to one wire end and insert the other wire end through the same two beads, crossing the wire ends through the beads. Pull both wire ends taut, keeping them of equal length.

3. Referring to the beading chart, continue adding rows of 4 mm beads in the same way until you have added all nineteen 4 mm beads as shown.

4. Add a row of three 3 mm gold beads the same as before.

5. Add a gold bead to each wire end, leaving the ends uncrossed. Then add another gold bead by crossing both wire ends through it, completing the top row of gold beads.

6. Twist the wire ends together above the top beaded row, leaving a small space between the wires and the center bead. Clip excess wire.

7. Slide the twisted wire end of the beaded light bulb onto the gold wire earring hoop. To use the charm, close the hoop around the stem of a glass.

BEADING CHART

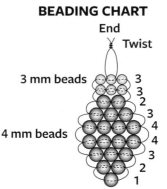

Stamped Clay Earrings

Your girlfriends are sure to love unique earrings made from moldable polymer clay. Jacquelyn Edkin, of Williamsport, Pennsylvania, used a rubber-stamp pattern to customize her designs. Have some extra time? Create a matching pendant.

CRAFT LEVEL: BEGINNER

FINISHED SIZE: Varies.

MATERIALS:
Polymer clay
Desired rubber stamp
Small piece of Plexiglas or other hard,
    flat surface
Foil-lined baking sheet
Waxed paper
Acrylic paint in desired color
Sponge brush
Paper towels
Toothpick
2 earring wires
Two 3 mm closed jump rings
Two 7 mm open jump rings
Ultrafine sandpaper
Long-nose pliers
Standard oven

DIRECTIONS:
1. Condition the clay by rolling and kneading it in your hands until it is pliable.
2. Make two same-size balls of clay and shape each into a slight cylinder.

Lay the clay cylinders on a piece of waxed paper. Use Plexiglas or other surface to flatten the cylinders into same-size ovals.
3. Press the rubber stamp in the clay, making a similar impression on both clay ovals.
4. With toothpick, make a hole at the top of each oval bead.
5. Place the oval beads on a foil-lined baking sheet and bake in the oven following the clay manufacturer's instructions. Let cool.
6. Use a sponge brush to apply paint on the stamped pattern. Wipe off excess paint with a paper towel, leaving paint only in the stamped impression. Let dry.
7. Lightly sand top of each bead to remove any remaining paint that is outside the impression. Buff with paper towel. Place the beads back in oven at manufacturer's recommended temperature for 10 minutes to set the paint. Let cool.
8. Use pliers to open 7 mm jump ring by carefully twisting ends sideways. (Do not pull apart.) Slip open jump ring through the hole on an oval bead. Slide on 3 mm jump ring. Use pliers to close larger jump ring. Add jump rings to remaining bead in same way.
9. Use pliers to open the hoop of an earring wire. Slip 3 mm jump ring onto it and close hoop. Add earring wire to remaining earring in same way.

Peekaboo Ornament Card

What's the secret to this festive, one-sided greeting? The top ornament rotates to the side, revealing your message underneath.

CRAFT LEVEL: QUICK & EASY

FINISHED SIZE: Card is about 6 in. high x 4 in. wide.

MATERIALS (FOR ONE):
6-in.-high x 4-in.-wide. rectangle
    of solid-color card stock for card
Scraps of card stock—patterned and
    solid-color card stock for ornament
    and solid brown card stock for top
Colored brad
Holiday sticker or stamp with inkpad
2¾-in. circle punch
Glue dots or glue stick
Awl or pointed scissors
Marker or pen for writing message
Paper trimmer (optional)

DIRECTIONS (FOR ONE):
1. Using punch, cut one circle from patterned card stock and one circle from solid-color card stock .
2. Using paper trimmer or scissors, cut a 1-in.-high x ½-in.-wide rectangle from brown card stock for the ornament top. Glue ornament top centered on the back edge of the solid-color circle.
3. Place the large rectangular card vertically in front of you. Glue the solid-color circle centered about ⅞ in. from card bottom, positioning the ornament top at the top.
4. Align the patterned circle on top of the solid-color circle. Holding the patterned circle in place, use an awl or pointed scissors to poke a small hole through all layers of card stock where the ornament top and circles overlap.
5. Insert brad into the hole and open the prongs on back, securing patterned circle on top of the bottom circle.
6. Either attach a holiday sticker or use a holiday stamp to write a message above the ornament on the card.
7. Rotate patterned ornament circle to the side and write a message on the solid-color circle. Move patterned circle back over solid-color circle.

3. Beginning at the twisted area by the beads, wrap the long wavy wire around the perimeter of the bead cluster 8-10 times, wrapping loosely and holding the wrapped wire in place with your fingers as you go.

4. To secure the wrapped wire, thread the end of the wrapped wire between two beads from the bottom to the top and pull tight. Thread wire a few more times between the same two beads in the same way. Repeat between the next two beads and continue until you have secured the wire in all three gaps between the beads.

5. Repeat Steps 3 and 4, wrapping the wire around the perimeter 8-10 times and then securing the wire between the bead gaps.

6. Wrap the remaining 6-in. end of wire a few times through the center back of the nest, then wrap it a few times over either the base of a pin back or the end of a kilt pin, securing it on the back of the nest. Wrap wire again through the center back of the nest a few times.

7. Use needle-nose or round-nose pliers to create coils in the remaining ends of wire on the top of nest. Use wire cutters to trim off excess wire.

Wire Bird's Nest Brooch

Let creativity take wing with an adorable gift for the bird lovers you know. Small blue beads form the eggs in the little wire nest, which makes a distinctive accessory when you attach a pin back or kilt pin.

CRAFT LEVEL: INTERMEDIATE

FINISHED SIZE: Excluding a kilt pin, nest is about 1¼ in. wide.

MATERIALS:
6-ft. length of 20-gauge wire
Three 8 mm round blue beads or pearls
¾-in. pin back or 2-in. kilt pin
Wire cutters
Needle-nose pliers
Round-nose pliers
Wood pencil or ¼-in. dowel rod

DIRECTIONS:
1. For the eggs, string the beads or pearls onto the wire, placing them together about 6 in. from one end of the wire. Bend the wire so that the beads form a triangular cluster. Secure the beads in place by twisting the wires together a few times where they meet.

2. Wrap the long end of wire around the length of the pencil or dowel rod, creating a spiraled wire. Pull the wire out to create loose waves along the length of the wire.

Beeswax Lotion

This luxurious, skin-soothing treat is easier to make than you might think. It contains just four ingredients—beeswax, olive oil, coconut oil and shea butter—and requires basic kitchen tools. Whip up a few batches to give away and an extra one to pamper yourself during the holiday season.

CRAFT LEVEL: QUICK & EASY

FINISHED SIZE: Makes about 1¾ cups lotion.

MATERIALS:

1 cup shea or cocoa butter
¼ cup coconut oil
¼ cup olive oil or grapeseed oil
2 tablespoons beeswax pellets or finely grated beeswax
Double boiler
Wire whisk or hand mixer
Desired containers with lids

DIRECTIONS:

1. In a double boiler, combine the shea or cocoa butter, coconut oil, olive or grapeseed oil and beeswax. Stir frequently to melt until mixture is completely liquefied.
2. Place mixture in the refrigerator for about 1 hour or until mixture has hardened but is soft to the touch.
3. Using a whisk or hand mixer, whip mixture for about 5-10 minutes or until creamy and smooth. (If it is too hard to whip, warm it in the microwave for 15-20 seconds.)
4. Place lotion in one or more lidded containers. Store away from moisture and sunlight.

Chalkboard Play Mat

Ideal for keeping little ones occupied in the car, a waiting room or church, these simple play mats roll up for easy transport. An eraser and chalk tuck neatly inside.

CRAFT LEVEL: BEGINNER

FINISHED SIZE: Unrolled play mat is about 14 in. square.

MATERIALS:
16-in.-square piece of duck cloth in desired color
12-in.-square piece of chalk fabric
36-in. length of ⅜-in.-wide ribbon
Standard sewing supplies
Iron with pressing cloth
Chalk

DIRECTIONS:

1. On all sides of the duck cloth square, fold a ¼-in. hem with wrong sides together. Use iron with pressing cloth to press in place, then fold a 1½-in. hem with wrong sides together and press hem in place.

2. Unfold both the 1½-in. and ¼-in. hems. Cut out the small square crease at each corner. Fold in cut corner edges diagonally and press in place to form mitered corners.

3. Refold ¼-in. and 1½-in. hems. Press in place. (The diagonal corner edges should meet, forming a line. Adjust mitered corners if needed for alignment.)

4. Insert the chalk fabric right side up and centered under the folded edges of the duck cloth. Smooth the chalk fabric so it lies flat on the duck cloth with the folded edges overlapping.

5. Using a straight stitch, sew ¼ in. from inner edge of duck cloth around perimeter of chalk fabric. Using a zigzag stitch, sew along each mitered corner where duck cloth forms a diagonal line.

6. Fold ribbon in half. Place folded end of ribbon so it overlaps straight stitch about ½ in. on center of one side of the mat. Sew ribbon in place on top of existing straight stitch to form a loop for the chalk. Use remaining length of ribbon to tie mat in a roll.

7. Before using, prep chalk fabric by rubbing with the side of a piece of chalk and wiping with a dry cloth.

Cuffed Knit Mittens

Warm up youngsters throughout the winter season with cozy knit mittens. Feel free to use recycled cuffs from old sweatshirts—or even the tops of socks—in place of purchased cuffs.

CRAFT LEVEL: BEGINNER

FINISHED SIZE: Children's small mittens measure about 7 in. around x 5½ in. long without cuff. Changes for medium and large mittens are in parentheses. Slight variation in gauge may change finished size a bit.

MATERIALS:

One skein each of worsted-weight yarn in desired color and 3-ply yarn in coordinating color (mittens shown were created with Lion Brand Yarn Vanna's Choice in Denim Mist and Bernat Softee Baby Yarn in White)

Set of four size 8 double-pointed needles (or the size needed to obtain the correct gauge)
Stitch marker (optional)
Stitch holder
Tape measure
Purchased knit cuffs in coordinating color
Matching all-purpose thread
Standard sewing supplies

GAUGE: 8 sts and 11 rows = 2 in.

DIRECTIONS (MAKE TWO):
HAND

1. Working with two strands of yarn as one, cast on 28(30,32) sts. Distribute sts on three double-pointed needles. Add stitch marker if desired and join into a round, being careful not to twist the sts.
2. K around until piece measures 1¾ in. (or desired length) to base of thumb.
3. K 2 sts, place next 5 sts on holder, cast on 5 sts on needle and continue to k around.
4. K around until piece measures 5½ in. (or desired length) from start.
5. Decrease for top of hand: Rnd 1: [K2tog, k2] around: 21(22,24) sts.
6. Rnd 2: K around: 21(22,24) sts.
7. Rnd 3: [K2tog, k1] around: 14(15,16) sts.
8. Rnd 4: K around: 14(15,16) sts.
9. Rnd 5: K2tog around. Cut yarn, leaving a tail. Using yarn or tapestry needle, draw yarn through remaining sts and drop them from the knitting needles. Pull yarn to close and fasten off on inside of mitten.

THUMB

1. Place the 5 sts from stitch holder, 5 cast-on stitches and 1 st from opposite sides of thumb opening on three needles: 12 sts.
2. K around until thumb measures 2¼ in. (or desired length).
3. K2tog around: 6 sts.
4. Cut yarn, leaving a tail. Close the opening of thumb the same as for top of mitten.

FINISHING

1. Weave in all loose yarn ends.
2. With right sides facing and making a narrow seam, machine-sew a knit cuff to the opening of each mitten. Overcast edges to finish and reinforce seam.

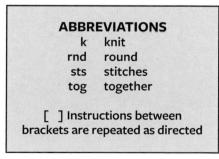

ABBREVIATIONS	
k	knit
rnd	round
sts	stitches
tog	together

[ ] Instructions between brackets are repeated as directed

Memory Wire Bracelets

Stacked together or worn individually, these stylish accessories are fun-to-wear accents in any season. Plus, the versatile bracelets are simple enough for beginners to create—without an entire jeweler's toolkit or unlimited budget.

CRAFT LEVEL: BEGINNER

FINISHED SIZE: Varies.

MATERIALS (FOR ONE):
Plated memory wire (large bracelet size)
Desired beads or crystals
Round-nose pliers
Wire cutters
Beading board (optional)

DIRECTIONS (FOR ONE):
1. Using wire cutters, cut a piece of memory wire about 4 loops long for a 4-strand bracelet (or cut a longer or shorter piece as desired).
2. Grasp one end of memory wire with round-nose pliers and curl wire tightly around one side of pliers. Wrap a few times to form a sturdy closed circle.
3. If desired, use a beading board to create the desired pattern for beads. String the desired number of beads onto memory wire, starting at the end without the circle.
4. When all beads are in place, trim the memory wire about ½ in. from the base. Grasp the end of wire with round-nose pliers and wrap wire around pliers a few times as before, forming a sturdy closed circle that is snug against the last bead.

Silhouette Ornaments

Making silhouettes used to be a long, laborious process. With today's digital cameras and photocopiers, it's easy to create a silhouette of even the most active toddler. Start a tradition of displaying your family's images on the tree.

CRAFT LEVEL: QUICK & EASY

FINISHED SIZE: Varies.

MATERIALS (FOR ONE):
Photocopier
Side profile photo
Tracing paper
Black card stock
Additional card stock or scrapbook paper in desired colors or patterns
Compass
Ruler
Scallop-edge or other decorative scissors (optional)
Glue stick
8-in. length of ribbon

DIRECTIONS (FOR ONE):

1. Use photocopier to make a copy of the side profile photo, enlarging or reducing the size of the side profile as desired. Trace around outer edge of profile on tracing paper and cut out to use as silhouette pattern.

2. Place silhouette pattern on black card stock and trace around outer edge with pencil. Cut out silhouette.

3. Use compass to make circles of varying sizes on card stock or scrapbook paper for the ornament, making the smallest circle at least ½ in. larger than the widest part of the silhouette. Cut out circles with standard or decorative scissors.

4. Center and layer the circles, working from the smallest to the largest, and adhere with glue stick. Before gluing the bottom two circles, place ribbon ends between them to form a hanging loop.

5. Center silhouette on the smallest circle and glue in place. Let dry.

Crocheted Jeweled Afghan

The look of the traditional granny square afghan inspired this intermediate-level project from Louise Puchaty, of Indian Harbour Beach, Florida. Customize the colors as you wish to suit a friend's home or to coordinate with your own decorating style.

CRAFT LEVEL: INTERMEDIATE

FINISHED SIZE: Afghan is about 44 x 57 in. Slight variation in gauge may change finished size a bit.

MATERIALS:
Caron Simply Soft Yarns—8 oz. Blue Mist (light accent),
  12 oz. Pagoda (dark solid) and 20 oz. Oceana (variegated)
Size G/6 (4.25 mm) crochet hook (or size needed to obtain
  correct gauge)
Tapestry or yarn needle

GAUGE: 16 dcs and 7 rows = 4 in.

DIRECTIONS:

1. Row 1: With Pagoda, ch 5, tr in fourth ch from hook, [ch 5, tr in fourth ch from hook of ch-5 just made] 11 times. Count: 12 trs and 12 ch-sps.

2. Rnd 1: Ch 4, in fourth ch from hook of ch-4 just made work (2 dcs, ch 2 for corner, 3 dcs, ch 2 for corner, 3 dcs), sc around post of last tr made in Row 1, * work 3 dcs in next ch-1 sp in Row 1, sc around post of next tr in Row 1, repeat from * to first ch made in Row 1, work (3 dcs, ch 2 for corner, 3 dcs, ch 2 for corner, 3 dcs) in first ch of beg ch-5 in Row 1; working across other side of Row 1, [sc in next ch-sp, work 3 dcs in next ch opposite 3 dcs of rnd] around to last ch-sp, sc in last ch-sp, join with a sl st in third ch made of beg ch-4. Count: 84 dcs and 4 ch-2 corner sps.

3. Rnd 2: Sl st to ch-2 corner sp, ch 3 (counts as first dc here and throughout), work 2 dcs, ch 2, 3 dcs in same ch-2 sp (corner made), ch 1, (work 3 dcs, ch 2, 3 dcs) in next ch-2 sp (corner made), ch 1, [work 3 dcs in next sc, ch 1] to next ch-2 sp, [work 3 dcs, ch 2, 3 dcs in next ch-2 sp (corner made), ch 1]

twice, [work 3 dcs in next sc, ch 1] to beg ch-3, join with a sl st in third ch of beg ch-3. Count: 96 dcs and 4 ch-2 corner sps.

4. Rnd 3: Sl st to ch-2 corner sp, ch 3, work 2 dcs, ch 2, 3 dcs in same ch-2 sp (corner made), ch 1, [work 3 dcs in next ch-1 sp, ch 1] to next ch-2 sp, * work 3 dcs, ch 2, 3 dcs in next ch-2 sp (corner made), ch 1 [work 3 dcs in next ch-1 sp, ch 1] to next ch-2 sp: repeat from * around to beg ch-3, join with a sl st in third ch of beg ch-3. Fasten off Pagoda. Count: 108 dcs and 4 ch-2 corner sps.

5. Rnd 4: With RS facing, attach Blue Mist with a sl st in ch-2 corner space. Ch 3, work 2 dcs, ch 2, 3 dcs in same ch-2 sp (corner made), ch 1, [work 3 dcs in next ch-1 sp, ch 1] to next ch-2 sp, * work 3 dcs, ch 2, 3 dcs in next ch-2 sp (corner made), ch 1 [work 3 dcs in next ch-1 sp, ch 1] to next ch-2 sp; repeat from * around to beg ch-3, join with a sl st in third ch of beg ch-3. Count: 120 dcs and 4 ch-2 corner sps.

6. Rnd 5: Repeat Rnd 3. Fasten off Blue Mist.

7. Rnd 6: With RS facing, attach Oceana with a sl st in ch-2 corner space. Repeat Rnd 4.

8. Rnds 7-11: Repeat Rnd 3. Fasten off Oceana at the end of Rnd 11.

9. Rnd 12: With RS facing, attach Blue Mist with a sl st in ch-2 corner sp. Repeat Rnd 4.

10. Rnd 13: Repeat Rnd 3. Fasten off Blue Mist. Count: 228 dcs and 4 ch-2 sps.

11. Rnd 14: With RS facing, attach Pagoda with a sl st in ch-2 corner sp. Repeat Rnd 4.

12. Rnd 15-19: Repeat Rnd 3. Fasten off Pagoda at the end of Rnd 19.

13. Rnd 20: With RS facing, attach Blue Mist with a sl st in ch-2 corner sp. Repeat Rnd 4.

14. Rnd 21: Repeat Rnd 3. Fasten off Blue Mist. Count: 324 dcs and 4 ch-2 corner sps.

15. Rnd 22: With RS facing, attach Oceana with a sl st in ch-2 corner sp. Repeat Rnd 4.

16. Rnds 23-27: Repeat Rnd 3. Fasten off Oceana at the end of Rnd 27.

17. Rnd 28: With RS facing, attach Blue Mist with a sl st in ch-2 corner sp. Repeat Rnd 4.

18. Rnd 29: Repeat Rnd 3. Fasten off Blue Mist. Count: 420 dcs and 4 ch-2 corner sps.

19. Rnd 30: With RS facing, attach Pagoda with a sl st in ch-2 corner sp. Repeat Rnd 4.

20. Rnd 31-35: Repeat Rnd 3. Fasten off Pagoda at the end of Rnd 35.

21. Rnd 36: With RS facing, attach Blue Mist with a sl st in ch-2 corner sp. Repeat Rnd 4.

22. Rnd 37: Repeat Rnd 3. Fasten off Blue Mist. Count: 516 dcs and 4 ch-2 corner sps.

23. Rnd 38: With RS facing, attach Oceana with a sl st in ch-2 corner sp. Repeat Rnd 4.

24. Rnds 39-43: Repeat Rnd 3. Fasten off Oceana at the end of Rnd 43.

25. Rnd 44: With RS facing, attach Blue Mist with a sl st in ch-2 corner sp. Repeat Rnd 4. Count: 600 dcs and 4 ch-2 corner sps.

26. Rnd 45: Sl st to corner ch-2 sp, ch 4 (counts as hdc and ch-2), hdc in same corner ch-2 sp, hdc in each dc and in each ch-1 sp to next corner ch-2 sp, * work (hdc, ch 2, hdc) in corner ch-2 sp, hdc in each dc and each ch-1 sp to next corner; repeat from * around to beg ch-4, join with a sl st in third ch of beg ch-4. Fasten off Blue Mist.

27. For edging, with RS facing, attach Oceana with a sl st in any ch-2 corner sp, ch 2 for first hdc, dc in same ch-sp, ch 2, sl st in top of dc, hdc in same ch-sp, ch 2, (hdc, dc, ch 2, sl st in top of dc, hdc) in same ch-sp, * sk next hdc, sc in next hdc, [sk next hdc, work (hdc, dc, ch 2, sl st in top of dc, hdc) in next hdc, sk next hdc, sc in next hdc] to next ch-2 corner sp, work (hdc, dc, ch 2, sl st in top of dc, hdc, ch 2, hdc, dc, ch 2, sl st in top of dc, hdc) in ch-2 corner sp; repeat from * around to beg ch-2 corner sp, join with a sl st in second ch of beg ch-2. Fasten off Oceana.

28. Use tapestry or yarn needle to weave in all loose ends.

PATTERN ILLUSTRATION

ABBREVIATIONS

beg	beginning
ch	chain
dc	double crochet
hdc	half double crochet
rnd	round
RS	right side
sc	single crochet
sk	skip or skipped
sl st	slip stitch
sp	space
tr	triple crochet
WS	wrong side

* or [ ] instructions after * or between brackets
are repeated a given number of times

( ) instructions in parentheses are all worked
in one stitch or space as indicated

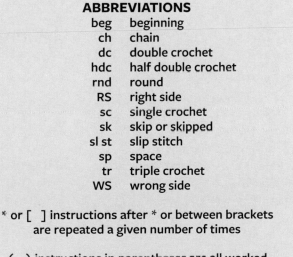

General Recipe Index

This index lists every recipe in the book by food category, major ingredient and/or cooking method, so you can easily locate recipes to suit your needs.

CHEESE

SIDE DISHES *(continued)*
Orzo Timbales with Fontina
    Cheese, 86
Parmesan-Baked Mashed
    Potatoes, 32
Parmesan Kale Casserole, 94
Stilton, Bacon & Garlic Smashed
    Potatoes, 24
Three-Cheese Hash Brown Bake, 73
Triple-Mushroom Au Gratin
    Potatoes, 84
SOUP & SALAD
Brie Mushroom Soup, 98
Layered Christmas Gelatin, 32

CHEESECAKES

Apple Cobbler Cheesecake, 126
Butterscotch-Cappuccino Cream
    Cheese Pie, 117
Creole Shrimp & Crab Cheesecake, 123
Glazed Strawberry Cheesecake, 121
Italian Chocolate-Hazelnut
    Cheesecake Pie, 114
Muffuletta Cheesecake, 116
No-Bake Oreo Cheesecake, 115
Peppermint Cheesecake on a
    Stick, 119
Pineapple Cheesecake-Topped
    Cake, 120
Sweet & Savory Mini Apple
    Cheesecakes, 122
White Chocolate Cheesecake with
    Cherry Topping, 124

CHERRIES

Amaretto Cherries with
    Dumplings, 106
Apple-Cherry Cream Cheese Pie, 156
Cherry Bounce, 166
Cherry Citrus Pastries, 165
Cherry Cranberry Punch, 82
Meatballs in Cherry Sauce, 11
White Chocolate Cheesecake with
    Cherry Topping, 124

CHICKEN

Chicken Wild Rice Soup with
    Spinach, 103
Honey Mustard Bacon-Wrapped
    Chicken, 6

Pineapple Chicken Sliders, 67
Plum-Glazed Roast Chicken, 44

CHOCOLATE

Chocolate-Covered Peanut Butter &
    Pretzel Truffles, 173
Chocolate-Dipped Orange Spritz, 132
Chocolate Drizzled Maple-Nut
    Tart, 160
Chocolate-Peanut Butter Cookies, 137
Chocolate Pecan Pie Bars, 159
Cranberry Cashew Fudge, 147
Cream Cheese Mocha Cupcakes, 125
Flourless Chocolate Torte, 158
Fudgy Mint Cookies, 129
Gooey Peanut Butter-Chocolate
    Cake, 110
Hazelnut Chocolate Cookies, 128
Italian Chocolate-Hazelnut
    Cheesecake Pie, 114
Layered Chocolate-Raspberry
    Triangles, 150
Marzipan Yule Logs, 142
Mint Chocolate Bark, 163
Mocha Macaroon Cookies, 137
Mocha Nut Balls, 138
Orange Cocoa Sandies, 138
Peppermint Cheesecake on a
    Stick, 119
Peppermint Puff Pastry Sticks, 132
Raspberry & Cream Cheese
    Pastries, 26
Red Velvet Candy Cane Fudge, 167
Rudolph Cupcakes, 79
Triple Chocolate Cookie Mix, 168
White Chip Peanut-Pretzel
    Clusters, 144
White Chocolate Cheesecake with
    Cherry Topping, 124
White Chocolate Cran-Pecan
    Cookies, 140

COCONUT

Almond Macaroon Tart, 145
Almond Macaroons, 130
Coconut Caramels, 162
Creamy Coconut Rice Pudding
    Parfait, 148
Lime & Coconut Cream Pie, 69
Mocha Macaroon Cookies, 137
Pecan-Coconut Sweet Potatoes, 105

COFFEE

Butterscotch-Cappuccino Cream
    Cheese Pie, 117
Cream Cheese Mocha Cupcakes, 125
Mocha Macaroon Cookies, 137
Mocha Nut Balls, 138
Sweet Kahlua Coffee, 100

COFFEE CAKES

Brown Sugar Glazed Coffee Ring, 49
Overnight Cranberry-Eggnog Coffee
    Cake, 61

CONDIMENTS

Baked Pearl Onions, 46
Fresh Cranberry Relish, 87
Seasoned Salt Mix, 162

COOKIES *(also see Bars)*

Almond Macaroons, 130
Cheesecake Sandwich Wafers, 124
Chocolate-Dipped Orange Spritz, 132
Chocolate-Peanut Butter Cookies, 137
Cinnamon-Sugar Crackle Cookies, 140
Cranberry-Raspberry Window
    Cookies, 14
Creme de Menthe Cheesecake
    Cookies, 139
Fudgy Mint Cookies, 129
Gingerbread Fruitcake Cookies, 138
Hazelnut Chocolate Cookies, 128
Lemon-on-Lemon Iced Cookies, 135
Mocha Macaroon Cookies, 137
Mocha Nut Balls, 138
Orange Cocoa Sandies, 138
Peppermint Puff Pastry Sticks, 132
Raspberry Almond Strips, 131
Shortbread Cutouts, 134
Thumbprint Butter Cookies, 131
Toffee-Almond Cookie Slices, 128
Triple Chocolate Cookie Mix, 168
White Chocolate Cran-Pecan
    Cookies, 140

CRANBERRIES

Apricot, Cranberry & Walnut
    Pilaf, 90
Cherry Cranberry Punch, 82
Cranberry Cashew Fudge, 147
Cranberry Meringue Cake, 155
Cranberry Pork & Sweet Potatoes, 104

MIXES

MUSHROOMS

NUTS & PEANUT BUTTER

APPETIZERS & SNACKS

BREADS

CANDIES

COOKIES & BARS

DESSERTS & CAKE

MAIN DISH

PIES & TARTS

SIDE DISHES

OLIVES

ONIONS

ORANGES

PASTA

PEARS

PEPPERONI & SALAMI

PEPPERS

PIES & TARTS

Alphabetical Recipe Index

This index lists every recipe in the book in alphabetical order. Just search for the recipe titles you want to easily find your favorites.

Craft Index

This index lists every craft project in the book by craft category, technique and/or main materials, so you can easily locate the types of projects you want.